MW01030535

GEORGES AND PAULINE VANIER

Footprints Series
Jane Errington, Editor

The life stories of individual women and men who were participants in interesting events help nuance larger historical narratives, at times reinforcing those narratives, at other times contradicting them. The Footprints series introduces extraordinary Canadians, past and present, who have led fascinating and important lives at home and throughout the world.

The series includes primarily original manuscripts but may consider the English-language translation of works that have already appeared in another language. The editor of the series welcomes inquiries from authors. If you are in the process of completing a manuscript that you think might fit into the series, please contact her, care of McGill-Queen's University Press, 1010 Sherbrooke Street West, Suite 1720, Montreal, QC H3A 2R7.

GEORGES AND PAULINE VANIER

Portrait of a Couple

MARY FRANCES COADY

McGILL-QUEEN'S UNIVERSITY PRESS

MONTREAL & KINGSTON • LONDON • ITHACA

ISBN 978-0-7735-3883-2

Legal deposit second quarter 2011
Bibliothèque nationale du Québec

Printed in Canada on acid-free paper that is 100% ancient forest free
(100% post-consumer recycled), processed chlorine free.

McGill-Queen's University Press acknowledges the support of the Canada Council for
the Arts for our publishing program. We also acknowledge the financial support of the
Government of Canada through the Canada Book Fund for our publishing activities.

Image on the title page: Georges and Pauline Vanier, Library and Archives Canada/
George P. Vanier Fonds, credit: Ashley and Crippen Photography, Acc. No. 1971-311,
Box 5821.

Library and Archives Canada Cataloguing in Publication

Coady, Mary Frances
George and Pauline Vanier : portrait of a couple / Mary Frances Coady.

(Footprints series ; 15)
Includes bibliographical references.
ISBN 978-0-7735-3883-2

1. Vanier, Georges P. (Georges Philias), 1888–1967. 2. Vanier, Pauline, 1898–1991.
3. Governors general–Canada–Biography. 4. Governors general's spouses–Canada–
Biography. I. Title. II. Series: Footprints series ; 15

FC621.V35C62 2011   971.064'20922   C2011-900523-9

Designed and typeset by studio oneonone in Sabon 10.3/14

For Patricia Cain and Margaret Holubowich

CONTENTS

GEORGES AND PAULINE VANIER

PROLOGUE

14 September 1959. The afternoon train from Montreal drew up alongside the Rideau Canal and pulled to a stop at Ottawa's Union Station. From the train alighted Canada's new governor general, seventy-one-year-old Georges Vanier. He climbed carefully onto the platform with the help of a walnut cane, a white cavalier moustache giving his face an old-world distinction. His wife Pauline, a tall woman ten years younger, stepped down with ease behind him.

The following day, Georges Vanier was formally installed in Parliament's senate chamber amid pomp and splendour, becoming the first person of French descent and only the second native-born Canadian to hold the office of governor general. In Quebec, the popularity of Prime Minister John Diefenbaker's Conservative government rose, albeit briefly, by ten percent at the news of this appointment.

Although most Canadians outside Quebec did not know them, the Vaniers had been at the centre of most of the nation's momentous events of the first half of the twentieth century. Georges Vanier was one of the founding officers of the famed francophone Royal 22nd regiment, known as the "Van Doos," part of Canada's expeditionary force heading into the First World War, and his need for a cane was the result of losing a leg after three years of fighting that war. Georges and Pauline Vanier were both confidants of Governor General Julian Byng during the historic constitutional crisis of the 1920s. As a Canadian representative, Georges Vanier had seen first-hand the futile efforts of the League of Nations; as a diplomat in England he had tried to aid the depression-era sale of Canadian wheat; and as the Canadian minister to France in the early months of the Second World War, he had been among the first to recognize Charles de Gaulle as the leader of the Free French. In devastated postwar France, the Vaniers had become the face of Canadian compassion. Throughout the personal crises, inevitable setbacks and disappointments during these years, they had come to a profoundly spiritual view of the world and their place in it.

The comfortable 1950s were coming to a close by the time Georges Vanier was installed as governor general. In the decade ahead, the postwar boom would gradually dissolve into societal upheaval. Familiar institutions and long-held traditions would be challenged, among them those that reflected Canada's imperial ties to Britain. The role of the governor general would be questioned. Quebec nationalism would emerge with a resolve not previously realized, terrorist violence erupting in its wake. As Canada looked forward to its centennial celebration, its very existence as a nation would, at times, seem to be in jeopardy. And just when the country needed strong federal leadership, Diefenbaker's historic majority would be succeeded by a series of shaky minority governments.

In the turbulence of the years ahead, the quiet wisdom of the governor general would become an asset.

* * *

During the final months of the Second World War, a soldier once said of Georges Vanier that meeting him "makes me feel proud just to be a Canadian." The story of the Vaniers is, in a sense, the story of the best that Canada can offer, and it, too, should make Canadians proud.

1

"GENTLE AND DEAR SOUL"

Four-year-old Georgie Vanier, ringleted and bedecked in lace, gazes out from the brocade chair on which he stands like a little aristocrat, as if his ancestors were of the highest nobility and his own destiny paved with glory.

The year is 1892. The brocade chair belongs to a Montreal studio photographer. The blonde ringlets and frilly attire reflect the waning years of the nineteenth century, the last vestige of the Victorian age. Indeed, Queen Victoria has just entered the final decade of her long reign. The Dominion of Canada is twenty-five years old, and Montreal is celebrating its two hundred and fiftieth birthday. It is the largest city in Canada, with a thriving business district. Its harbour is a hub for sea traffic, and the streets are lit with newly installed electric lights. An electric streetcar has replaced the horse-drawn ones. As the twentieth century approaches, both the old city and the new nation are coming into their own.

And the ancestors of this princeling? They had come to Canada in the humblest of circumstances and for the most ordinary of reasons: to improve their lot. A mere six decades after Samuel de Champlain had built a small fort on the high cliffs overlooking the St Lawrence River, Guillaume Vanier, a young man in his twenties, left his home in Honfleur, on the French coast of Normandy, in the late 1660s or very early 1670s. He landed in Quebec, a fortress city with a fortified wall standing high upon a cliff, with tin-roofed buildings and houses of rough stone built tightly together on irregular streets, in the land known as New France.

In 1672, at the age of twenty-seven, Guillaume married Magdeleine Bailly, a *fille du roi*, one of the young women sent over to become wives for the habitants, adventurers, and fur traders who had been arriving on New France's shores as single men. This young woman had arrived from Paris the previous autumn. Of the couple's two sons and one daughter, one boy died in infancy, and thus it was through the second son, Pierre, that the Vanier name continued to exist in Canada. Guillaume eventually became part of a corps of soldiers charged with maintaining public order. He was killed as a result of a skirmish with the Iroquois – not, however, by a bow and arrow, but by his own gun, which misfired, the bullet somehow hitting him rather than his intended target.

At some point in the following century, perhaps after the Seven Year War between England and France, which culminated in *la conquête* of Canada by the British in 1763, some of the Vanier progeny settled near Montreal. Five generations later, and two centuries after the young Guillaume set out from France, Philias Vanier was born in 1860. The youngest of a family of eight children, Philias set out for the big city in the early 1880s. He had received very little schooling and was probably close to illiterate, but he had ambition and a certain canniness about business that soon would work to his benefit.

In due time, he found employment in a grocery store owned by an Irishman named John Maloney. The Irish entry to Canada, triggered by massive poverty in Ireland, had come about in successive waves over the previous sixty years. It is not known when John Maloney had arrived in Montreal, nor is it known exactly when Philias first began noticing Maloney's daughter, Margaret, a young woman with long wavy hair, or when he finally summoned the nerve to broach the subject of marriage (the French and the Irish both being parochial in their insistence that their children marry their own kind). Despite whatever resistance there may have been on both sides, Philias Vanier married Margaret Maloney on 31 May 1887, at the Church of St Patrice.

Not quite a year later, on 23 April 1888, the feast day of St George, their first child, Georges Philias, was born. He was baptized the following day at St Joseph's church on rue Richmond, with an uncle and aunt, David Maloney and Josephine Vanier, as godparents. They and his father signed his baptismal certificate. His mother was not present at his baptism (the reason probably being that, according to the Catholic custom in Quebec and some other places, a woman who had just given birth did not enter a church until she was ready to be "churched," or purified, usually forty days after the birth). On the birth certificate Philias's profession is given as a grocer, but it was not long before he discovered a talent for other kinds of business as well. He quickly bought up land, and was soon managing a burgeoning real estate business. The family lived modestly at first, but with increasing prosperity they moved into larger quarters, and eventually settled into a large house on Dorchester Street, acquiring the services of a maid, known as Sophie, who became a beloved member of the family.

When Georges was five years old, his sister Eva was born. In quick succession, his brother John arrived, and then Wilfred, who died at the age of five. Philias had a rough-and-ready personality, born of hard work on the land, little education, and none of the refinements of culture. His wife, by contrast, although herself not well-educated, seems to have had intellectual gifts, a tender heart, and a zealous ambition for her children. Philias tended the business, which provided a comfortable living, and Margaret established a warm and secure family life. It is likely that their first-born son found her to be the more sympathetic parent. Years later, Georges wrote to her from the trenches of France, "when poor Wilfred died and you were dangerously ill, Aunt Kate ... said, 'How much worse it would be if it had been mother.' And looking back I see how right she was, because I cannot conceive how we could have lived without you."[1]

The Vaniers seem not to have been particularly caught up in the political or social issues of the day: labour unrest, women's suffrage, or the ever-present struggle of the francophones to maintain their language on an English-speaking continent. They lived in an anglophone milieu, and because English was the language of the business elite, it was a pragmatic move on Philias's part to maintain an English-speaking household. Thus "Georges," known as "Georgie" as a child, became "George," a quintessentially English name. His gradual return to spelling his name with an "s" traces his trajectory in identifying himself as a French Canadian.

As business continued to prosper, Philias and Margaret took extended train trips to the United States, and Philias was among the first automobile owners in Montreal. Not bothering to learn to drive himself, he hired a chauffeur. The car took the family every summer to a farm on Lake Memphremagog in the Eastern Townships, and to Cacouna, on the shore of the upper St Lawrence River.

The factor that drew the family together more than any other, both among themselves and within their circle of friends, was religion. Religious zeal had always been an integral part of the French endeavour in Canada. Jesuit missionaries had sent enthusiastic reports back to France about converting the natives, and in response, a devout layman, Paul de Chomedey de Maisonneuve, had arrived at the Ile de Montréal for the express purpose of establishing a Christian outpost. The Jesuits, and later the Sulpician Fathers, had laid

strong groundwork. By the end of the nineteenth century, Roman Catholicism
was not only an integral part of Quebec culture but also, in the collective
body of its clergy, a powerful social and political force. The particular historical form it had absorbed was a phenomenon known as ultramontanism.

Ultramontanism, from the Latin *ultra montes*, "beyond the mountains,"
originally referred to European territory outside of Italy – to any place that
was across the Alps separating Italy (and Rome) from the rest of the world.
After the sixteenth century Counter Reformation and the rise of Protestantism,
"ultramontanism" took on the meaning of allegiance to the Catholic Church
as embodied in the teachings and person of the Pope. And after the French
Revolution and the rise of French anti-clericalism, the term implied a con-
demnation of liberalism and the nineteenth-century rush to modernity. In
1864 the Vatican issued the *Syllabus of Errors*, a compilation of heresies,
which included liberalism and socialism.

The Act of Union in 1840, by which Upper and Lower Canada became
united, provided the ground for ultramontanism to flourish in Canada.
French culture was now in danger of being overwhelmed by the British presence, and this danger extended to the Roman Catholic religion. The Church
felt itself under siege, and so how better to defend itself than to demand
unshakable loyalty from Catholics? During the middle decades of the nineteenth century, ultramontanism found a champion in the person of Bishop
Ignace Bourget of Montreal, who worked to strengthen ties to the papacy
and to establish unquestioning submission to the Church's teachings. Intellectual reaction in the form of a group called the Institut Canadien, which
called for freedom of thought for French Canadians, eventually dissipated
under Bourget's increasingly powerful governance.

The ultramontane movement brought a unifying element to the Church,
with ecclesiastical power centralized in Rome. Local initiatives were discouraged in favour of religious uniformity. Rituals established by the Vatican
were encouraged – not only Sunday Mass, but also practices such as recita-
tion of the rosary, novenas, and the Benediction of the Blessed Sacrament.
Devotions in honour of Mary sprang up, bolstered by the apparition in
Lourdes in 1858. Catholic shrines sprouted, and Ste Anne de Beaupré, Cap
de la Madeleine, and later, St Joseph's Oratory in Montreal, became re-
nowned places of pilgrimage. Processions took place amid much pomp and
enthusiasm. Parishes were the centre of social activity, and within these
spheres, Vatican-approved confraternities and pious associations were formed,
as well as interlocking networks of charitable organizations, with priests

acting as spiritual directors. Fire-and-brimstone preachers were brought in for parish retreats, known as "missions," to revive religious fervour whenever it was thought to be waning. Emphasis was placed more on devotional practices and less on the intellectual study of church doctrine. The bishop was the ultimate authority within the diocese, and the priest within the parish, but all bowed to the absolute authority of the Pope. (The Pope's infallibility was promulgated during the First Vatican Council in 1870.)

As a result of all this religious revival, Catholic institutions flourished in Quebec. The humble institutes established by Marguerite Bourgeoys and Jeanne Mance two centuries earlier expanded into large religious orders of nursing and teaching sisters. Church-run hospitals and schools abounded, young men flocked to seminaries in order to become priests, and the diocese of Montreal prospered. In the last decade of his long tenure as overseer of this flowering of Canadian Catholicism, of which Montreal was the undisputed centre, Bishop Bourget supervised the planning and building of a new cathedral: a scaled-down replica of St Peter's Basilica in Rome. Called St James Cathedral, later raised to the status of "Basilica," it was consecrated in 1894, nine years after his death.

Catholic Quebec also contained remnants of a movement known as Jansenism. Named after a Dutch theologian called Cornelius Jansen, this teaching emphasized the corrupt nature of humanity and envisioned God as angry, rigorous, and vengeful. Jansenism had been formally condemned by the Church as a heresy in the seventeenth century, but strong traces of it remained among many of the French clergy, who carried its influence across the Atlantic. The sense of personal unworthiness became entrenched in people's consciences.

One of the effects of Jansenism was a pervasive belief that confession was necessary immediately before receiving communion, because any hint of sin would mean that the person had received communion unworthily, and such an act invited Satan deeper into one's soul, beginning the slide into eternal damnation. As a result, some of the Catholic faithful received communion only minimally – the Church's requisite once a year. This was to become Georges Vanier's practice for many years, the result of a religious outlook that was driven by fear. (When he eventually reached the trenches of France, he would carry in his pocket a list of stern religious exhortations that ended with a terrifying description of hell: "If I commit one mortal sin and die without repentance, I will be hurled to hell for all eternity for millions of years. I will have to spend as many millions of years in hell's fire as there have fallen or will fall till the end of the world, drops of rain from the skies. As many millions of years as there are leaves on all the trees that ever existed and that ever will exist! As many millions of years as there are grains of sand on the sea-shore and when I have spent this number of years my torments will begin anew."[2])

In all other respects, however, the Vanier family life was bourgeois and prosperous, and young Georgie was a happy, well-adjusted child. The first glimpse we have of him is a letter to his Aunt Katie Maloney written at the age of nine while on holiday, probably at Cacouna. This childish document suggests he still had much to learn in the matter of spelling and punctuation, but it also demonstrates his familiarity with the formalities of letter writing and the dry and quirky sense of humour that was to be a hallmark of his adult personality. There is also, in spite of an ability to have "lots of fun," an intense earnestness and a desire to do the right thing.

> Montreal, July 17, 1897
> Dear Auntie Katie,
> I received your letter last night I went to the post as soon as I got the letter I suddenly ran into the house and cried out loud I got a letter from Auntie Katie. I did not expect the letter so soon and I see that the thought made your hair turn gray at first I doubted it but I see that it is true. So I see that uncle Dave said my letter was very nice but I think he will be better pleased with this one as it is longer than the other. I am having lots of fun down here."

He signs the letter, "Your loving nephew, Georgie."[3]

The following fall his parents enrolled him in Loyola College, which had been established by the Jesuits a year earlier as a school for English-speaking boys. Jesuit education entailed a strict adherence to the classics and to English literature, as well as a solid grounding in religious education. The Society of Jesus, the official title of the Jesuits, had been founded over three centuries earlier by St Ignatius Loyola, who sought to spread the word of God through the education of youth. "God in all things" was one of their mottoes, signifying a broad religious outlook that would become a way of life rather than a mere Sunday devotion.

At school there was study of the Latin texts of Virgil and Livy and intensive reading of literature, especially the hefty nineteenth-century English novels and the romantic poets. Georges was to gain lifelong pleasure from the poetry of Keats and Shelley. During his early adolescence he entertained literary ambitions and modelling his writing on that of his favourite poets, he gave himself a pseudonym, "George Raymond," under which name he sent plays and poetry to the "Young People's Corner" of *The Siemens Magazine*, published in Toronto. His essay style was somewhat florid and youthfully opinionated, as an excerpt from an English composition called "The Pleasures of the Imagination" shows: "Poetry is one of the principal pleasures in which the imagination revels, for as poetical effusion is the highest form of literature, so also is it if not the highest, at least one of the many things that please the mind by its sublimity and grandeur."[4]

He was a conscientious student, and scored well in Loyola's weekly competitions. In his first year, out of a class of forty-one pupils, he came in second place in geography, and in April 1898, he "merited the note VERY GOOD for application, class standing and conduct."[5] In 1904 he took second place in Ethics, and in 1905 he placed first in Trigonometry, Rhetoric, and Philosophical Essay. An essay on Darwinism shows a leaning toward both open-mindedness and desire for truth. It also indicates his lingering fondness for flowery phrases: "The soul, we know from Psychology, is the great and immortal principle that animates the body – that stirs in every limb, that throbs in the overburdened heart, that strives in the seething brain. The soul is that immaterial substance that looks out of its prison house of clay and gazing beyond this puny earth, interprets the signs in the heavens, measures the distance and magnitude of the stars.[6] (A later, somewhat sheepish pencilled inscription in Georges's handwriting to an unknown correspondent reads, "Written in 1906 and not revised. Be indulgent svp.")

Outside of class, he was reserved, but well liked by the other boys. He enjoyed boxing and had a passion for hockey that lasted until nearly the last day of his life. Years later, he remembered that his proudest moment during his eight years at the school was when he scored the decisive goal for Loyola's intermediate hockey team one minute before the end of the game. A less happy memory was of an impromptu three-round boxing match under the railroad bridge on Guy Street, where his opponent turned out to be a superior fighter.

As he progressed through his teen years, it is not surprising that his Jesuit teachers began to regard him as a possible recruit for the priesthood. In 1903, he received a long letter from a former teacher, a Welsh Jesuit who had returned to his home country. "George, do you know what God loves, I may say, *most*, in a young man, indeed in any man for that matter ... is

gratitude," the priest wrote. "It is evident that you, my boy, are grateful –
even to an old master who was dreadfully exacting and a veritable old
scold. Be grateful to God too ... Another thing that God loves to find in a
man – He finds it only too rarely – is generosity." He urged the fifteen-year-
old boy to read a section from *The Imitation of Christ*, a medieval text
intended for monks and used as spiritual reading by novices in religious
life. He concluded the letter, "You had better make a short retreat of three
or four days at the Sault. This is the proper time."[7]

The priest's final allusion was to a retreat generally undertaken by
Loyola boys at the Jesuit retreat house at Sault au Recollet, near Montreal.
These retreats were based on the Spiritual Exercises of St Ignatius, a system
of Christian meditation that was intended as a guide for deepening a person's prayer life. In particular, in the case of young men, these exercises
were meant to help them discern whether they might have a calling to the
priesthood or religious life. Georges did not take the priest's advice right
away, but his youthful piety, no doubt nurtured at home by his mother, was
obvious. For the years 1904–05 he was named the prefect of the day in the
pupils' section of the Sodality of the Blessed Virgin Mary, a confraternity
that fostered devotion to the mother of Jesus and a prayerful way of life
through works of charity. Membership in the sodality appealed to idealistic young people, especially those from devout households and those who
were contemplating entrance to religious life.

At some point during his adolescence, he came under the spiritual tute-
lage of a Jesuit from France called Pierre Gaume. Père Gaume taught French
at Loyola, and it was he who first chided Georges for not having fluency in
French in spite of his stellar French Canadian pedigree. This blunt throwing down of the gauntlet awakened in him not only a stirring of pride in
his nearly three-century-old French Canadian heritage, but also a sense of
belonging to the far-off land of his forebears. He sought out a tutor, and
found one in a man from France of mysterious background by the name of
Camille Martin. Martin was a person of obvious culture and sophistication,
and although the reason he had come to Canada as a lowly tutor was never
known, his influence on Georges Vanier was enormous. The tutor lived in
a house he called "The Hermitage" on Mackay Street, not far from the
Vanier home, and he not only taught Georges to speak fluent French, but
the two also discussed matters of literature and culture – subjects that were
close to Georges's own interests.

In 1906, after nine years at Loyola, Georges was the valedictorian at his graduation ceremony. An examination report of February that year shows that he obtained a respectable 696 marks out of a possible 900 (the highest was 814). He was a cultured young man of eighteen, quiet and serious, respected by his friends. His tiny world of Montreal's English Catholicism had been widened by his study of the French language, his increasing passion for French culture, and the romantic idea of the French fatherland. His graduation photograph shows a slender-faced young man with a clear and serious gaze and with a tight-lipped mouth, suggesting a cerebral inclination and a tendency toward being both aloof and opinionated.

Another side of Georges Vanier is not so evident in the photograph. The early years of the twentieth century had seen the Vanier family augmented by two more children, Anthony and Frances. Fifteen years separated Georges and Frances, and the presence of a baby in the home as he was passing through adolescence brought out a tenderness and playfulness in him. As Frances grew older, he liked to tease her, and together they made up a baby language that revealed in both of them a sense of the ridiculous. A favourite nickname for her during her childhood was "Goo," and she in turn called Georges "Snooky-ookums."

In May of 1906, just before his graduation from Loyola, he made a retreat at the Sault au Recollet, presumably with the express purpose of determining whether or not he felt called to the priesthood. The outcome of this retreat seems inconclusive, and it is also unclear exactly what activities occupied Georges during the next two years. There are indications that he may have had some bouts of illness. Perhaps he felt a certain amount of pressure to join the Jesuits, or to enter a seminary when he felt no inclination for it, and the resulting uncertainty did not allow him to make a decision about what, exactly, to do with his life. He seems to have continued his French tutorials with Camille Martin and his reading of French literature. Père Gaume was concerned about him, writing from St Boniface, "Are you sick? I've sent you at least three cards and I haven't received a response ... I'm waiting for a letter from you by return mail to explain your silence and give me news."[8]

In 1908 Père Gaume sent him a letter from Quebec City. The priest had previously reproved Georges for his lack of emotional openness, and his letter quotes Georges's response: "Intimate feelings of joy, sadness, desires, aren't something to write about. They can be spoken about, and in fact are more often understood, with gestures, looks, and tone of voice." The Jesuit wondered if Georges could come for a visit to Quebec and went on to comment on the young man's reading material. "You've bought books, and I approve, but not without reserve. Molière, for example, isn't to be read completely. He has written some abominable things, and I count on your good taste and refinement to leave them in the oblivion that they merit. But perhaps you've bought an expurgated edition – in this case, very good."[9] This advice reflected the kind of ultramontane thinking that might have cast a chill on Georges's high school education: criticism of any aspect of Catholicism (Molière's satirical portrayals of hypocritical devotionalism, for instance) was regarded as an attack on the Church as a whole and therefore a danger to the Catholic faithful. Perhaps by now the position of priests like Père Gaume, that one should steel oneself against the wider world of ideas, had begun to clash with Georges's own growing interests.

In May 1908, now twenty years old, he made another five-day retreat at Sault au Recollet, and emerged from it with a definitive answer: he did not have a calling for the priesthood, and was now at peace with the conviction. Père Gaume responded graciously to this news, but with just a hint of disappointment:

> I waited impatiently with as much discretion as possible in order to prevent myself from questioning you, and I'm happy to finally be finished with the uncertainty that weighed on me almost as much as it did on you.
>
> So now a very grave question has been decided, and I congratulate you, my dear Georges, for finally being able to set the course of your life in the light of faith and the Exercises.
>
> I thought that you perhaps had a vocation and I would have been happy to see you called, but God prefers you in the world. It is perfect.
>
> Remember what I said to you two years ago on one of our last walks: that whatever decision you took, I would approve it if I knew that you had taken it seriously, discerning for and against before God, and you have done that. I therefore approve your choice completely.
>
> You have conducted yourself honourably and reasonably, so leave regrets behind. You are going resolutely along the well marked path that God, through your director, has opened up for you.[10]

The retreat of 1908 – and no doubt Père Gaume's letter – took a mountain of pressure and uncertainty off him, and Georges now decided to take a degree in law. On 8 June, he signed a contract with the law firm of Alexander Chase-Casgrain. He was to remain with the firm until he had finished his studies and was called to the bar. He seems to have made the choice of law as a career with little enthusiasm, but what was clear to him was that he wanted to do his studies in French, and to this end he decided on Laval University. (He may have been aware of the irony of his decision, which was the opposite of that taken by Wilfrid Laurier, who had become the first French-Canadian prime minister ten years earlier: Laurier had deliberately learned English ways and had taken his law degree in English at McGill University.)

Sometime in 1910 Georges fell ill, and in spite of a Christmas blessing from Père Gaume that year ("May God give your body perfect health and maintain your soul in the excellent supernatural atmosphere where it has lived up till now"[11]), his illness returned in 1911. No record remains as to the nature of these illnesses, but they seem not to have interfered unduly with his studies, and he was able to graduate with a law degree in the early summer of 1911.

During these years he developed a friendship with a fellow student by the name of Paul Morin, who was a year younger in age and a year ahead in studies. Morin was a budding poet of considerable ambition, and it is very likely, given their common literary interests, that Georges accompanied him to readings by a loosely knit group of young poets called "École littéraire de Montréal," which had been seeking to burst through the bonds of Quebec's artistic provincialism. Culturally, Montreal was considered a backwater by these new bright lights of the French Canadian literati and they looked to France, and in particular to Paris, as the inspiration for all things cultural and artistic. Those with the means to do so moved there, hoping that life in a rich cultural milieu would help to give substance and energy to their literary art. The son of a wealthy family, Paul Morin moved to Paris in 1910 to work on his doctorate and write poetry.

In June 1911, Chase-Casgrain recommended Georges for the bar ("during all the time he was so under indenture with me his conduct was good and gentlemanly"[12]), and on 6 July his mother received a telegram at Lake Memphramagog: "Got through the bar exam."[13] With that hurdle behind him, he too began making plans to travel to Paris. He wrote to Paul Morin about his plans and received an enthusiastic reply. Morin's letter is striking in allowing a glimpse of young Georges through the eyes of a close contemporary. His letter begins, "*Alma soave e cara* ('gentle and dear soul') – or in other words, my very dear George, how happy I was to receive your nice newsy letter! I shall not go into details and try to explain my satisfaction and relief, because my very words would, I am afraid, sound too frenchy to your very English ears, but I jolly well feel it all the same." Georges had apologized for his "boorishness" in not writing sooner, to which Morin replied, "I did not 'think anything of my friend's 'boorishness', because my friends, being my friends, can have no boorishness." The letter refers to the "nervous depression" which Georges had written about – the only mention anywhere of Georges's illnesses during these years. Morin makes light of it, wondering if the condition came about from too much studying or too many affairs of the heart or as he puts it, "Heart troubles or super-tension of the grey matter?"

Morin's letter continues in the same light-hearted manner, giving details of his doctoral thesis on Henry Wadsworth Longfellow – "This Longfellow beggar," he declares, is "very little of a poet (I hope I am not hurting any of your opinions?)" – and then regales his correspondent with news of his own "heart troubles": "the Swiss girl is gone to the Isle of Wight, and I don't mind a bit, being deeply interested in a Denver girl who goes to school in Neuilly, and belongs to the Club. But for all that, I do not forget the little Westmount girl who – wonderful to relate – wrote to me at least twice a week since I left home. I call that marvelous and very sweet. Such *fidelité* in a little morsel of humanity astonishes me and touches me very much – she has a good time with the boys, I do the same here with the girls."[14]

Georges left for Europe on the RMS *Franconia* at the end of January 1912. He visited Paul Morin in Paris, and was no doubt introduced to literary salons as acclaim rained down upon Morin's book of poetry, *Paon d'Email*. The poems, one of which was dedicated to Georges Vanier, had been published to enthusiastic reviews the year before. The reviewers had praised the technical brilliance of the poetry, which drew its inspiration from Greek and Roman antiquity, and had lauded Morin as one of a new generation of literary promise.

In June, Georges's sister Eva and his father, Philias, joined him, after some concern that they might not make it because of the latter's reluctance to travel and his desire that the trip be made with no fuss or social fanfare.

The Vanier household received postcards from Paris, Rome, "where I saw His Holiness Pius X," Venice, Dublin, and London. All three returned together to Montreal at the end of August.

In a sense, this trip marked the end of Georges Vanier's youth. He had had a closely guided upbringing in the midst of increasing material prosperity and a loving family life. He remained a committed Catholic, and although his youthful pieties probably waned in the wake of new interests, he was still punctilious in his observance of Catholic teaching and such ritual requirements as Sunday Mass and Lenten fasting. He had been given enormous educational advantages and had come into contact with both sides of his family background, falling particularly in love with his French heritage. Studies had posed no particular hardship, and if he wasn't entranced with his chosen profession of law, at least it provided prestige and a good future. He had seen something of the world, and at the age of twenty-four, the time had come to settle down and look ahead.

2

THE CALL TO ARMS

Was Georges aware of the gathering forces in central Europe that would soon explode into war and thereby change his life? Probably no more than the average well-educated Canadian. Noises in far-off Germany, Austria, and Serbia were not of immediate concern and did not dominate newspaper headlines. Besides, political affairs seem not to have captured Georges's imagination, and certainly he had no interest in military matters. In May 1913, he turned down an offer of a commission in the 6th artillery brigade of the reserve army.

Soon after his return from Europe, he went to work for the law firm Dessaules and Garneau, and settled into the staid life of a Montreal lawyer. Montreal was not Paris, where he had become smitten with the food and wine and the intellectual ferment taking place in the salons, and where he felt the pull to become a citizen of the world – but it was home. He continued his discussions about French literature with Camille Martin, and resumed his interest in sports, especially hockey and boxing. He became a member of the University Club. He lived in the family home, the big comfortable house at 861 Dorchester Street West, where he resumed his position as the dutiful eldest son, increasingly worldly wise, but still conscientious to a fault.

He also took up the role of responsible big brother, quietly admired by John and Eva, and revered by young Anthony, with whom he shared a bedroom. With baby Frances, who was by now a schoolgirl, the teasing relationship resumed, and her childish playfulness continued to soften his edges. Naturally reserved, he may have been shy with women, but as a highly eligible bachelor he was likely not lacking for female companionship. If there were "heart troubles" of the kind Paul Morin wrote about, they have been lost to posterity. The life of abundant prosperity flowered, especially during the summer holidays at the idyllic Lake Memphramagog, in day after day of sunshine and yachting, and hours of poetry reading and quiet conversation on the veranda.

Life changed when, on 1 August 1914, Germany declared war on France and then invaded Belgium. Within two months, the Canadian Expeditionary Force was formed and thousands of volunteers, mostly young men of British birth, had signed up, and the first division had sailed for training in England. Support in Quebec for the war effort was not unanimous – French Canadians were not themselves threatened, and therefore many could see no reason to join a European war – but both the Catholic hierarchy and the press were in favour of the call to fight. Sensing the mood of the moment, a medical officer by the name of Colonel Arthur Mignault sought to form a battalion made up entirely of French-Canadian soldiers.

At a historic gathering in Montreal's Parc Sohmer, which Sir Wilfred Laurier (by now leader of the opposition) attended with great enthusiasm, the battalion was formed. It was named the 22nd battalion, soon popularly known as "the Van Doos." Georges was one of the first to join up; at age twenty-six one of the older recruits (the average age was twenty-four).

What prompted him to be among the first to say "yes" to the government's call for volunteer soldiers? He was a young man with a deep sense of duty, and perhaps this was sufficient for him to put his comfortable life on hold. But it was without doubt his feeling of kinship with France, its history and its people, that propelled him to act. There was, as well, his sense of justice. "I could not read the harrowing account of Belgian sufferings without feeling a deep compassion and an active desire to right, so far as it was in my power, the heinous wrong done," he wrote much later to his sister Frances.[1]

One also wonders whether he felt his youth slipping away in the soft and easy life of the Montreal bourgeoisie. At the Jesuit-led retreat he had made six years earlier, he had determined that he did not have a vocation to the priesthood, but a sense of personal mission probably continued to pursue him. During that retreat he had been presented with a spiritual either/or question called the "two standards," representing the necessity of choosing between good and evil; it is likely when the call came to save the French and the Belgians from the clutches of the enemy, the choice became clear. At any rate, when he shucked off his tailor-made suits and silk socks and donned the rough brown serge uniform and khaki leggings of the 22nd battalion it was with the conviction that on the road ahead lay another vocation.

This decision to join in with the conflict half a world away was to change the whole course of his life – not only physically and professionally, but also in more profound ways. It set the seal on his personal identification with France as the land of his ancestors and, more importantly, it brought out

leadership qualities that lay just beneath the surface. The stripped-down life
of discipline and intense focus in the face of extreme danger, the realization
that the lives of millions depended upon him and his comrades, the constant pushing himself to the limit: all of this contributed to the making
of the man. He was to blossom in this severe milieu, and the increasing
desperation as the war progressed did nothing to dampen his enthusiasm
for it. The notion of sacrifice, of giving himself to help his spiritual kin in
the land of his ancestors, never left him – not when the shells were bursting around him, or when his body was limp with exhaustion and sinking in
mud, or when he viewed the horror of the carnage around him.

The nightmare ahead was still unknown when, two months before the
end of the year 1914, over a thousand recruits of the 22nd battalion set out
on the first leg of their new life. The training camp of St Jean had been built
to house and train only one hundred and twenty, but in its cramped and
makeshift quarters, the effort began to convert a group of civilians – students,
businessmen, engineers, lawyers – into soldiers. They did arduous physical
exercises and went on extended marches, some as long as thirty kilometres,
in which they were expected to step in perfect unison, eyes front, about turn.
The winter weather made no difference to their routine; the marches continued day after day in freezing temperatures and knee-high snow. There
was little equipment to practise with, and even a scarcity of rifles for the
men to learn how to shoot. The commanding officer, Colonel F.M. Gaudet,
a fierce-looking man with a thick moustache, kept a sharp, stern eye on the
fledglings he would soon be leading into battle.

On 10 February 1915, Georges passed the required examination and thus
qualified for the rank of Lieutenant. Branch of service: Infantry. Regiment:
80th. He stood a lean six feet, one-half inch in height, his weight one hundred and sixty pounds. Still a military greenhorn, he was nonetheless put in
charge of training a group of recruits. Thus continued the ad-hoc preparation for war.

The Montreal papers kept an upbeat tone in informing readers of the
progress of the military training. *The Standard* published photos of the 22nd
battalion on the barrack square in St Jean, "where the regiment is now under-
going an arduous training for service with the Allied Armies in Europe."[2]
In the photos, more than a dozen lines of soldiers wearing great coats with
brass buttons stand at attention. The ground is covered in snow and at the
back can be seen the Spartan buildings of the barracks. The faces are indis-
tinct, and the general impression given by the stiffly standing bodies is of a

determined willingness for self-sacrifice in the face of a common cause, mingled with bewilderment at the strangeness of it all.

On 12 March 1915, they assembled in long rows, now looking less like ragtag trainees and more like disciplined soldiers, and prepared for the next step on their road to the front lines of Europe: the training ground of Amherst, Nova Scotia, where the 22nd arrived amid considerable local excitement at the sight of the young men in their khaki uniforms, a thousand strong. The new inhabitants immediately took over the town, filling stores and barber shops, and packing the streets with good cheer and robust friendliness. The *Amherst Daily News* was pleased to report that there had been no rowdiness among the "brave lads," only gentlemanly behaviour. On Sunday morning "the thrilling notes of the bugles, with the rattle of the drums"[3] announced the march in parade to church.

At Amherst they received more advanced training. They continued the marching practices, walking for hours in mud and rain, and also began learning the rigorous methods of trench warfare. On 20 May, the thousand-plus men marched past the cheering crowds that lined both sides of the street waving flags and banners, and boarded the train for Halifax. There, the ship HMT *Saxonia* waited, and within an hour the men had embarked, and to the brass band's rendering of "Oh Canada," the ship pulled away from the Canadian shore. As the vessel silently glided into the Atlantic, the crowd waved flags and hats and handkerchiefs: poignant gestures of pride and hope, as well as, perhaps, a slight shudder of fear for the safety of the smartly uniformed young men. After a scant four and a half months of training, the soldiers of the 22nd were steaming into war. For Georges, it was romance all the way. "It is a privilege ... to be of this age, when instead of mediocre, colourless lives we can forget the dollars and the soil, and think of principles and the stars," he wrote to his mother. "We have been looking at the ground so long that we have forgotten that the stars still shine."[4]

Nine days later, under the escort of two British destroyers, they sailed into the port of Plymouth. They travelled by train through the pleasant green countryside to East Sandling Camp, near the towns of Shorncliffe and Folkestone, in Kent. More rigor ensued: five thirty am rising, a whole day of training, and bedtime at ten pm. Georges immediately embarked on a course in map reading. "Our work has become very much more interesting," he added in a letter to his mother. "We pay particular attention to bayonet work, musketry and machine-guns."[5] He was soon also taking a special machine gun course, and then a bomb-making course. "The work is very interesting," he wrote to his mother of the latter activity. "At the front there are officers who carry bombs instead of revolvers."[6] One wonders how such news from her poetry-loving son was received at 861 Dorchester Street.

At East Sandling, the 22nd joined three other Canadian battalions to form the 5th Infantry Brigade, which was soon to become part of the 2nd Canadian Division. There were brief periods of escape from the intense training – short trips to London and Brighton, a quick dip in the frigid waters of the English Channel, Georges's first experience of flying in an airplane (which he described as close to an out-of-body experience). He assured his mother that his purchases in London were necessary for the front and not extravagances – a heavy raincoat with a detachable fleece lining was one of them – as if, like a schoolboy on holiday, he had to account for his expenditures. A visit in July from Prime Minister Robert Borden and Minister of War Sam Hughes, and some weeks later a visit from King George V, lifted the men's spirits and confirmed their determination to do Canada proud. As the hot weather ground on through the summer, rumours circulated that they would soon be heading for France. In a letter of 20 July, Georges told his mother that the censor might black out this information if the rumours proved correct, and so he suggested a code: "How is Arthur?" was to mean that he was leaving for the front.

On 13 September, the first of the 22nd troops embarked for Southampton, and from there to Le Havre. Georges, now a machine-gun officer, was in a state of exhilaration combined with nervous excitement. Spending the night on the wharf, with a horse blanket as a mattress, could not be topped by any sleep anywhere, he declared. "I shall begin to get very fat, I'm afraid, with this outdoor life."[7] On 16 September, the Vanier household in Montreal received a cablegram that read, "How is Arthur?" The beloved first-born son was soon to be in the thick of war.

* * *

Throughout the ten months of intensive training, nothing in Georges Vanier's correspondence indicates the casualties suffered by the ill-prepared Canadians who had arrived in France several months earlier. By January 1915 they had reached the Western Front, the system of trenches heavily fortified with barbed wire that snaked diagonally across France and into Belgium from Switzerland to the North Sea. Canadian forces had been consolidated in the area around Ypres, the only Belgian town not yet captured by the Germans. Refugees streamed along the roads throughout the countryside. In April, a new weapon, chlorine gas, had been unleashed by the Germans, and soldiers as yet unequipped with gas masks gasped, spat blood, and writhed on the ground in agony as waves of the green poison rolled over them. Two thousand Canadian soldiers had been killed in a single April weekend in the battle for Ypres, and the town had been left in ruins. Here, in the section of Belgium known as Flanders, was the destination of the 22nd battalion after their arrival in the port of Le Havre. They arrived at the trenches on 20 September 1915.

Nothing could have prepared them for what they saw there. The land all around them had been torn up and churned into mud, impossible to walk on without sinking up to the ankles; trees had been twisted into grotesque shapes and stripped of foliage; and over all lingered the sickening odour of chlorine gas and the stench of rotting bodies. Thousands of soldiers from both sides of the conflict had sunk into the mud or lay decaying in No Man's Land, the divide separating the Allies' trenches from those of the Germans. Clouds of flies swarmed about the corpses. And in the trenches themselves, there were infestations of rats, fleas, and lice.

Thus the trench routine began: six days in, six days out. While the soldiers were in the trenches, they remained in their uniforms the whole time, sleeping only for a couple of hours at a stretch, on ledges or sandbags. Orders were given that they were to be kept busy so as to avoid melancholy. The approach of winter brought a new problem: "trench feet," painful swelling caused by constantly standing in cold water. Georges Vanier emphasized in his letters home the necessity of wearing woollen socks, the thicker the better, and commented wryly on the silk and cashmere socks of his former life.

Intelligence Summaries were circulated daily, with accompanying notes sizing up the enemy and revealing the strategies to be taken. Excitement could be generated by these ongoing updates, but then there was the dreariness of the weather – a constant grey drizzle – and the fatigue, the ennui of nothing happening for hours and days on end, and the depression of being surrounded by dirt and filth and barbed wire. A sporty newsletter of the 7th Canadian Infantry Battalion, *The Listening Post,* captured the strange polarity of emotions in the trenches: "On a fine night, with a full moon, dry ground and a good view. Fine! A regular picnic. All the universe and the myriad stars to remind you of your future happiness. But on a wet night, a thin, drizzling, slush of a night, your knees a sponge, your elbows a marsh, your tummy a morass, nothing to be seen, heard or smelt but wet, damp and misery. Then's the time you think of your past sins."[8]

In the midst of it, Georges wrote unfailingly gracious letters, full of cheery optimism, in English to his mother (his main correspondent, with whom he obviously felt a strong link, both emotional and intellectual) and siblings, and in French to his father. In the trenches he wrote, as likely as not, while sitting on a wet sandbag, sometimes in pencil, sometimes in blue-ink pen, usually on lightly lined graph paper. His writing sloped to the right, the letters large. The penmanship was on the whole readable, the spelling and grammar almost perfect, an accomplishment for someone writing on his knees and in cramped positions, with danger around him and the sound of artillery in his ears.

A continuous stream of letters had followed him ever since he had left home almost a year earlier, keeping Georges, in his straitened circumstances, up-to-date with the family's minutiae as well as landmark news. From Frances he heard about her tonsillitis and her little rabbit Jack, her studies and her music lessons. When the news reached Montreal that Georges was going overseas, she wrote, reflecting general Canadian pride in the call to arms, "when people ask if you have a brother at the front or going, we can answer yes and I bet you we say it with proud emphasis."[9] And then, trying to conceal her anxiety behind the teasing rapport with her much older brother: "Be as prudent in the trenches as you can for when you are careless for a moment it is just the time you may be hit with a sharpel [sic]. *Obey me.*"[10] He responded with a teasing comment on her misspelling of "shrapnel" and a playful twist on her worried plea: "Be as prudent in the streets of Montreal as you can, for when you are careless it is just the time you may be hit by a streetcar. Obey me eh?"[11] He learned that Anthony had graduated from short pants to long trousers. The letters from Anthony reveal a combination of languid adolescent sensibility and intense brotherly pride. In sentences filled with spelling errors and sloppy grammar, the young teenager wrote of the heart-bursting thrill he felt in his older brother's achievements and self-sacrifice. He wrote that Georges's letters were "very nourishing," adding, "I did not write you sooner because their bright gems of thought, whole treasures of wisdom and golden vein of language were too much for me."[12]

His sister Eva wrote with shy affection, assuring him that she was pasting newspaper clippings, postcards, and letters into an album, as Georges had requested. Montreal was now a quiet city, she reported, except for regiments marching in parade. She was helping raise money for refugees in Europe and volunteered her time in wrapping bandages to be sent overseas. "I can't tell you, dearest, how minutely we follow you up and how deeply we are with you, in spirit."[13]

In November came the news that Eva was now engaged to be married; "the other party is Mr Trudeau," Frances informed him with childish solemnity.[14] On hearing of his sister's engagement, Georges's reaction, declaring his approval of her decision to get married as soon as possible, revealed his position as the oldest brother, the second man of the family. "You are quite right to be opposed, as I am, to long engagements," he wrote to his mother,[15] as if it seemed only right that as a twenty-seven-year-old bachelor he should be considered an expert on the subject. In the same letter (perhaps because he really believed it, perhaps to ease his mother's sense of loss) he suggested that he would be home soon, in the unmarried state that he expected to be in for the rest of his life. In a later letter he added further advice, wading into the dangerous waters of wedding plans, telling his mother to advise Eva to finish planning well ahead of time – again with the aplomb of someone who knows much about the matter – because "most girls worry and work themselves to shadows before their wedding day, and many remain nervous wrecks for some months after."[16]

In December, he received a letter from a young cousin, George Pelletier, who wrote with adolescent male enthusiasm and naiveté: "I wish you would write me a letter describing the battlefields of Europe. How do you like it etc ... I also often think of you when I have nothing else to do."[17] Georges replied with typical graciousness and understated humour, describing trench life: the closeness to the enemy, the necessity of venturing forth from the underground only at night, the crash of the shelling, the waiting and watching, the knee-deep water. "We are very well fed in the trenches and we usually have enough left over for the thousands of rats and mice which invade our dugouts. Of course sometimes we witness disagreeable sights, but one must get used to them."[18] His diary entry for the same day gives a hint of how in fact he kept himself sane in the long days and nights: "A light rain is slowly falling, the weather makes one feel melancholy. I have to react somehow – dream of the smiling spring, of friends back home."[19]

It may have seemed to Georges that, along with other Canadian soldiers, he was living in two parallel worlds – the real one in the trench, sitting on a ledge in the fading light, perhaps under a tarpaulin to keep the rain away, feet soaked with mud, the sound of shells above, the monotony and then the paralyzing fear as the explosions started and shells landed. And the other world, also real, but a universe away, that he entered when the mail arrived and he could sit on an earthen ledge, his hands grimy, and open a letter from home. He might picture around the dining room table his sister, Eva, pasting newspaper clippings, his brother, Anthony, writing him a letter with tortured effort, the whimsical Frances. The domestic scene: clean, safe, innocent.

But there was worry across the ocean as well. Every day the papers printed news of casualties, and the news was now close to home. In October, word had reached Montreal that an officer of the 22nd, Major Adolphe Roy, had been killed when an unexploded bomb suddenly blew up as he was trying to throw it out of harm's way. The news heightened the family's anxiety. And for Georges, it was the first of many deaths that would threaten to shatter his resolve.

1916 ushered onto the plains of Flanders one of the coldest winters in memory. Georges's New Year's letter home, however, was upbeat, noting that cheers and shouts and bugle calls had sounded from the German dugouts at midnight and that 1916 had come in like a lamb. What he did not tell them was that he had received word from Lieutenant Colonel Thomas (Tommy) Tremblay, who had taken over from Colonel Gaudet as commanding officer of the 22nd, that a secret dangerous patrol would be taking place in a few days. Georges was to lead the patrol, which took place on the night of 2 January. The *Christian Science Monitor* described the success of the operation succinctly under the headline "Canadian Exploits in Flanders Region." Vanier, the article said, "volunteered to lead a small detachment against a German timbered outwork, which was obviously designed to hold a machine gun or a trench mortar, in unpleasant proximity to our lines. They crawled out in the night, cut the German wire without discovery, and blew the work up."[20] The Montreal papers noted the exploit as well. Anthony told him that one of the Jesuit priests at his school, College Ste Marie, read about Georges's success with pride. As for the priest, his brother added, "from then on I have always liked him."[21]

On the morning of 15 January, he sent a telegram to Eva and her new husband for their wedding day. On the same day he received word that he had been promoted to the rank of Captain. He joked about the new rank with mock haughtiness using baby language in a letter to Frances: "Me is awfuts person, horribits proud and terribits captain ... me wouldn't 'peak wif you," adding, "The thing, you see, is very serious."[22]

But the elation was short-lived. Six days later, he received the worst news yet since his arrival in Europe: Adrian McKenna, the son of close family friends and a fellow Loyola graduate, had been killed in action. Five years younger than Georges, Adrian had earlier been wounded in the shoulder and returned to the trenches only to suffer problems with his eyes. He had been offered a permanent disability discharge, but refused it and wrote home enthusiastically about returning to the front. Of the nearly one hundred Loyola boys who enlisted, Adrian was the first to be killed. Georges recorded his death with sadness.

Meanwhile, he was due for a week's leave, which he spent in Paris, noting the sombre tone of the city, even in the theatres, and remarking on another side to the sober reality of war: the large number of women wearing black in mourning. But the grand cause of the European struggle continued to enthral him: "Ah, the sheer joy of it – to visit Paris on leave from the trenches where we are all trying to do our bit for the triumph of civilization," he wrote while on leave.[23] From Paris he sent home a postcard showing a picture of the Cluny Museum and with the message, "Affectionate greetings from Paris, centre of civilization."[24]

As winter slowly melted away, he spoke in letters of new positions: second-in-command of "C" Company; temporary command of "A" company. Spring began to arrive at the end of March, and when he was out of the trenches, he revelled in the green of the land and the birdsong and the brightness of the sunshine. The warm weather was especially welcome, as it dried out the mud in the trenches. Parcels arrived from home. The thick woollen socks he had received during the winter were now followed by food – maple syrup, tinned meat, cake. There was also tobacco and a supply of *Mutt and Jeff* cartoons.

Letters continued to keep him up to date with news from Montreal. From his friend and fellow lawyer Walter Shanks, he heard about boxing and wrestling matches as well as news of the current court cases. He was transported back to the family on Dorchester Street for a few moments when he opened a letter from Anthony that began, "It is now nine thirty pm and in our big room, I have your dressing gown on, and it gives me great consolation, for it has that clean smell that is always around you. I am writing on the old desk, that you once soaked me [for], for carving my initials on it ... I think a great deal of you, George, and feel rottenly lonely, and I think of how many times I was mean to you."[25]

After receiving in the mail a piece of Eva's wedding cake with instructions to put it under his pillow so that he might dream of his own true love, Georges reported to Frances: "Tell Eva I slept over a piece of her wedding cake three nights in succession without any results. I could dream of nothing and of nobody. I am afraid I shall remain a bachelor."[26] Further letters brought news of his brother John's engagement, which gave him a feeling of wistfulness: "I congratulate him and in a way envy him."[27]

April brought the rains, and once more the fields of Flanders became a morass of mud. Fighting intensified around the area known as the Ypres Salient, the small parcel of land jutting into the territory captured by the Germans, and the village of St Eloi, where the 22nd had been stationed since coming to Flanders. Perhaps feeling the possibility of death for the first time, Georges wrote out his will and placed it in an envelope:

12 April 1916
I believe in God and in the holy Catholic Church.
I believe in eternal rest and in divine mercy.
I confide my soul without fear to the Lord Jesus Christ.
I renew all the promises made at my baptism and confirmation.
I believe in the sanctity of our cause and the triumph of justice.
I believe in the future of French Canada.
At my death, I leave all my possessions to those I love the most:
   to Maman, Papa, Marie Eva, John, Anthony and Frances, to be
   divided equally among them.
I name my father as executor, with complete power and without
   obligation to report.
I entrust this task to Papa at the time he considers best.
Pray for me.[28]

He came through the heavy bombardment unscathed. By the time he celebrated his twenty-eighth birthday on Easter Sunday, the weather had turned warm and sunny again, but the hours of bombardment only increased. The craters littering the battlegrounds remained full of water from the rains, some as large as ponds. In early June, Georges received the news that he had been awarded the Military Cross for his bravery in blowing up the German machine gun hut in January. His pleasure at this recognition was dampened, however, with further news of the deaths of friends and comrades. And then, on 10 June, the Vanier family in Montreal received a telegram that read, "Shaken by shell no wound don't worry." A day earlier, a German shell had exploded beside him on the front line, and he was knocked unconscious and had to be carried out of the firing line.

Suffering severe shell-shock, he was taken to a Trappist monastery on the Flanders plain that had been converted to a convalescent hospital. Here, although dazed and suffering from nervous headaches and numbness in his fingers and toes, he was still able to write lucid letters home. He proclaimed his approval of John's decision, like Eva's before him, to get married soon, and perhaps feeling older than his twenty-eight years (or thinking that his end was near), he wrote to his mother for her birthday with the declaration, "It is only late in life that one understands the importance of a mother."[29] He described his peaceful surroundings: the hospital was situated on a high hill known as Mont des Cats, and "far below, villages here and there dot the ground and the bricks of the buildings look like red spots against the green of the fields."[30] Most of the monks had been conscripted into the French army, but the few older ones who remained could be heard chanting their prayers in the chapel or seen tending the gardens. There was a silence and peace about the large tree-filled grounds a world away from the distant sound of the shelling. His diary, however, records a side of his inner disposition that he did not allow his family to see: depression and sleepless nights.

At the end of the month, while he was on leave in England, the effects of the shell-shock on his nerves overcame him once again, and he was admitted to the Perkins Bull Hospital for Convalescent Canadian Officers in the London suburb of Putney Heath. This was a large mansion with ivy-covered stone walls that had once been the home of the explorer Sir Ernest Shackleton. The property had been bought by Toronto lawyer William Perkins Bull who – having no sons to offer to the combat – turned it into a hospital in April 1916 as his contribution to the war effort. He supplied the staff and equipment and maintained the hospital himself, and the Canadian army paid a daily rate for each convalescent officer. The mansion was surrounded by hedges, and the officers' dining room overlooked a sunken garden. Vine-covered arbours formed archways along paths and over seating areas, providing a tranquil milieu for recuperation. A tennis court at one end provided exercise for those officers on their feet again.

Back in Montreal, Georges's parents elicited help from people of influence to authorize his return to Canada. To his parents' disappointment, when the authorization came through at the end of July, he turned it down. "I can't go back to Canada now," he explained to his mother, "with the boys fighting in France. I should be as unhappy as I was in the early months of the war before I enlisted."[31] In a subsequent letter he explained that he wanted "to see this sacred war through," and he went on in a vein that was somewhat detached from the reality that faced him: "At some time or other we have all wished that we had lived in Napoleonic days, but the present days are fuller of romance, of high deeds and of noble sacrifices."[32]

With the idealistic Anthony, he shared the reasons he was content to endure the filth and vermin of the trenches, the discomfort of mud-soaked legs and feet, the loud bursts of shells, the screams of wounded soldiers, and the constant stench. His reasons were summed up in a postcard showing a drawing of Edith Cavell, the English nurse who had been shot in Brussels the previous October for hiding escaped Allied prisoners of war. The drawing depicted a German officer pointing a pistol at the prostrate nurse, her cape and veil draped around her. Underneath Georges wrote, "To dear Anthony, This is the sort of thing that makes one glad that he enlisted."[33]

The idea of the "holy war," as a means of keeping up troop morale, was not unknown, especially among those who tended to be more religious and less cynical than others. For Georges, it was a holy crusade and more. He sent Anthony a clipping of an article in the *Spectator* in which the writer speaks of heroic knights going into battle. The article describes the song of the nightingale and reminds readers of all those who have gone into battle before – including mythological heroes as far back in the mists of time as Hector and Achilles. Here was the spirit and inspiration behind Georges Vanier's cause: the brave warrior, pure of mind and heart and body, giving his all to preserve an idealized freedom in the fight against tyranny.

In early September 1916 he received the Military Cross from the hands of King George V at Windsor Castle: a fleeting re-creation of the knighthood of yore. Then, in October, it was a return to the hardened world of twentieth-century warfare.

3

SAD COMMAND

Georges knew, of course, that while he rested in the soothing confines of the English convalescent home, the 22nd had moved south from Flanders to the vicinity of the Somme River, near the town of Albert. Fighting had been fierce during the summer and early fall of 1916, with massive killing on both sides. He had heard about the 22nd's moment of glory in capturing the village of Courcelette, north of Albert. They had advanced upon the village in successive waves, over a welter of shell holes and shattered trenches. They had fought their way house by house, stepping past fallen bodies, smashing their way with bayonets, and finally, on 17 September, those still standing saw the enemy running over the crest of the village, throwing away their rifles as they fled. Typically, Georges expressed mixed emotions: sorrow at the loss of yet more friends and comrades, and regret that he had not fought alongside them. He wrote, "The Battalion has been doing such big things lately that we who have not been with it are a bit ashamed of ourselves."[1]

Throughout 1916, newspapers in Montreal had praised the heroism and courage of the 22nd battalion, their fighting spirit in the land of their ancestors, and their ability to downplay fear. The fact was, however, that support for the war had fallen off in Quebec. Henri Bourassa, publisher of the influential newspaper *Le Devoir*, had initially supported the war, but now questioned the necessity for French Canadians to participate in it. Some priests also spoke disparagingly of the European conflict, and the numbers of volunteers had dwindled. By the time Georges returned to the trenches in October, hundreds from the 22nd battalion had been killed or wounded, including three-quarters of the officers, and the need for replacements was desperate. New recruits were rushed in, many of them ill-trained and poorly disciplined.

The winter of 1917 was even more savage than that of the year before, and the Canadian Corps was at the breaking point. Those who had not been killed or permanently wounded were exhausted and worn down. Back in

Canada, the possibility of conscription had been introduced and was being furiously debated. In the midst of this bleakness, Georges was named adjutant of the 22nd, first assistant to the commanding officer, a position that gave him responsibility for the day-to-day details in the running of the battalion. He was also promoted to the rank of major.

Another new development was the appointment of Lieutenant General Sir Julian Byng as the commander of the Canadian Corps, which by now numbered four divisions. Byng was a British aristocrat, a childhood friend of King George V, and one of those legendary military leaders who first learned tactics on the playing fields of Eton College. He was a seasoned fifty-four-year-old war veteran, and his heavy moustache and the deep pouches under his eyes, combined with his slightly hunched shoulders, gave the initial impression of a brooding presence. Initially, he had grumbled about his appointment: "Why am I sent to the Canadians?" he wrote to a friend. "I don't know a Canadian. Why this stunt? ... However, there it is. I am ordered to these people and will do my best."[2] In a few years, he was to come to know Canadians very well and was eventually to become one of Georges's lifelong friends. For now, he was faced with Canadian troops who had gained a reputation for raw courage and spirited enthusiasm, but whose lack of proper military discipline had too often led to unnecessary deaths on the battlefield.

As it turned out, the match between commander and troops fit perfectly. Belying first impressions, Byng had a friendly and approachable manner that was unusual in a military man with an aristocratic pedigree. He tried to live as much like the ordinary soldiers as possible, choosing Spartan accommodation, eating the same food as his men, and taking no more leave than they did. He treated his soldiers with respect and always said a prayer for their safe return when they were sent out to battle. He was known to be concerned about every aspect of his soldiers' welfare, including the amount of rations they received. (One example of his concern for the troops occurred when, immediately after the battle for Courcellette had been won, he passed a group of bedraggled Canadian soldiers returning to the trenches from the front line, some of them carrying wounded comrades. They all saluted, and Byng, returning the salute, hesitated as if to speak, and then moved on. He then told the officer accompanying him that he had wanted to say something to the men, but was so moved that he feared he would break down.)

His reputation as a taskmaster, however, proved well founded; outwardly affectionate and easygoing, he drove the men hard, while applying a sharp mental focus to the problem at hand. Nothing in the training of a soldier was unimportant to him: he insisted that such matters as clean uniforms and the proper method of saluting, seemingly insignificant in themselves, led to the discipline required for successful military action. The Canadians, who soon became known as "Byng Boys," thrived under his command.

During the early months of 1917, the 22nd battalion was billeted near the village of Vimy, north of the ancient town of Arras, once a Roman settlement. In a château situated at the nearby town of Camblain l'Abbé, the Corps headquarters, Byng plotted the next big offensive. For the first time, all four Canadian divisions were to move in one furious barrage along a four-mile front, to capture the ridge behind Vimy and drive back the German front line. Vimy Ridge was regarded as the most formidable defensive position along the entire western front. The attack was set for Easter Monday, 9 April. Byng ordered each soldier to be provided with a hot meal and a ration of rum before setting out.

After months of exercise and practice that pushed them to the limit, the Canadian troops had rallied and were ready for the offensive. At four am, amid snow and sleet driven by a sharp northwest wind, the first wave of Canadians crept along in the darkness. At five thirty, led by the pipers, they charged up the ridge with their bayonets, moving forward in one great thrusting force. In three days the victory was complete and the Canadians beheld the wide plain on the other side of the ridge. Georges wrote, "The morale of our troops is magnificent." He added, in a burst of misplaced confidence, "the war will be over in six months."[3]

In the weeks following the victory at Vimy Ridge, Byng managed to evade two attempts from higher command to remove him from the Canadian Corps. But in early June he received a direct order to leave the Canadians and take command of a British unit. The commander, who a year earlier had reluctantly taken charge of the nondescript troops from across the Atlantic and transformed them into an elite corps, now wanted to slip away quietly to avoid the prospect of making a public display of his emotion. Instead, he visited each of the divisions separately, and as the men stood silently at attention in rigidly straight lines, he spoke a brief, dignified farewell, looking down so as not to make eye contact that might cause tears. The deep affection he had developed for the Canadians had been fully reciprocated, and the accounts of his goodbye speeches indicate that they were all the more moving for the attempt on the part of everyone to maintain a stiff upper lip. Georges does not mention Byng in his letters or diary of the period, and thus there is no foreshadowing of the friendship that was to blossom between them within a few years.

Spring rains continued into the summer of 1917, the wettest summer in memory, making the fields of northern France and Flanders, already pock-marked with shell holes and littered with rats and decomposing bodies, a sea of mud. Lieutenant-Colonel Sir Arthur Currie, a native of Victoria, BC, who was known as a master tactician, was named commander of the Canadian Corps. In July, Georges was awarded the Cross of the Legion of Honour from the government of France for his help in establishing the first French-Canadian force to fight on French soil since the battle of the Plains of Abraham in 1760.

There was more news from Montreal: the next generation of Vaniers had begun, with the birth of Eva's baby daughter. His mother wrote about her worry over Anthony's poor showing in school and general inability to apply himself. Georges responded with his usual oldest-son advice, delivered with a "tut-tut" fustiness: "There is hardly any excuse. 334 marks out of 900. I can understand 550 or 600 marks, but not 334. I am afraid he will have to 'buck up.' Then if he did not work very hard during the year, with a little 'cramming' (of which I do not, of course, approve) he could have done very much better."[4]

A letter from a friend to Margaret Vanier gave her a picture of her son after almost two years of war. "He is quite the tallest and largest of the officers and is quite stout. You would have to look twice to be sure it was he. He has filled out, and says that he enjoys his life here. Certainly he looks as if he did." Noting Georges's promotion some months earlier to the position of adjutant, the writer added, "he seemed to be a general favourite with the other officers notwithstanding the fact of his being adjutant, which appointment requires endless tact and diplomacy to fill properly."[5] Another Montreal friend wrote to say that physically Georges had never been so robust, and that he had retained his characteristic sincerity and warmth.

In September 1917 he went on leave to London, hoping to find respite from the sound of explosions, but to no avail. Zeppelin raids on England's capital took place nearly every night, leaving many dead and wounded among the devastation. This interruption of his leisure time, however, did not prevent him from playing tennis, shopping, going to the theatre, and meeting friends. A cryptic and intriguing entry in his diary for 26 September noted, "Lunch with Miss Doris Robson ... Tea with Miss Elsie Moore. Dinner very much alone at Simpson's."[6] Neither "Miss" makes any further appearance in Georges Vanier's diaries, nor did either make her way into the determined bachelor's letters home. Who they were? Where were they from? Indeed, did either make any further appearance in his life? As in similar cases, the questions are left discreetly unanswered by history. And the dinner consumed "very much alone" – did this imply a welcome solitude? a searing loneliness? a touch of boredom? Again, it is impossible to speculate. It is clear, however, that his leaves comprised rather more than solitary theatre-going and visits with old comrades.

By October, the 22nd had moved back north to their former location near the Ypres salient in the flat wilderness of Flanders. Four days later came the order to capture a village from the Germans. Situated to the northeast of Ypres, the village was called Passchendaele. After three years of war and weeks of rain, the landscape surrounding Passchendaele was a lunar morass. Huge craters were filled with water, and a network of planks was set up, across which the men had to walk in single file. With one slip of the foot off the slick wood, a soldier sank into the mud and drowned. The final assault took place on the night of 6 November. The fighting was fierce, and the victory came at the cost of thousands of lives. The nightmare of this experience was to haunt those who participated for the rest of their lives. Georges made no mention of the battle of Passchendaele in his letter home afterwards, but almost fifty years later, in a speech to mark the fiftieth anniversary of the 22nd, he described it as the battle that weighed on his memory more than any other of the war.

Back home in Canada, the talk of possible conscription grew. Recruits for the front continued to dwindle, and the government introduced a nation-wide inventory of the male population called the National Service. Prime Minister Sir Robert Borden had visited Canadian troops in England earlier in the year and returned to Canada in May determined to introduce conscription. In July, the Military Service Act came into being. Borden proposed a coalition government composed of Liberals and Conservatives, but Sir Wilfred Laurier, opposed to conscription, refused. Some of the Liberals crossed the floor, and the Union government was formed. In the months leading up to the December election, conscription became the main issue, and a battle raged in Quebec along the ethnic lines of French versus English. For the first time in Canadian history, certain women were allowed to vote – those in the employment of the armed forces and those who, like Margaret Vanier, had relatives at the front. The Unionists under Borden won an overwhelming victory. Georges made scant mention in his letters of this election, and it could be that his family kept from him such morale-defeating details as those of the conscription controversy.

Everything significant that happened to him made the Montreal papers, which continued to show pride in the exploits of the 22nd. Early in 1918, a glossy four-page insert in one of those newspapers featured photographs under the caption "Young Canadians Who Are Doing Their Bit." One of the photographs was of a hatless Major Georges Vanier, looking idealistic and grave, "who was decorated with the Military Cross in 1915 and last year was made a Chevalier de la Legion d'honneur." (On another page, under the caption "Flowers from Canada's Field of Fair Women," the publication showed pictures of four lovely young women. In one of the photographs, the so-called "flower" was swathed in tulle, delicately arranged to reveal a bare shoulder. The camera had caught, under a mass of dark hair, a hint of seduction in her eyes. The young woman was identified as Miss Pauline Archer of Sherbrooke Street.)[7]

The first two months of 1918 were relatively quiet, and Georges spent a February leave in Paris and the south of France, visiting places he had seen with his father six years earlier and attending films and theatre productions. In typical fashion, he pronounced judgement on the opera *Mignon* in a letter to his mother: "The roles of Mignon and of Philine were very well sung and that of Meister very badly (I hear Eva saying 'What does *he* know about singing and how does *he* know Meister sang badly?')" Clearly at least one of his siblings had already noted that scanty knowledge of a subject did not deter him from making confident pronouncements on it; perhaps Eva had received too much big-brotherly advice in the past. He continued picking apart the performance of the hapless singer, with cheerful disregard for his sister's possible scorn: "If I were wealthy I'd settle him down in the butcher business. He should be able to fell an ox, if not with an axe, certainly with his voice." The Riviera's warmth did him good, he told his mother, and he concluded the letter: "I will go back to my work with a reserve of energy and of buoyant spirits."[8]

On 6 March, the sunshine and leisure behind him, he returned to the damp, cold barrenness of the north of France and rejoined his battalion near Arras. Almost immediately they marched farther north to their billets in Auchel, a dreary coal mining town northwest of Lens. A week later, on 14 March, he made a grim entry in his diary. He had already suffered through many of the war's horrors but as adjutant, he had that afternoon officially informed a deserter that a court martial had found him guilty and had sentenced him to death. He noted that the man, Arthur Degassé, received the message calmly. "I have been told to take charge of the troops that will be present at the execution tomorrow morning," Georges wrote, concluding his terse diary entry with the words, "Sad task, sad command."[9]

Executions of soldiers were an uneasy reality that the general Canadian public back home knew nothing about. The harsh "ultimate penalty," as it was known, existed under the authority of the British Army Act, which had established certain criminal offences as punishable by death. These offences included not only obvious crimes such as murder and treason but also acts of desertion and cowardice in the face of enemy fire. If a court martial found a defendant guilty and recommended the death penalty (an unusual occurrence), the sentence in each case was reviewed at every level in the chain of authority, from the man's commanding officer up to the commander-in-chief of the Allied forces, Sir Douglas Haig. If the sentence was not accepted at one of the levels, it was commuted, a situation that occurred in ninety per cent of the cases. For the few who were executed, most had been charged with desertion and cowardice rather than the more serious offences.

When the death penalty was carried out, the purpose was not punishment for the condemned soldier as much as it was a warning to those still in the trenches: *if you run away from the front line, you risk meeting your death in shame at the hands of your own comrades.* (Ironically, the bitterly sarcastic phrase that Voltaire had coined in his play *Candide* and that has come to symbolize this policy, *"pour encourager les autres,"* referred to the case of John Byng, a great-great-uncle of Sir Julian Byng, an eighteenth-century British admiral who was executed on a flimsy charge.) As casualties had mounted over the months and years of the war, those in high command worried that increasing numbers might lose courage and refuse to go into the front line; the appearance of leniency was thought to encourage this risk. Some officers recognized the symptoms of shell shock for what they were and sent the afflicted soldiers for rest and treatment so that they could be rehabilitated and sent back to the trenches in fighting form. But everyone's highest priority was to win the war, and victory depended on military discipline.

Problems with military discipline had dogged the 22nd battalion since its inception. The battle of Courcelette, at the end of the Somme conflict of 1916, had been a turning point for the 22nd in more ways than one: while they were honoured in Quebec for their courage and perseverance in capturing the town, the troops had been horribly depleted through deaths and

injuries and those who survived had returned exhausted and frightened. Disillusionment had begun to undermine morale. The new replacements brought
in from the camps in England toward the end of 1916 were ill-prepared,
with insufficient training behind them and with a lax sense of discipline.
Threats did little to deter them from deserting.

Thomas Tremblay, the thirty-one-year-old commanding officer of the
22nd, one of the youngest commanding officers among the Allies and one
of the few soldiers trained prior to the war, had taken ill at the end of 1916,
and when he returned in February 1917 he was shocked to see how many
of the men had gone absent without leave. As a commanding officer he felt
a double obligation not only to secure the reputation of his battalion, which
was already gaining legendary status, but also to display the valour of French-
speaking Canadians. He immediately began recommending the death penalty
for deserters from the 22nd battalion. One man was shot by firing squad in
April 1917, and two more on the same day in July. In a memo of 12 July
1917, chilling in its starkness and clarity, Tremblay recommended the death
penalty for yet another unhappy deserter and explained his reason for this
new severity: "The crime of absence without leave was very prevalent in my
Battalion until 2 [sic] men were shot a short time ago. The prevalence of this
crime was due principally to the extraordinary leniency of the previous Courts
Martial, especially at the end of last year and during the first 2 or 3 months
of this year. Conditions in the Battalion are much better now with respect
to absences without leave, since the two men were shot ... I recommend, in
order to stop altogether absences without leave in my Battalion, that the
extreme penalty be carried out and that the execution be public."[10]

Arthur Degassé, the man visited by Georges Vanier in the makeshift prison
cell near the town of Auchel on 14 March 1918, likely knew that his number was up even before the awful news was delivered to him. Degassé (whose
name has also been variously spelled Degasse and Dagesse) was thirty-one
years old. He had enlisted in Valcartier, Quebec, in September of 1914, giving "Cook" as his trade. His birthplace was New Bedford, Massachusetts,
and on his attestation paper he named his mother, a resident of Montreal,
as his next of kin. He had sailed for England with the 1st division of the
Canadian Expeditionary Force in October 1914 and been placed as a cook
in Southampton's No. 1 Canadian General Hospital.

In March 1915, Degassé began a pattern of absences without leave for
which he not only forfeited pay but also spent some time in detention.
On at least one of these occasions he was drunk when he was caught. In

September 1915, he received permission to marry a woman who lived in Wimbledon, near London, and at some point they had a child. Less than a month after his wedding, he was admitted to hospital with a venereal disease. Such diseases, which some soldiers were said to have contracted deliberately as a means of avoiding the trenches and the front line, were considered not only an illness but also an indication of bad morals and poor discipline. A soldier diagnosed with VD was isolated as if he were a leper and treated with stern disapproval. The cure was almost as bad as the disease, consisting of an arsenical compound that caused side effects such as violent cramps and vomiting.

Degassé's sorry conduct continued throughout the next year – absence without leave, then agonizing treatment for venereal disease, then the same sequence over again. In October 1916 he was transferred to the 22nd and sent to France, where the battalion was in the last ferocious throes of the Somme battle. It is unclear whether he spent any time at the front line, and indeed the question may have been raised as to whether he was ultimately more of a hindrance than a help to the army. In December, and again the following March – in the midst of massive preparation for the assault on Vimy Ridge – he went absent without leave. Each time, after being caught, he spent nearly a month in detention.

Released from detention in early April 1917, he absented himself again but was caught in Paris on 29 April. On 8 May he escaped while awaiting trial and managed to elude arrest for nearly six months (during which time his wife, probably unaware of his escapades, sent a letter to headquarters asking that he be granted leave, as it had been a long time since he had had one). On 4 October he was finally captured in Paris, wearing the uniform of the Royal Army Medical Corps. (The discovery of a soldier out of his own uniform was typically seen as concrete evidence of his intention to desert.) Adjutant Georges Vanier noted in a memo that Arthur Degassé was under arrest and awaiting court martial. The court martial was held on 26 February 1918. Degassé was convicted and the sentence of death was confirmed, first by Tremblay and then up the line of command by Arthur Currie, the commander of the Canadian Corps, and finally, on 10 March, by Sir Douglas Haig.

After completing his unwelcome duty in announcing to Degassé that he was to be executed the next day, Georges left him in his grimy prison cell in the company of the chaplain, Father Rosaire Crochetière, a native of Nicolet, north of Montreal, who was much loved in the battalion for his gentleness of spirit. Chaplains were never more welcome than when a soldier faced the threat of death. We do not know what transpired between these two on the night of 14 March, but a chaplain was allowed to spend the whole night before an execution in the condemned man's cell, and it is likely that Father Crochetière did so.

The next morning, 15 March, Georges rose at five o'clock while it was still dark. On the square in front of the heavy stone Norman church in the centre of the town, the "public" demanded by Tremblay assembled: a platoon from each company in the battalion, plus men from company headquarters and prisoners under guard, over two hundred in all. They lined up in silence and Georges led them in the march to the execution site.

The firing squad consisted of ten men from the 22nd. One of the rifles had been fitted with a blank round so that each man might hope he had been spared the unsettling task of shooting a comrade. They formed two ranks and faced away from the target, the front rank kneeling and the rear rank standing. Then, blindfolded and guided by two guards, Degassé appeared, a short and stocky figure at five foot three and one hundred and sixty-five pounds, his hands cuffed behind his back. He was led to a chair that had been fixed to the ground. A thick rope bound his legs and another fixed his shoulders to the back of the chair. A medical officer pinned a white marker to his uniform, marking the location of his heart. Father Crochetière stood beside him and the two prayed together. The chaplain then moved quietly away. The men from the 22nd who had marched the distance to the execution stood at attention in straight lines. Georges heard Degassé's last words, "*Chapelain, Chapelain.*" The officer in charge of the firing squad gave a signal to the ten men, and they turned to face the prisoner. At another signal, they raised their rifles. At a third signal, they fired, the shots sounding sharp and clear in the early morning air. Then there was silence. Degassé slumped against the rope, his head dropping heavily to his chest. The medical officer came forward and declared him dead. Everyone present filed past the body as the blood spread across the front of his uniform. The time was noted as six thirty-seven am.

Nothing more is known about the last hours of Arthur Degassé. Chaplains who assisted condemned soldiers have noted that often the bravery that wilted on the battleground somehow emerged in the form of a quiet dignity as they went to their ignominious death. The final written comment from Georges on the death of Arthur Degassé was a brief diary entry two days later, on Sunday, 17 March. At Mass, he noted, Father Crochetière (who himself was to die from a bursting shell in less than three weeks) had read a moving farewell letter from Degassé. The man who had failed as a soldier proved capable, in the end, of eloquence and courage in facing his death.

Anecdotal reports from members of the 22nd in subsequent years suggest that Georges continued to be haunted by this experience, and given the sensitivity of his temperament, this is not surprising. Out of twenty courts martial that handed down the death penalty to recalcitrant members of the 22nd, only five were carried out, but even this small number exceeded the numbers of executions from other Canadian battalions.

* * *

The Allied cause had been given a boost when the United States joined the war, but heavy fighting continued, amid which Georges celebrated his thirtieth birthday. He remained optimistic that the conflict would soon be over. In the early summer of 1918, a rumour reached Montreal that Georges had been killed, and Eva received a letter of sympathy from one of his friends in England. "As a civilian I always admired him *so* much as a gentlemanly, scholarly young man, and who could but help admiring his splendid spirit in putting his career (for the present) in the background and in spite of his poor health, offering his services to do what he could to beat off the common enemy," the friend wrote. "You have no idea how he was thought of in his battalion, always kind, just, fair."[11] In a flurry of anxiety, the family chased down whatever official channels they could. After an agonizing month during which they continued to receive letters from the supposedly dead Georges, they were officially informed that the rumours were false. Upsetting news, however, was soon to come.

Georges did not indicate in his letters home the gravity of the situation as the spring of 1918 turned to a summer of renewed ferocity from the German side. Reinforcements had arrived from the eastern front, and the Germans launched furious surprise attacks, moving dangerously close to Paris and the coast. The Canadian divisions were ordered to charge the Hindenburg Line, the Germans' main line of defence, in a counterattack. They marched in stealth, night after night, south toward the line near the city of Amiens. Georges noted in his diary the sight of the spire of the city's great medieval cathedral against the setting sun. The summer heat was oppressive and the general feeling of uncertainty intense, but when night fell and they were on the move again, he revelled in the moonlight marches.

On 8 August, the 22nd was ordered to take some villages. Several days later, Tremblay cited Georges Vanier's fearless leadership and bravery in the successful capture. German strength had waned, and the Canadians were able to advance more than the Allied forces had for the four previous years. The feeling of gaining so much ground was exhilarating, and although the fighting remained fierce and good friends were dying, they could taste victory. Georges wrote to his mother, "I have seen some of my comrades fall beside me and I have had so many narrow escapes myself that I am beginning to think that one should not worry much about possible eventualities."[12]

On the morning of Monday 26 August, the Canadian Corps woke to a drizzling rain and prepared to attack at three am. They advanced through the wooded plain south of Arras, over shell holes and broken down trenches, toward the road leading southward toward Cambrai. By noon, the day's objective had been met and prisoners rounded up. Georges had been unsure of his role in the day's fight and was told only at one am, when he rose, that he would be a liaison officer with another unit. The day's work over, he bolted down some "bully beef," the soldier's staple, that he found in an abandoned trench. The next objective, he was told, was the capture of Cagnicourt, a village beyond the Arras-Cambrai road.

The following day, 27 August, the fighting began at four thirty am in pouring rain. Sleep had been almost impossible for several days, and the Canadians were near the end of their endurance. The church steeple of the village of Chérisy rose in the grey distance, and it was toward this village that the 22nd advanced. They had just reached the narrow Sensée River on the eastern outskirts of Chérisy when the major in charge of the 22nd was blinded in one eye by a bullet, and no sooner had they crossed the river and gained the ground on the other side than the next in command was also wounded. It was late afternoon, and Georges was now in charge of the 22nd. Further fighting was impossible: the losses had been enormous and they had encountered uncut barbed wire that hampered their advance. The odds were overwhelming against the men of the 22nd and those of the 24th, alongside whom they had been fighting. Georges spent the evening planning the next day's attack with Lieutenant Colonel William Kennedy, who was commanding the 24th.

The next morning they received orders to attack shortly after noon. The plan was for the 22nd and 24th to continue pushing north and east, past the Arras-Cambrai road, and take the village of Haucourt. The two officers surveyed their miserable, depleted troops: filthy, sleep-deprived, done in by day after day of deadly struggle. They examined the pockmarked territory ahead of them. The barbed wire still remained, through which they would have to fight their way. Kennedy looked over at Georges, his face expressionless. "I think the attack ought to go very well," he said. (Kennedy was later to receive the Victoria Cross for continuing to fight while wounded.) At twelve thirty pm the signal was given, and their attack began. Georges led his battalion, and almost immediately received a bullet in his right side. As a stretcher-bearer was dressing the wound, a shell burst beside them, killing the stretcher-bearer and shattering Georges's legs. "This was to be one of my bad days," he wrote to his mother some time later.[13]

It was worse than bad. It was the end of Georges Vanier's war. The date was 28 August, a day that would have significance for the rest of his life. In seventy-four days the Great War would end. Others were to return home and write about torn limbs and headless bodies and numbing exhaustion and the frightened eyes of enemy soldiers whom they recognized as human beings like themselves. Georges had seen it all too. As the war had continued to claim young men by the thousands, commanders in the field often seriously questioned the strategies and tactics of the high command, and he may have questioned them himself. Yet there is no written evidence of such criticism from him. In fact, when the conflict was all over and others turned their backs on the army, he would eagerly choose it once again. Perhaps the extremity of his situation for three years – the stripping down to bare essentials, the primitive trench life, the daily fear – brought him a clarity, a sense of purpose that on a deep level he knew he could not have achieved in any other way.

Mystery and paradox lie at the heart of every human life, and perhaps this is the only answer to why Georges Vanier, a man of peace and poetry and contemplation, was to continue embracing the military life.

4

"UNFIT FOR SERVICE"

War is full of grim irony. In the case of Georges Vanier, the irony was that the wound he received in the thick of the battlefield was relatively minor, the revolver strapped to his side preventing the bullet from entering his abdomen, whereas the wound he received in the relative safety of the medical sidelines changed him permanently.

The Vanier family on Dorchester Street in Montreal received the news from Tremblay by telegram ten days later: GEORGE WOUNDED LEGS HOSPITAL DOING WELL. The basic facts were all there, and the details, more or less, would be filled in as the weeks progressed. The same day, 6 September 1918, Georges himself wrote home from the British Red Cross Hospital in Boulogne. His letter gave the family a superficial overview of his final battle and assured them that "My present state is more than satisfactory – temperature and pulse normal, sleep coming back to me etc ... I am really making rapid strides to complete recovery. Remember there is NO CAUSE FOR WORRY."[1]

In fact, his right leg had been amputated above the knee the day before, and contrary to the assurances he made to his family, his "present state" was far from satisfactory. On the same day that he wrote this letter, he noted in his diary that he was unable to sleep in spite of the morphine he had been given. The heat and pain were intolerable. Day after day, his diary entries consisted of one-word exclamations and sentence fragments, terse and distress-laden. Although he never wrote about it directly, one can decipher between the lines his grief at the loss of a limb after three nearly unbroken years of activity, danger, and life-and-death responsibility. Physical agony had become his only companion, replacing the heady, adventure-filled rush to combat that had filled his life and given it meaning.

Four days after the amputation, he suffered a massive hemorrhage. A blood donor was rushed to the next bed and a tube connected the two men. Almost immediately, Georges's temperature and pulse returned to normal. His letter home to his mother and his private diary entry that same day are polar opposites. To his mother he wrote, "My normal sleep is returning very quickly."[2] But to his diary, "A long night of insomnia. God! The nights are long!"[3] His cheerful letters home continued almost daily ("My condition continues to be most satisfactory ... In a month I shall be as fit as a fiddle"[4]), speaking only generally of "wounds." It was not until the 18th of September that he broke the full news in a cablegram: "General health excellent right leg amputated above knee fortnight ago."[5]

The following week his general condition was deemed stable enough for him to travel to England for the next phase of his recovery, and he caught a last glimpse of the French coast as the boat carried him across the English Channel. He was taken to the Third London General Hospital in Wandsworth, London. "The loss of the leg does not affect me in the least,"[6] he wrote rather over-confidently the next day. The fact was, as he admitted to his mother a few weeks later, he was not even able to walk with crutches at this time because the injuries to his remaining leg had left it too weak to support his weight.

His strength was returning, however, and he had the mental stamina to spend much of his time reading books and making brief comments in his diary about them (*With the Turks in Palestine* by Alexander Aronsohn: "A pitiful picture of the condition of the Jews in Palestine." *A Royal Tragedy*, the story of the assassination of the king and queen of Serbia: "What struck me most was the hypocritical and criminal politics of the Russian factions and the horrible cruelty the Balkan officers were capable of." *Literary Lapses* by Stephen Leacock: "Very amusing. A little ludicrous in some places.") He also resorted to his old whimsy when describing to Frances a new occupation he had acquired: "They have put me in a sort of summer-house outside the regular ward and when I woke this morning I found four spiders industriously spinning beautiful, regular webs outside my four windows."[7] The letter did not mention that he still could not lift himself up without help.

But he was able to give his family good news in early October: he had been awarded a bar to his Military Cross and also the Distinguished Service Order. With typical modesty, he did not repeat the statements made by Tremblay and others in recommending these honours. Tremblay had written that in the battle of 9 August, "the leading companies found themselves confronted with very serious opposition, and it was largely due to his leadership and magnificent courage that the enemy was overcome and the objective reached." A statement from another officer noted Georges Vanier's "fearlessness and determination" and his "qualities of great bravery."[8] In an equally moving vein, Margaret Vanier received a letter from a family acquaintance who wrote, "I have spoken to a few of his battalion and they all speak well of him; they say he was strict but he was loved."[9]

In early November, he was moved to a Canadian hospital run by the Imperial Order of Daughters of the Empire (IODE) in Hyde Park Place, London. By now it was clear that the war was nearly over. The German Kaiser had abdicated, and the conditions for an armistice had been laid out. Georges noted with gratitude the kindness and attention that Tremblay had bestowed on him, but admitted that he regretted his inability to "carry on with him in France until the victorious end."[10]

There were still further troubles of his own, however: his amputation had taken place in haste in order to save his life, and the bone still protruded, with insufficient flesh to fold over into a clean stump. A medical examination determined that a further operation was necessary to cut off a piece of the bone so as to smooth out the stump. This surgery took place on the early morning of 11 November. As he was coming out of the anaesthetic, he heard the sound of cannons booming in celebration of the armistice. Omitting any mention of his second surgery, he noted in his letter home the next day that London had gone wild with excitement. The streets were packed with celebrating citizens, King George V and Queen Mary appeared on the balcony of Buckingham Palace to deafening cheers, and in the general revelry, the statue of Nelson at Trafalgar Square was damaged.

As for the Canadian officer whose second amputation had coincided with the end of the war, he lay in his hospital bed on 11 November 1918 in a state of groggy happiness and pride mingled with pain and disappointment at his inability to taste the victory on the battlefield. His medical record describes in cold, clinical language the physical fallout from his contribution to the glorious victory: "Amputation of right leg at a point 12 inches from the great trochanter of the femur, giving a stump of 9 ½ inches long. Stump conical in shape."[11]

* * *

The year 1919 dawned, and with it – now that the guns had fallen silent and the armistice celebrations had given way to sober post-war reality – the question of future prospects. By now the muscles in Georges's left leg had become sufficiently strong for him to walk for short periods on crutches.

In January, he was fitted with a "peg leg": a round wooden stick attached to an iron bar that fastened to a girdle-like garment held in place by shoulder straps. He was moved to a hotel that had become a rehabilitation hospital in Buxton, Derbyshire, for the necessary therapy in preparation for his permanent artificial leg. The attending nurses at this hospital were graduates of the Winnipeg General Hospital School of Nursing. With characteristic cheerfulness, he wrote that he could "hobble fairly well"[12] on the peg leg, and he regaled his family with details of his daily routine of massages, rowing, and bag-punching for muscle development, and his lessons in walking with his new prosthesis ("I am put through such antics as walking on a narrow strip of wood, walking backwards and sideways upstairs, downstairs and in every imaginable fashion").[13]

But the peg leg was not satisfactory, and he hated the English winter, with its depressing grey skies and bone-chilling dampness. Lack of central heating meant that coal was a precious commodity and, making light of his discomfort as usual, he joked about the lengths to which he and his roommate, Captain J.P. Cathcart, went in obtaining heat for their room. "Recently a new orderly came on duty, and Captain Cathcart and myself decided that we must have a confidential talk with this important personage. We called him in and informed him that his two most important duties in the hospital were firstly to see that a fire was at all times blazing in Room 23 (ours) and secondly that the coal box in Room 23 must be filled at all times to overflowing ... The result has been miraculous. The rest of the hospital patients are allowed to freeze (more or less) but Room 23 sometimes presents the aspect of a Turkish bath."[14]

Future employment prospects also entered his narrow world of invalidism and rehabilitation. Having done nothing to solicit attention except for his outstanding skill and leadership on the battlefield, Georges had become known to no less a figure than Canada's prime minister, Sir Robert Borden. Borden now approved a request from Canada's commissioner in Paris, Philippe Roy, that Georges be invited to fill the position of secretary on his staff. "I hope you will convey to Major Vanier my congratulations upon his fine service and my deep regret that his injury was so serious as to necessitate the amputation of one leg,"[15] the prime minister wrote.

Georges was torn; the offer was obviously attractive; as he wrote to his parents, "the year 1919 in Paris will be full of momentous events, really unprecedented in the history of the world and I would get in touch with men of mark and of ability."[16] But there were also drawbacks: he longed

to return to Canada, and it was possible that he was emotionally unpre-
pared to take the next step in his career. So he accepted Roy's offer with
stiff conditions, including a generous salary (he asked for five thousand
dollars a year, more than twice the amount the previous secretary had been
paid) and short duration (the appointment was to be temporary).

He told his parents he was indifferent to the outcome. He did not add,
but could not have been unaware, that while he awaited Roy's response, he
stood at the crossroads of his future. The answer came at the end of February: with regret, Roy was unable to accept Georges's conditions. If Georges
had second thoughts about softening his conditions and making a counter-
offer, or if he felt pangs of regret that he would not be part of the historic
Paris Peace Conference, such sentiments have not survived in his letters or
diary. All that is recorded in the spring of 1919 is his anticipation of returning to Canada and such weighty domestic questions as which bedroom he
would like in the house on Dorchester Street. "I am quite satisfied with my
old room filled with books and it will seem like returning to old friends
when I see them all smiling down on me,"[17] he wrote at the end of March.

But there were still two other matters to settle. The previous September,
while recuperating from his wound, he had received notification that although he had been promoted to the rank of major in 1916, it had been,
in the obscure wisdom of the army, as an "Acting Major," with "the apparent rank and pay of a Major but the substantive rank of a Captain."[18] His
permanent withdrawal from fighting meant that his pay had reverted to
that of a captain. This mindless bureaucracy rankled, and with Tremblay's
support he protested both the illogic and the injustice of it.

The other matter related to his artificial leg. He had been informed that
Canadian soldier amputees would have their new limbs fitted in Canada.
This meant returning home on crutches. Georges explained to his mother
that English fitters of prostheses had greater experience, because of war casualties, than their Canadian counterparts, and he asked to be fitted in England.
Besides, he wrote, "it will give me great personal satisfaction to be quite
crutchless before I reach Montreal."[19]

In mid-April he received good news on both counts: his rank had been
changed from acting major to major retroactive to August 1918 and his pay
had been adjusted accordingly, and in addition, he received permission to
remain in England to be fitted with his new leg. He moved to the Perkins Bull
Hospital in Putney, where he had spent weeks of recuperation three years

earlier. Here, in the welcoming atmosphere created by the Perkins Bull family, he spent his thirty-first birthday. His spirits rose considerably. He sent home a cartoon postcard featuring a woman and a young military dolt with one arm in a sling and the other leaning on a cane. "Is there a soldier here with one leg named Smith?" asks the woman. "Dunno, Mum," replies the soldier. "What's the name of his other leg?" This hoary exchange was to be the first of many man-with-one-leg jokes that Georges was to collect and use to regale increasingly large audiences for the rest of his life.

Throughout the spring, his own pressing concerns now settled, he followed Canadian and world affairs closely. He noted the death of Sir Wilfred Laurier, who, because he had opposed conscription, had lived his final years in an atmosphere of unpopularity and even hostility. Georges wrote to his mother that obituaries in the British newspapers had been cool because "they cannot forgive him for his attitude during the war. Without a doubt he will rank among the ten or twelve greatest Canadians."[20] More personally, he received with sadness the news of his old French tutor Camille Martin's death. Commenting on world events, he noted that the war that had so recently finished was just the beginning of trouble for Europe, and that the revolution in Russia had been inevitable: "I don't defend Russian Bolshevism – far from it," he wrote to his father, "but I do realize that violent reaction necessarily follows an autocratic regime where people are kept in ignorance of their rights and responsibilities." He added, "I agree completely with your pessimistic outlook on the question of Europe and even the whole world."[21]

On 10 May 1919, the 22nd battalion sailed for Canada. Georges had hoped to be on board with them, but being fitted with the new leg meant that he had to stay in England. In Montreal, the *Illustrated Supplement* republished the same photo that it had proudly displayed four years earlier, of the 22nd battalion arrayed in lines on the barrack grounds as they prepared to go overseas to fight in the European war. The publication noted the grim fact that only a handful of the men standing at attention in the photo would be returning. (The battalion disbanded on 19 May, three days after its arrival back in Canada.)

The ship transporting the 22nd battalion also carried a trunk that contained Georges's torn, blood-stained army tunic and the boots that had been taken from his feet after he was wounded. They were boots that had been bought for him by his mother at Dangerfield's store in Montreal. Still clinging to them was the mud from the field near the village of Chérisy where his final battle had been fought. That date – the last on which his two feet had trod the ground, 28 August 1918 – had already become sacred to him, and its meaning would deepen as the years progressed.

It was a matter of weeks before Georges himself would be returning home, and he began to prepare his family. Up to this point he had given a rosy picture of his state of health and had joked about his disability; he had even written in February that the physical therapy had "put me *on my feet again* (unfortunate metaphor!)."[22] Now he had to prepare them for the distress of seeing a pale, underweight invalid. "I need not tell you that after the shock of losing a leg and the consequent inaction I *am not* in good condition,"[23] he wrote to his mother on 13 May. He had left Canada weighing one hundred and seventy pounds. By early 1918 he had gained thirty pounds, but because of the heavy activity of that year, he had lost most of it. Now his frame of six feet and one-half inch carried only one hundred and fifty pounds, notwithstanding the loss of a leg. "I *do not* look well, so expect to be disappointed in my appearance,"[24] he repeated a week later.

On 15 May he was fitted with his artificial limb, and two months later, on 14 July, he stood on two legs at Buckingham Palace to receive from King George V the bar to the Military Cross and the Distinguished Service Order. The king, he wrote, "was very considerate to me, wishing me not to stand and questioning me at length about the condition of my stump and the comfort of my artificial leg."[25]

Four days later, on 18 July, he boarded the *S.S. Minerva*, waved goodbye to the English coast, and set his face homeward. His medical report indicated that the prosthesis was not yet comfortable; it was too heavy, the pressure was too great on the stump, and the limb could be worn for only short periods. The report concluded, however, that he was a "well built, well nourished male of good colour,"[26] and it is likely that pain and discomfort were disregarded as he walked off the ship, upright and proud, keeping his limp as slight as possible, back on Canadian land.

At home, he found the family changed. Eva was now a "little matron" with two small children. Anthony had become a serious-minded young man embarking on law studies, and Frances – whom George still thought of as "Goo"– had grown into a beautiful teenager, "with a row of pearls for teeth."[27]

Now that he had returned home to his family, there was no need for letters, and so no written record exists of the weeks following Georges's return to Canada from the Great War. From England he had given precise – one might say almost military – instructions regarding his return: "I do not intend to remain more than a few days in Montreal after which I mean to go to Magog to recuperate."[28] This is no doubt what happened. The hero whose welfare had been the family's anxious concern for four years spent the remaining summer weeks in idyllic repose at the cottage with the long veranda on the shores of Lake Memphramagog. The malady afflicting battle-worn soldiers was still decades away from having the designation of "post-traumatic stress disorder," but one must still wonder: were there nightmares? Cold sweats? Bouts of depression? Recurring images of mutilated comrades and joyless spectres of bayonets thrust into the youthful bodies of enemy soldiers? As with many other personal matters in Georges Vanier's life, if such terrors recurred they remained private, and only tiny snippets of memory are recorded to suggest that the war continued to haunt him.

When the fall came and the family returned to Montreal, the question of his future yawned before him. His battalion no longer existed, and although a confidential report had indicated that he was "an officer of the highest order in every respect,"[29] the final word on his service record was a rubber-stamped notation: "Unfit for Service. Category B."[30] There had been some talk that the 22nd battalion might be reorganized as a permanent regiment, and Georges expressed his interest in continuing to serve with it to Sir Arthur Currie, who had become inspector general of the Canadian forces. In a letter several decades later, he recalled his exchange with Currie: "He laughed – nicely – but he laughed. He said, 'You have lost a leg.' I said, 'I know that, but don't you want a few officers with brains as well as legs?' What he really liked, I think, was my modesty."[31] The story may be somewhat exaggerated, because in the last week of September he received an admiring letter from Currie who wrote, "I appreciate fully your qualifications as an officer, and I give you this assurance that if the 22nd Battalion is constituted as a permanent regiment that you will not be overlooked. In fact there may be some other place in the militia organization of Canada where your great services can be recognized and your ability made use of."[32]

As it turned out, in early 1920, the permanent 22nd Regiment was formed and Georges found himself back in uniform at the regiment's new home, the Citadel in Quebec City, as second in command (the following year the regiment was to have the title "Royal" attached to it in recognition of its action in battle). But in the meantime, he resumed without enthusiasm the practice of law. After four years of excitement and action, office work proved tedious and uninspiring. Life was soon to become more interesting, however, in an unexpected way.

The next event that would profoundly change Georges's life took place towards the middle of September, 1920. He was having tea at Montreal's Ritz Hotel when suddenly his former superior from the 22nd battalion, Thomas Tremblay, stood before him. Accompanying Tremblay was a tall, slender young woman with dark hair swept up around her face. She held herself with the cool grace and elegance of a Gallic princess, and yet her smile radiated friendliness and warmth. Tremblay introduced her as Pauline Archer. She was twenty-one years old. The one-legged soldier who had returned from the war convinced he would remain a bachelor was transfixed.

5

AN UNLIKELY ROMANCE

Unlike Georges Vanier, Pauline Archer had grown up in a perfectly bilingual household, speaking French to her mother and English to her father. In Montreal society, the Archers occupied a place that was, if not on a higher level, at least in a different league from that of the Vaniers. Pauline's father, Charles Archer, unlike the uneducated, nouveau riche Philias Vanier, had studied law at Laval University, winning the Tessier Gold Medal for general proficiency, and had risen to become a judge of the Quebec Superior Court. Charles Archer belonged to a Quebec City family that had prospered in the coal and construction businesses. His grandfather had come to Canada from Brixham, Devonshire, in 1833. His father married a French-Canadian woman and converted to Catholicism, and thus Charles found himself an oddity in Quebec: a Catholic who was neither Irish nor fully French.

Pauline's mother, Thérèse de Salaberry, counted among her ancestors Charles-Michel d'Irumberry de Salaberry, who had distinguished himself by commanding the Canadian troops at the battle of Châteauguay in the war of 1812 against the United States. The de Salaberry family had come to Canada in the eighteenth century, and in the pre-Confederation custom of property-holding, established themselves as seigneurs. At the age of three, Thérèse lost her mother to tuberculosis, and when she was nine her father died. For the remainder of her childhood she was brought up in the Pensionnat d'Hochalaga, a convent school in Montreal. Here, as a lonely orphan with a nervous temperament and fragile health, she came under the spiritual influence of a kindly middle-aged Jesuit priest by the name of Almire Pichon, who had come to Montreal as a retreat preacher from France several years earlier, and who was to have a profound influence on her life. Thérèse eventually went to live with an aunt in Kamouraska, on the south shore of the St Lawrence River, where she met and married Charles Archer. Shortly after Pauline was born, on 28 March 1898, they settled comfortably into a large sandstone house on fashionable Sherbrooke Street in Montreal.

Pauline grew from babyhood to childhood as coddled and protected as a little princess, with a prettily appointed nursery and a large array of toys. A nanny and a succession of maids waited on her. At the age of eight she began school at the Convent of the Sacred Heart, and the school's records show that almost immediately she began winning pink ribbons, the prizes given to children in the lower grades. She was confirmed in the Catholic Church at the age of ten, and six weeks later received first communion. Then, shortly after her eleventh birthday in April of 1909, she left the convent school. She had attended the classes there for only two and a half years, and this was the end of Pauline Archer's formal schooling.

It is unclear why she withdrew from the school so abruptly. In later recollections, she spoke of having outgrown her strength due to a growth spurt. She had nearly reached her adult height of five feet ten inches by her early teens, and it could be that with hormonal changes, an excitable, nervous temperament was beginning to manifest itself and the normal give-and-take of the school atmosphere demanded more energy than her constitution could handle.

A classroom was set up for her in the Archer home and governesses were hired in an attempt to complete her education. The school notebooks from her early teenage years record a daily schedule that included French, English, and Italian lessons as well as piano and singing practice. The local parish priest, Georges Gauthier (later to become auxiliary bishop, and eventually, archbishop of Montreal), came regularly to the home to give her catechism lessons. He was to remain a family friend for the rest of his life. At some point in Pauline's mid-teens, a professor from McGill University, Germaine Grétrin, introduced her to literature. This exposure opened up new worlds for her, causing some anxiety in the household (her protective mother hastily pinned pages together when the girl started reading Marcel Proust). Pauline's meagre education was to be a source of insecurity and lack of confidence for the rest of her life. But her intellectual capacity was considerable, and probably without realizing it, she drank in knowledge readily.

It was a lonely life for a girl who was maturing into a vivacious young woman. Her parents were aware of her need for friends, and there were skating parties and frequent outings with cousins. The days spent alone, however, led to the introspection revealed in her diaries, which began in January 1914 ("I am 15 years and 9 months"). Her attraction to religion was intense and emotional: "Tomorrow I'm going to receive my dear Jesus," she wrote in fervent anticipation of Sunday Mass and communion, and then the next day, "How good God is ... what a beautiful communion I made this morning. Thank you, my dear Jesus. I love You – that is the only thing I can say to You." Still only fifteen, she worried about her future, and then chided herself for being worried. "Why am I tormenting myself? I'm so silly. Oh, God, hold me, I'm feeling so weak! My soul feels empty and I need You."[1]

The gushing tone of these teenaged diaries is reminiscent of that of a young Carmelite nun who had died at the age of twenty-four in 1897 in the French town of Lisieux. The nun's name was Soeur Thérèse; she was canonized in 1925 and, known as the "Little Flower," she would eventually become one of the most popular saints in the Catholic Church. In fact, there was a direct link between the adolescent Pauline and the French nun. Almire Pichon, the Jesuit priest who had taken Pauline's mother under his wing, had also nurtured Soeur Thérèse's spiritual development and that of her family before being posted to Montreal. His influence, however, went much deeper than sentimental language.

Père Pichon's approach to those whom he counselled was to regard God as someone who loved them. Known as "a way of the heart," this approach belonged to a spiritual stream that had always existed in Christianity, and had been particularly exemplified in the lives and writings of medieval mystics such as St John of the Cross and Julian of Norwich. It emphasized the goodness of creation, and offered a spiritual path that was marked by simplicity, trust, and confidence in God. Such an attitude contrasted sharply with the spirit of Jansenism, which had infiltrated much of Quebec and which emphasized a corrupt human nature and the necessity for fear in the face of an angry God who threatened the eternal fires of hell.

Pauline's mother had also learned from Père Pichon the injunction to care for the poor. Although she was in frail health and suffered frequent migraine headaches, and also betrayed a lifelong streak of elitism (she loved high society and fancied herself to be descended from French nobility), Thérèse Archer nevertheless befriended a woman who lived with her young daughter in the slums of Montreal's lower town. Pauline often accompanied her and played with the child, becoming acquainted with a slice of life that had nothing in common with her own experiences.

How exactly did Pauline's father fit into this scenario? The de Salaberry-Archer marriage was a strange one. The two had little in common – Charles Archer was a brusque and robust man of the world: a man's man. He had a great love of sports (especially golf), little regard for literature or the arts, and scant interest in religion. His sense of fairness however, was such that when he was named a judge, he withdrew from the club he had frequented and gave up many of his friendships in the legal profession so as to maintain a professional impartiality. The couple had separate bedrooms – a fact that may explain Pauline's status as an only child. His desire to visit western Canada was thwarted on at least one occasion by his wife's claim that train travel gave her a headache. Ships were much more pleasant, she insisted, and besides, if they travelled to Europe she could visit Père Pichon, who had returned to France in 1907.

If Charles Archer felt that the elderly Jesuit intruded on their marriage, there is no record that he said so, and he seems to have taken his wife's spiritual zeal with a certain amount of equanimity. He took his family to Europe on two occasions, in 1911 and again in 1913. On both trips, his wife often pleaded a headache and stayed in her hotel room or attended Père Pichon's retreats, leaving her husband and daughter to sight-see together. Charles Archer had a down-to-earth manner and a droll sense of humour that offered some balance to his highly strung daughter, and it is likely thanks to him that Pauline's spiritual intensity and religious passion were tempered by a sense of the ridiculous and a ready inclination to laugh at herself, especially as she matured into adulthood.

Nonetheless, she fretted in her diaries about her place in the religious and spiritual scheme of things. When she was sixteen, Pauline began making an annual spiritual retreat at the convent of the Society of Marie Réparatrice. This order of nuns had been founded in France in the nineteenth century and had come to Montreal in 1910. The retreat house stood on Mount Royal Boulevard, a large structure surrounded by gardens and shrines. There, for five days every year, Pauline lived in a small, austere room with a narrow bed, a small desk, a hardback chair, and a washstand with a jug and basin. The whole time was spent in silence, and the daily program was not unlike the religious routine of the nuns themselves: Mass, meditation, way of the cross, and three instructions a day delivered by a Jesuit priest. The days were ordered along the lines of Jesuit retreats everywhere: retreatants were asked to consider creation, sin, the life of Jesus. There were exhortations to examine their lives, and in particular their faults. In her 1915 diary, seventeen-year-old Pauline explained to herself one method of doing this: "The particular examen is the examination of only one fault. That is to say, when you want to correct one fault in particular, you pay special attention to how many times in the day you commit that fault." Then she marked down in a list the number of times she had succumbed to vanity, presumably the fault she had chosen to concentrate on.

Part of the worry that consumed her was the question of whether or not she should become a nun. She liked the nuns of Marie Réparatrice and was attracted to their life of prayer and dedication as well as their pretty habit (a long white serge dress with a pale blue shift called a "scapular," a blue veil, and a regal white cloak which they wore in chapel). She was enthralled by the idea of giving herself entirely to a life of service. She fretted upon the question until one day, during her 1916 retreat, she approached the Mother Superior. After this meeting she wrote with obvious relief, "She thinks I should wait with patience for God's will to be made more clear and precise. She is so good, so kind, that it seems to me that whenever she speaks, it is truly the voice of God speaking."[2] The Mother Superior probably saw in front of her a girl who possessed not only a deep desire for prayer and a spirit generous enough to throw herself into a life of self-sacrifice, but also a fragile ego and an unrealistic view of the rigors of convent life. The wise nun's assurances gave her some peace of mind, but the idea remained. She continued her regimen of prayer, daily Mass and communion, and annual retreats at the convent of Marie-Réparatrice.

As she grew into her late teens, her statuesque beauty and vivacious personality drew admiration on all sides. Her father's position and her mother's tendency to social climb helped to make her one of the outstanding young women to emerge on Montreal's social scene during the World War I years. Parties and balls, outings and soirées, tea at the opulent Ritz Hotel and summers at country houses with endless games of tennis – such activities filled her days, while of course servants did all the work at home. The sculptor Alfred Laliberté chose her as the model for the woman symbolizing civilization on the Jacques Cartier monument in Montreal. She was invited to a ball at Rideau Hall in Ottawa during the duke of Devonshire's term as governor general, and she caught the eye of the elderly duke himself, who chose her as a dance partner.

While enjoying all these activities with the effervescence of youth, she was not blind to their essential shallowness, and in her diary she continued to upbraid herself for her vanity and for what she perceived as her imperfect temperament. At the age of twenty, finally beginning to consider a way of life for herself other than that of a nun but still unsure what to do with her desire to be of service, she wrote, "I think I'm beginning to understand what God wants from me. It seems to me that my place is in the world where I'll try to know and love God."[3]

In the meantime, she was not oblivious to the war raging in Europe that had drawn some of her male acquaintances and cousins to join up. The overall mood of Montreal was sombre, and the daily newspapers were full of stories about soldiers who were distinguishing themselves, as well as lists of those who had been wounded or killed. In later years she would remember a comment her father made in late 1914: he had heard a young lawyer by the name of Georges Vanier argue his last case before joining up, and he feared that the tall young man, who looked thin and pale and unfit, would never make it. At some point during the war, Pauline joined a program of morale-boosting for the soldiers at the front and became a *marraine*, or "godmother" to two Belgian soldiers. She kept up a correspondence with both of them and sent them regular parcels of cigarettes and socks, as well as pictures of herself.

In 1917, a chance for real service presented itself. She learned that the Red Cross was in need of volunteers to tend wounded soldiers who were being sent home, and without her mother's knowledge, she took a rudimentary nursing course and worked in a Red Cross hospital among these men until the war was over and the worst of the Spanish flu of 1919 had passed. This experience was a giant step for the sheltered and cosseted Pauline who had never even heard of gonorrhoea – let alone tended a man afflicted with the disease – and who now had to face death on a daily basis.

Perhaps through her nursing work, or perhaps through the *marraine* program, Pauline agreed to join a committee of young women whose task was to entertain the returning soldiers after the November armistice of 1918. She was thrilled with the glamour surrounding the brave and dashing young heroes in their splendid uniforms. She joined the triumphant fanfare hailing the return, in May 1919, of the 22nd battalion. It was as part of this welcoming committee of young women that she made the acquaintance of Thomas Tremblay, the celebrated commanding officer of the 22nd. Having tea with Tremblay at the Ritz Hotel one day in mid-September, she noticed him smiling at the occupant of another table. She followed his gaze and saw a man with a pencil moustache and slightly graying hair. A pair of crutches leaned against the man's chair. Tremblay told her that he was Georges Vanier, a distinguished officer of the 22nd, who had lost a leg in battle. Tremblay invited her to come with him to meet the wounded soldier.

* * *

George's immediate reaction to the tall and vibrant young woman who stood before him is lost to history, but he asked her to lunch the next day. What transpired after that is not clear, although from her diary it is obvious that Georges told her about some of the places where he had fought and the ultimate sacrifice paid by many of his comrades. At any rate, there was little time for further acquaintance, because now that the war was over, the Archers were due to set sail for a six-month European trip. It was to include a tour of the battlefields, and upon hearing this, Georges presented Pauline with his army maps, precisely marked with his wartime whereabouts. She was touched by this gesture, but whether she actually took the maps with her is doubtful. In later recollections, she claimed to have already been smitten with Georges, but other matters were also on her mind: the correspondence from one of her Belgian soldiers, Captain Michel Laury, had turned into love letters as the war had come to an end. The missives were flattering and romantic, and uppermost in her mind was the question of what would transpire after she had met the man in person.

The Archers set sail on 16 September. The gallant Georges, obviously taken with Pauline, ordered flowers to be sent to the ship, but they failed to arrive. As the ship steamed away, Pauline felt giddy with anticipation, but also faced the trip with some misgivings. She wrote in her trip journal, "I'm a bit afraid for the coming six months; I'm especially afraid of myself."[4]

The family made Paris their base and in early October, Pauline and her father left on a guided tour of the battlefields of northern France. The countryside remained devastated, and she was overcome by the sight of fields covered with white crosses. At Courcellette, where the 22nd battalion had made a name for themselves and had sacrificed many of their numbers, she saw, on the site where a sugar refinery once stood, the shelter used by Tremblay. She stood amid the rubble and described the experience in her journal: "There was a lump in my throat and I felt heartsick – it was there, as Major Vanier said, that I made contact with all those who had died; it felt as if the earth was trembling beneath my feet!" At the nearby cemetery, she recognized several names and prayed for a few moments: "It's the only thing one can do for those who sleep beneath the soil of France."[5]

Her first face-to-face meeting with Michel Laury took place on 12 October in Paris. A handsome war hero, he had lost an arm in battle. He came from an aristocratic family and although they had become impoverished, his father's position as a marquis was sufficient to win Madame Archer's approval. "We spent a charming afternoon chatting together," Pauline wrote in her journal. "It was extraordinary the number of things we had to tell each other, and it seemed rather strange to actually see each other after corresponding for three years. He is very nice and extremely interesting."[6]

Her journal records nothing more about this new encounter for almost two months, during which the family toured Italy. The highlights were a Pontifical High Mass and an audience with Pope Benedict XV in the Sistine Chapel. The delights of Paris beckoned, however, and on 18 December, she wrote, "In an hour we'll be on our way to la belle France. I'm sad, very sad to be leaving the wonderful Italian sun, but so happy to be returning to Paris!!! for plenty of reasons." She renewed her acquaintance with Michel and spent one deliriously happy day after another in his company. On Christmas Day they pledged themselves to each other. "Great happiness," she wrote. "I'm all upside down; I don't know what I'm saying or what I'm doing, and I'm also very tired."[7]

On 9 January, Michel presented Pauline with a ring, and two days later a reception was held to celebrate their engagement. Moving among the titled guests, Pauline's mother shook with excitement at the prospect of her daughter marrying into the nobility. Her father, however, threw a dose of reality into the fairytale romance by pointing out that Michel, a student at a military college, was not earning any money. This cold-water treatment may have brought Pauline up short and lifted her from her romantic trance. By the spring of 1920, the engagement was called off and the Archer family returned to Montreal.

It was likely sometime in the autumn of 1920 that Pauline was staying with relatives at Percé on the coast of the Gaspé Peninsula when she met Walter Shanks, a friend and former colleague of Georges Vanier. He suggested – had he perhaps heard that Georges had been disappointed in love and hoped to play Cupid? – that they write a joint postcard to him. Georges, by now with the Royal 22nd at the Citadel in Quebec City, immediately responded to the postcard, writing, "Miss Archer, if you come through Quebec, do let me know. I'd like to take you out to tea."[8]

In Quebec City, an awkward courtship began, and Pauline soon learned that, unlike her former suitor, this hero of the Great War had no clue about how to woo a young woman. He tried a regimental approach at first ("He asked me to lunch and he asked me to tea and he asked me to lunch and he asked me to tea," Pauline recalled several decades later with exasperation still in her voice.) Unused to the smooth discourse of sweet nothings, he told her about the latest book he had been reading, a tome by the French philosopher Henri Bergson ("Oh dear, dear, dear, dear!") and then moved on to his favourite works of English literature ("He thought I was intellectual.").[9]

The courting bungled along through teas and dinners and rides in the country until Pauline announced that she would be returning home to Montreal the next day. With the desperation of someone forced to jump or forever stay put, Georges asked her to marry him. When she answered a prompt, "Yes," he told her the reason for his stammering-schoolboy hesitation: "he felt he had lost a leg and was inferior and he couldn't possibly marry someone like me."[10] The next morning, he phoned her to ask if he had really proposed, a question made half in jest and half in trepidation.

What did they perceive in each other during the waning weeks of 1920? Georges saw before him a spontaneous young woman who was intelligent but not cynical, sophisticated in some ways and innocent in others; a woman who combined religious intensity with a rollicking sense of humour, and a zest for life with a profound spiritual sensibility. She went to Mass and communion every day, and he was shocked and fascinated that her religious life was part of the fabric of her being, and yet there was a carefree spirit about her. Unlike him, she did not fear God or the fires of hell. Although a regular Sunday churchgoer, he never went to communion unless he had been to confession immediately before, and even then, only a few times a year. There was also something in her – an immense capacity for empathy – that allowed him to reveal the extent of his suffering. She had not flinched from it. Here was a woman who, far from recoiling from his mutilated body, was ready to embrace it.

And what did Pauline discern in this man ten years her senior, who had tried to win her hand with talk of philosophy and literature and whose descriptions of the war had shaken and unsettled her? "He is not like the others," she wrote in her diary. "He is so good."[11] In fact, there was none of the falseness that she might have seen in others who had wanted to court her. Georges was his own person, quiet and reserved, who, for all his seriousness and self-discipline, displayed a delightful teasing wit. He showed as well a depth that came not only from his wartime suffering but had perhaps lain dormant from the years he had been contemplating the priesthood. Like her, he wanted to give himself to some kind of service. He had found one vocation in the midst of war, but there was still the deeper call now that combat had come to an end.

His first gift to her was a small bottle with a silver top containing some of the dirt from the boot of his amputated leg. His wound had already become for both of them a sign of self-sacrifice, and also, more deeply, of human frailty. In later years, Georges would declare with a teasing smile that he already had one foot in the grave. If this was true in a literal sense, it was also true in an existential sense. This daily reminder of life's impermanence was eventually to deepen into a profound acceptance of the Christian paradox that strength is made perfect in weakness. The weakness was shared between them – for his part, the physical handicap coupled with his consequent fear of a diminished manhood; for her part, the terrifying realization that beneath her beauty and exuberant personality lay a crippling insecurity. The silver-topped bottle of battlefield dirt, the size and shape of a perfume bottle, became the symbol of their shared frailty and their love.

In the meantime, though, there was romance. By early January 1921 they were clearly in love. Although they became secretly engaged on 13 January (this date was one of the anniversaries they would keep), in her first letter to Georges, dated ten days earlier, we find Pauline delirious with happiness. Sitting in her bedroom, where she had spent years in worry and anxiety, she now saw everything in a new light. She could barely contain herself, and wondered if she was dreaming. "I am too happy," she wrote. "When I think of how I despised life, or at least was afraid of it, now it seems beautiful to me. With you, I fear only having an unlimited confidence ... I love you with all my heart, all my strength." [12]

The couple corresponded daily, with Pauline complaining to her new fiancé that she hated Sundays because no mail was delivered. Day after day the stoic army officer received ardent love letters from her, each as effusive as the last. 25 January: "Mon petit, how good it is to feel loved by you, understood by you, to have your whole confidence, to have the same desire for good, to be in such perfect communion of ideas and sentiments. With this, what things we can do, for example, to help poor human beings whose lives are so miserable, who need support. We have received much, and it will be necessary to give much." 26 January: "The more I see you, the more I love you and the harder it is to separate from you." 27 January: "I'm not only proud of your heroic actions, but proud of your heart which is mine, proud of your soul which is so truly beautiful and ardent." [13]

The engagement was formally announced in April. Georges wrote to J.P. Cathcart, his roommate from one of the convalescent hospitals in England, that he had become engaged to "the only girl in the world." Cathcart replied, "I knew nothing short of that would ever stir you out of that hermit's life you were leading ... of course my love affairs were a constant suggestion to you to do something yourself, hence the castles in the air."[14] And Maria Perkins Bull, the wife of the owner of the London hospital where Georges had recuperated, wrote enigmatically, "I feel sure your fiancée is comely in every way, as I know you, George ... through all your pain and suffering you were always chic Vanier."[15]

Others replied in a similar spirit. A friend wrote to Pauline, that "it was my good fortune to have met the Major at your house one Sunday afternoon. I noted well then a certain look on both your faces that indicated peace with the world and satisfaction with the situation."[16]

During the spring and summer, Pauline prepared for the wedding on the two levels where she had already begun to operate – living in two worlds as it were. There was the superficial activity of the typical bride-to-be: choosing the wedding gown, making invitation lists, going to engagement parties, planning a trousseau. Then there was the world of the spirit, which was not actually a world apart, but rather a sense of the deeper reality permeating the day-to-day events that filled her life. She continued her habit of making a retreat every springtime at the convent of Marie-Réparatrice. Writing to Georges from the convent, she set the scene for him: a completely white cell, a narrow bed, a table, a chair, and a crucifix. The only sound, the sandals of one of the nuns along the parquet floor of the corridor. "When I think that I might have become one of them," she wrote. "I love life, I love this world, I love heaven, because I find you everywhere, my beloved. I feel full of emotion this evening, and yet serene."[17] "Serene" was hardly the word to describe Pauline at this stage in her life – or, perhaps, ever. The ink had not even dried on this word than her anxiety rose to the surface. "You'll love me always, won't you? Even if I become ugly, even if I complain a bit? Because *cheri*, I am far from being perfect, I'm full of faults that you're not aware of yet!"[18] Thérèse Archer gave him ample warning of what he could expect in Pauline's personality (if he had not already found this out for himself): "You have her whole heart, and her soul ... is attached to yours, with all the intense ardour of her nature." And then, as a mother who knew her daughter well, "*Mon Dieu*, what lively exuberance of heart and of soul, what an impressionable nature, almost too much for her nervous system."[19]

On 24 August, Pauline wrote in anticipation of the third anniversary of Georges's wounding, "Next Sunday will be a painful anniversary for you, *mon cheri*, I would like to be near you to encircle you more than ever with the real and profound tenderness I have for you. A painful anniversary, yes, but also and especially a glorious anniversary. I am proud of you, proud to be the wife of a man who has not only suffered, but who can suffer with a smile on his lips."[20] From now on, until Georges's death, Pauline would write him an "anniversary" letter every year on the 28th of August.

She may have already become a puzzle for her future husband (Georges's engagement letters to her have not survived) because the explosive passion bursting forth in torrents was sometimes accompanied by an insatiable need for assurances (4 August: "You didn't tell me last evening that you loved me, *mon petit*"[21]). Yet she could pause amid the flurry of wedding plans and reflect on the basic purpose of their life together: that there were glorious years of service ahead of them, and that even as they gazed at each other in love, there was a wider and deeper calling to look outward.

As for Georges, the matter of his career had entered into the picture, three years of fighting the "war to end all wars" apparently being insufficient military training. A plan was set up whereby after the wedding he would begin a course at the Royal Military College in Kingston and, if he were successful, he would take the examination for the prestigious Staff College in England.

Then, as if the approach of one life-changing event were not enough, he received a letter toward the end of August, the envelope of which bore the insignia of the governor general of Canada. The letter was from the chief of general staff of Government House: "His Excellency the Governor-General has asked me to write to you, to ascertain if you would be willing to accept the appointment of aide-de-camp to him. It is an honour which you deserve in every way, and I trust that you can see your way clear to accept it."[22] The governor general in question was Sir Julian Byng, under whose brilliant leadership Georges had fought at Vimy. Lord Byng of Vimy, as he was now known, had arrived in Ottawa only a week earlier to take up the vice-regal position, and wildly cheering war veterans had gathered to greet him in front of the Parliament buildings. One of the new governor general's first acts was to break with tradition by appointing Canadian rather than British aides de camp. He particularly wanted one from French Canada who would not only assist him with his shaky use of the French language but help him navigate the waters of French-English relations.

Georges replied with "heartfelt thanks," and in the starched language in which he had become adept, informed the chief of general staff that he would be getting married on 29 September. "In view of this circumstance," he wrote, "I would require to be in Montreal on or about the 25th September until the day of the wedding."[23] "I received your letter ... and have communicated with His Excellency, who is agreeable to your marriage on the date arranged," came the reply.[24]

For Pauline there was no time or inclination for starched language in the days leading to their wedding, nor would there ever be. She made the final all-important visit to the couturier for the fitting of her bridal gown, which she hoped would be to Georges's liking, since "my vanity is only for you."[25] In her last letter before the wedding, during a rare moment of calm, she wrote, "Our love is so profound that nothing will shake it."[26] In fact, she was right: Georges's steady love for his temperamentally fragile bride would only deepen. And her obsessive love for him would diminish in intensity over the coming years, but the devotion would remain firm in spite of the rocky times ahead.

EARLY YEARS

The wedding of Pauline Archer and Georges Vanier had in all likelihood been planned for Saturday, 27 August 1921, so that their first day of marriage would coincide with the third anniversary of his wounding. This date had already assumed a nearly sacred position. Thérèse Archer, however, wrote to Georges to ask that the wedding be postponed for a month so that she would have more time to prepare for it. (She had approached him before speaking to her daughter, for fear of Pauline's angry reaction, since "the date she chose is so dear to her heart."[1]) Georges readily acquiesced, and the date was changed to 29 September.

The wedding, described rather insipidly by *The Standard* as "one of the most interesting of the season,"[2] was splendid in every respect. It took place in the Cathedral of St James,[3] which had been elevated to the status of "basilica" two years earlier. This enormous edifice, a scaled-down model of St Peter's in Rome, had been built by Montreal's Bishop Ignace Bourget and completed at the end of the nineteenth century, during the flowering of Catholic triumphalism and ultramontanism. The copper and gold leaf baldachin, a four-pillared, canopied piece of baroque magnificence – a replica of Bernini's original – stood over the high altar, forming the centrepiece of the interior.

On 29 September 1921, at ten o'clock in the morning, Pauline Archer came down the long aisle on the arm of her father to the full-throttled chords of the pipe organ, preceded by her two attendants, her cousin Lita Rohr and Georges's sister Frances, dressed identically in blue silk and velvet. The bride wore a white satin gown with a long train lined with pale pink georgette. Her tulle veil, held with a wreath of orange blossoms, fell to the end of her train. Her only jewellery was a diamond and platinum bar brooch, a gift of the groom.

The sanctuary was banked with yellow chrysanthemums, palms, ferns, and autumn foliage. The presence of members of the Royal 22nd regiment in their well pressed brown uniforms, their shoes shining and postures erect, added a measure of grit and an aura of heroism to the occasion. Indeed, the list of ushers read like a roll-call of the officers that Georges Vanier had fought beside in the trenches; nonetheless, one of the hardened veterans, given the responsibility for looking after Madame Archer when the wedding was over, declared himself incapable of coping with the weeping mother of the bride. The groom's best man was Thomas Tremblay, his former commander and the man responsible for bringing Georges and Pauline together. Two personages in particular added to the splendour of the occasion (and in retrospect, perhaps acted as portents of the future): an aide de camp sent by Governor-General Lord Byng as his representative, and the officiating priest, the pastor of Pauline's childhood and the man she dubbed her "spiritual father," now the auxiliary bishop of Montreal, Georges Gauthier. At the conclusion of the wedding, the newly married couple walked under the arch of swords held aloft by members of the Royal 22nd regiment, and into married life.

After the glamour of these nuptials their first home, a hundred and sixty miles down the road, could not have been more of a comedown. The Royal Canadian Military College in the old military city of Kingston stood on a small finger of land known as Point Frederick, surrounded by water on three sides: the St Lawrence River, Lake Ontario, and the Rideau Canal. It had been established as a military base more than a century earlier, and the stone building rose majestically against a backdrop of islands and watery channels. The college did not provide quarters for married students, and the best Georges and Pauline could find was a dingy boarding house on King Street. Georges, of course, was used to cramped accommodation, and the stripped-down life of the army gave him a sense of freedom and exhilaration. Scant details remain, however, as to how Pauline managed to cope with the abrupt change in her life, living in one room with a curtain separating their quarters from those of another couple. Their first night in the rooming house a cupboard fell over them, and the second night their bed collapsed. Some weeks later, when the new governor general came to visit, Pauline was obliged to borrow a teapot from a neighbour. In retrospect, their living situation provided fodder for laughter, and they were in the first throes of newlywed love, but for Pauline, it was probably a lonelier life than she remembered later. Two months after their wedding, she wrote in her sporadic journal that she was "swimming in serenity," thanks to the simple life she was living with her new husband, and a few lines later she reminded herself not to be "too egotistical." Georges's course at the college was dense and demanded hours of concentrated study, and although she declared herself to be happier than she had ever been, asking herself, "What would I do with a lot of strangers?"[4] an isolated life without friends was not Pauline's métier.

In December 1921, they were invited to Government House in Ottawa to meet Maréchal Foch, the supreme commander of the allied armies during the Great War. It was the one bright spot on Pauline's social calendar in the first months after her wedding. From there, they went on to Montreal where she came down with the flu, necessitating Georges's return to Kingston in early January without her. It is thanks to this confluence of otherwise inconsequential events separating the couple that we have an odd series of letters from Pauline to Georges beginning on 5 January 1922.

On that day she wrote that hardly had she left her sick bed than she was forced to return, weaker than ever. The reason: "Yesterday evening I had a moment of fear. After dinner I had a bit of hemorrhaging. I was afraid, but once I was in bed, it stopped, leaving me weakened and without energy. I stayed in bed as a measure of prudence today and it has nearly stopped completely." The doctor came the next day, and as soon as he left, she wrote to Georges, giving him the doctor's diagnosis: "He thinks that I had a small miscarriage – at least I am certainly not pregnant now. He is giving me a treatment to follow and letting me resume life as usual ... I don't feel very strong, but with rest, I'm going to regain my strength very quickly." She admitted, however, that she was sad and listless, and reproached herself for being a crybaby and for having gone through a half-hour weeping spree the afternoon before.

The strange combination of her own sadness and concern for Georges ("Don't study too much, my darling. Take the tonic that *Maman* gave you ... take care not to get cold, and eat well.") as well as her obsessive love for him ("*Mon petit*, I love you with all the ardour of my being"[5]), and little mention of the fact of the miscarriage itself sparks the question: did she realize that she was in fact pregnant, or did she think that what she had gone through was a prelude to pregnancy, or perhaps a false pregnancy? What did she mean by a "small" miscarriage (*une petite fausse-couche*)?

Three days after she rejoined Georges in Kingston, with her husband concentrating on his studies ("Right now Georges is too taken up by his studies to talk with me; he is totally preoccupied"), she poured herself into her journal. She fretted about her spiritual life: was she too taken up with newly married happiness to be concerned with the aim of the Christian life, to keep moving toward God? She upbraided herself for her fear of life, for her restlessness, for her tendency toward depression. "Depression: a sign of weakness, of selfishness." This was "a humiliating phase"[6] for her. Here was Pauline at a new low: fearful and turned in on herself, and although she was living in bliss with the most tender of husbands, his composure was an unwitting rebuke to her emotional turmoil. The small military city provided her with neither close friends nor the outlet of a social life. And to whatever extent she consciously realized it, she may have felt grief for her lost, barely formed baby.

Mercifully for Pauline, for whom introspection and isolation always led to depression and then on downward in a spiral of self-absorption and self-castigation, things changed when the couple moved to Ottawa, where Georges took up full time duties as aide de camp. Ottawa was still only a few decades away from being a small logging town, and was not sophisticated in the manner of either Montreal or Toronto. As the capital of the country, it bespoke a nation in relative infancy. Still, it had the distinction of being not only the seat of government but also the home of the sovereign's representative. A class system of sorts had developed, along with an attendant snobbery, thanks to the old guard of established families.

With the arrival of the post-war governor general, the social order began to change. His very presence signaled something new: in the mysterious parsing of social standing, Lord Byng's rank was low. In spite of his status as a decorated military hero and his aristocratic upbringing, he did not belong to the British peerage, and in upper-class society, this fact mattered. Moreover, Lord Byng loathed pomp and ceremony and pretension. He preferred simple human contact to grand occasions, and with the exception of his military uniform (which he kept in immaculate condition), he wore clothes that tended to be shabby. The tone of camaraderie and good fun that Byng established suited Georges and Pauline perfectly. "All their entourage is nice," Pauline wrote in her journal. "We are just like a big family."[7]

Rideau Hall, the governor general's residence, also known as Government House, was a world apart. Entering the grounds, the Vaniers came into a sprawling nineteenth-century English village-like compound of thirty-two hectares, with stately buildings, stables, tennis courts, greenhouses, and expanses of lawn, all surrounded by parkland and a forest of maples, oaks, pines, and fir trees. Rideau Hall itself had originally been built as an eleven-room country villa by Thomas McKay, a stonemason who had worked on the construction of the Rideau Canal. By 1922, eighty-four years later, several wings had been added to it. Pauline and Georges were given Rideau Cottage, which stood on a tree-lined avenue behind the main residence, and there could hardly have been a greater contrast between their first home as a married couple and their second. Far from being a "cottage" in the popular sense of the word, Rideau Cottage was a two-storey Victorian house. Constructed of red brick, it had fourteen rooms and a veranda on three sides. Its interior was classically designed with a hallway down the centre on both storeys, and airy, spacious rooms on either side. The house had been built as a home for the governor general's secretary, but since Lord Byng's secretary, Patrick Hodgson, was unmarried and lived in a room in the main residence, Rideau Cottage stood unoccupied when the Vaniers arrived in the early spring of 1922. It was a perfect honeymoon home for the couple after their rocky start in Kingston.

More than this elegant accommodation, what made their first stay in Ottawa most memorable was their unexpected friendship with Lord Byng. The Byngs were childless, and to some extent Pauline and Georges acted like surrogate offspring. Byng, who had won the Canadian soldiers' affection by the warmth of his personality and his desire to live in conditions as close as possible to those of ordinary folk, favoured people with whom he could establish bonds of affection based not only on the values of honour and integrity but also on a broad sense of humour. The young couple's relationship with Lady Byng, although always cordial, was not as close as that with her husband, due probably to the difference in temperament and interests of the two women; Pauline found the half-Greek Lady Byng, who was well-educated and an authority on flowers and gardens, to be exotic and somewhat intimidating.

Almost immediately the running joke with Georges was Byng's difficulty with certain hard-to-pronounce French words, especially *accueil*, which, meaning "welcome," was a word that was a necessary part of his vocabulary wherever he was called upon to speak French (in one letter he referred to "the warmest "accool," "acurl" – damn! I'll look it out – *accueil*. That's the one. I am getting better at it. I find a slight suspicion of a yodel, just where the vowels are thickest – u, e and i – adds wonderfully to the effect. I tried it on a French M.P. who said it reminded him of the noise he made to entice a kitten.")[8] And for Pauline, whose height emphasized her very slender frame, he exaggerated her name into "Poor lean."

The summer of 1922 brought two pieces of good news. First of all, Georges had passed the entrance examination and was therefore accepted to the two-year program at the Staff College, Camberley, England, where he was to present himself the following January. The official notice also informed him that "each officer is provided with a servant and horse whilst at the College."[9] This bit of information – the dispassionate coupling of a servant and a horse, as if they were two of a kind, like a knife and fork – may have given the couple an inkling of the class-ridden society they would soon be entering. The other news had much greater personal import: Pauline was pregnant again. When the news sank in, she was in a state of exultant happiness combined with fear. "When I feel this life awakening inside my body, I feel confused – is it joy or fear?" she wrote in her journal. Although twenty-four years old, she felt that she was still too young and irresponsible for motherhood. "Poor little thing, you have a mother who loves you tenderly already, but who is a bit afraid of you," she wrote, describing succinctly an emotional state that would never quite leave her. What made her most happy in her new condition was that here was a gift she could offer to Georges, "the most delightful of husbands," who would be an equally delightful father. As always, she would lean on Georges for support: "With such a father, I'm not afraid of seeing you come into this world."[10]

They left for England in November. Pauline had written to Lord Byng that she was contemplating the Bible passage in which two pregnant women meet each other – Mary, who is to give birth to Jesus, and her cousin Elizabeth, who is expecting a baby eventually to become John the Baptist – and having spiritual conversations with them. A bemused Byng, whose many life experiences most certainly did not include meditative talks with women of the Bible, wrote, "I am sure you are right – absolutely right. You and Elizabeth and Mary had many things to say to each other." He then went on, surer of himself: "Pauline dear, we miss you two dreadfully. We miss you inside and outside the house. We miss you the sunnyside and the blizzard side. It is bad for you to know this, but I can't help giving you what I know to be bad. We miss you greatly. Things go on like things do go on ... *But we miss you two!*"[11]

And to Georges: "I suppose an Englishman should keep his pipe of affection very carefully soldered. But somehow with you and Pauline I have allowed a leakage. I could not help it, and I feel I should like you to know how sincere my affection is for you both."[12]

He had words of advice for the Canadian neophyte setting foot in the hallowed bastion of British military might: "you may find my countrymen ponderous in thought but remember it is national, and our very ponderosity, though irritating, has led to some sound judgements and careful decisions." He drew Georges's attention to the photographic gallery of the "has beens," including himself. "You will notice we all wore ferocious moustaches in those days … I think it helped to win the war, at least something must have done so, and why not ferocious moustaches?" Knowing Georges's tendency to express his opinions freely (and perhaps without due discretion), he added some fatherly advice. "Don't be too keen to write your opinions for others to read. They frequently take the form of 'spasms' and everybody has a spasm occasionally, but invariably like their own spasms best and only lead the other fellows out of civility. Read all you can of other people's opinions before giving your own to the world."[13]

In Camberley, a town built on heath land in the lush county of Surrey, fifty-five kilometres southwest of London, the Vaniers settled in a house on Branksome Park Road, a street that wound up a hill brimming with flowering shrubs, horse chestnut trees, and hemlocks. Across the town stood the stately Royal Military College, the training institution for raw military recruits and adjacent to it, the Staff College, where officers came who, like Georges Vanier, had attained the rank of captain or major and hoped for a promotion. (The only other Canadian there during Georges's time, Harry Crerar, was eventually to become the commander of the First Canadian Army during the Second World War.) This was a more modest building of sandstone brick in what was known as the modern Italian style, with an ivy-covered façade, approached rather grandly by a wide walkway. An alumnus described the approach to the college deprecatingly thus. "For the thousands who pass by the Staff College by the London road each week there are very few indeed who know of its existence. It is quite commonly confused with the Royal Military College, while it has often been taken for a girls' school, and even mistaken for Broadmoor Criminal Lunatic Asylum."[14]

In the imposing entrance hall, a Roman bath was decorated with lances and pennons, armour worn during the fight against the Spanish Armada, pistols used at the battle of Waterloo, and on a stone plaque, the names of alumni who had fallen during the Great War. Two lakes stood on the vast college grounds, and in springtime when the rhododendron and azalea bushes were bursting with purple and pink blossoms, a favourite form of exercise was to walk along the lakeside path to the nearby village of Sandhurst.

It was a two-year course of study with sixty students in each year. The average age of the students was thirty-three. Lord Byng gave a fulsome projection of the initial proceedings: the new students would start off "smelling round each other and growling like a lot of dogs,"[15] but this phase would soon pass; the second-year students would lord it over the novice officers telling them things they already knew; the students and instructors (hardly distinct from each other in age) would be sizing each other up. The first-year courses were concerned with such minutiae of military life as the thoroughness of planning and analysis of strategies. There were also such basic courses as fundamental mathematics and map reading. Many of the examinations had to do with matters pertaining to the war in which most of the students had fought just a few years earlier. One can assume that Georges had sufficient background knowledge to answer such bloodless exam items as "Discuss briefly the military system, terms of service and organization of the military forces of any Dominion with which you are acquainted. In the event of the Government in question deciding, in a sudden emergency, to send a small contingent for service overseas to any theatre which you may elect, discuss."[16]

As Georges settled into the life of a student once again, Pauline, joined by her mother early in 1923, awaited the baby's birth. By the middle of February she had engaged both a midwife and a nanny, and the vigil began, as Thérèse Archer and the midwife sat on stools on either side of the fireplace, checking the unborn infant's progress from time to time. On 27 February, after a relatively easy two-hour labour, Thérèse Marie Chérisy Vanier was born. (Chérisy, the French village where Georges had been wounded, was now enshrined in the name of their first-born child.) The baby, Georges declared in a letter to his sister Frances, "is a dear: it isn't fair to her (who cannot defend herself), but everybody says she is the image of her daddy."[17]

From the start, the nanny took charge of the child. Her name was Isobel Thomson, and she was to remain with the family for more than a decade and a half, the mainstay of the household. She hailed from the Scottish border city of Berwick-on-Tweed, spoke with a soft Scots brogue, and was likely in her late thirties when she took on the job with the Vaniers. Pauline, an only child lacking experience with babies, did not take easily to motherhood, in spite of the sincere desires she had poured into her journal. She was in awe of the tiny human being she had brought into the world and felt helpless in the face of the squalling, needy infant. She marvelled at Nanny Thomson's effortless approach and common sense.

Starting a family within a British military milieu may have had a greater impact than the Vaniers realized at the time. The strictly hierarchical military system was a mirror image of the English class system, and the lives of officers contained a whiff of the aristocratic. Nannies were expected to look after the children while fathers supported the family and mothers furthered their husbands' careers by associating with the correct circles of society.

Neither of the Vaniers had a familial pedigree sufficient to impress the citizens of Camberley, but they did have an important aristocratic connection of the highest kind: not only was their friend Lord Byng a childhood playmate of the king, but Byng's nephew by marriage, Lord Stamfordham, was the king's private secretary. As soon as the Vaniers had left for England, Byng set the wheels in motion to obtain an invitation for them to dine with King George V and his wife, Queen Mary. This was the brass ring of English society. The invitation arrived in the spring of 1923: "The Master of the Household has received their Majesties' commands to invite Major G.P. and Mrs. Vanier to Dinner at The Royal Pavilion, Aldershot on Tuesday, the 22nd May 1923 at 8:30."[18] Dryly warned by Charles Archer that they might get "swollen heads,"[19] the Vaniers were sufficiently awed by the experience to record their conversations with the sovereigns.

Inside the drawing room of the Royal Pavilion in the nearby army town of Aldershot, ladies and men were separated, and they stood apart from one another like shy teenagers at a dance, while the royal couple walked around shaking hands. At dinner, King George spoke mostly with General Ironside, the head of the Staff College, and later, when the men had rejoined the ladies, the king and queen moved around the circle, asking questions. Queen Mary asked Georges if it tired him to stand. "No," replied Georges, and then he stood back as she moved on. Then the king inquired about Georges's leg. Did he ride? Were Lord and Lady Byng popular? A chair was brought for Georges out of concern for his leg, and he sat down.

King George fixed his eye on Pauline. What part of Canada was she from? "Have you been to Toronto? Aha ... You do not like Toronto. Aha. The rivalry between the two cities." Pauline, at her most prim, responded, "I hope you don't think we are so narrow-minded." The king replied jovially, "No, I was only teasing you."[20] And on it went, the ultimate society experience for anyone living on British soil. Both Vaniers managed to stammer their way through the wooden evening. Finesse would come with the years, and the polish that put one at ease in the upper reaches of society would gradually become second nature to them.

* * *

In the second year at the Staff College the workings of higher command were studied: the organization of a base, planning for an overseas expedition. There was also a tour to Europe's battlegrounds, and Georges's small group was slated for Czechoslovakia and Hungary. By the end of the two-year course, Georges, like many before him, felt that it had lasted too long, that it was too removed from active service, and that, especially for one who had fought a real war, it lacked any semblance to reality. He was now thirty-seven years old and wanted to get on with his career. In the summer of 1925, Georges, Pauline (once again pregnant), and two-year-old Thérèse took their leave of England and returned to Canada. Georges was promoted to the rank of lieutenant-colonel and given charge of the Royal 22nd, and in September the family moved into a newly renovated apartment in the Citadel in Quebec City.

In looking back at their two-and-a-half years as "colonials" in England, Pauline was to remember an initial snobbery towards them that ended once their invitation to dinner with the king and queen had stamped them worthy of inclusion in high society. But by the end of the two-year course, their reputation rested on their own merits. "You leave a great memory behind you and Canada owes to you a great debt of gratitude," wrote one couple. "No country was ever better served than has been Canada by you both."[21] Georges received glowing praise in the final Staff College report signed by General Ironside. The report described him as "a very hard working officer of high mettle and courage," with "an attractive personality and a deep sense of loyalty and good comradeship" as well as "marked grit and determination"[22] and a wide knowledge of the world outside of military matters. And as for his wife, whose "way with the male"[23] had already been noted by Lord Byng (a way that was to last for the rest of her life), one of Georges's fellow students wrote, "Tell Pauline that the whole of Great Britain is deploring the withdrawal of her radiance, and we've none of us been the same since."[24]

Already, four years into their marriage, the blend of their personalities was working its particular alchemy, and the Vanier star in the social firmament had begun to rise.

7

SETTLING DOWN

The grey-green St Lawrence River begins to widen as it reaches Quebec City and flows around the Ile d'Orléans, and then, past distant mountains, it fans out majestically toward the Atlantic Ocean. The vista, as seen from the four-hundred-foot cliff known as Cape Diamond, rivals that of Gibraltar. This, at least, was the boast of Georges Vanier, echoing Charles Dickens,[1] when, in 1925, he wrote to his fellow Staff College students who had been dispatched to the far-flung reaches of the British Empire. He did not add that Quebec had also once been called the coldest military post in the empire.

He could also have told them that the city itself, the capital of the province of Quebec, was spectacularly situated, rising up the cliffs in a maze of narrow streets and grey centuries-old buildings, with a railway terminus and a thriving seaport, the first stop of the steam ships sailing from Europe to Canada. The Citadel stood near the city's centre at a strategic point on top of the cliff, and yet was almost hidden because it had been constructed in the form of earthen embankments that seemed to sink into the cliff itself. Built as a walled fortress in the 1820s, the Citadel comprised a number of stone buildings and parade grounds within an area of over two square kilometres – in effect, a little world of its own.

Much had changed in George's life since he had said his good-byes to the Royal 22nd at the Citadel four years earlier. Then he had been a bachelor officer; now he had a wife, a two-year-old daughter, and another child soon to be born, and he had returned as the commander of the regiment's one hundred and four men and nine officers. The family moved into the commander's quarters, a long, grey, two-storey building that stretched lengthwise along the top of the cliff, facing north into the parade grounds. Attached on either side to the commander's quarters were the officers' mess and the Quebec residence of the governor general.

One of his first tasks, in the early summer of 1925, was to lead the Royal 22nd in helping to quell a labour dispute in Sydney, Nova Scotia, that had boiled over into violence. The powerful British Steel Corporation had taken ownership of the Caledonia coal mines five years earlier, cutting management jobs, lowering the wages of miners who already faced poor working conditions, and refusing credit to hungry families. The United Miners had gone on strike many times, and in a June showdown, the police responded with brute force. One miner was killed and several injured. The military presence helped restore peace: no further violent incidents took place, and the Royal 22nd troops were soon back in the Citadel.

In a circular letter Georges wrote at the end of December to his fellow Staff College students, he downplayed the incident: "We spent the whole summer there, most of the time behind barbed wire fences. Fortunately the weather was fine." This casual comment displays Georges Vanier's odd habit of sometimes writing in a light vein to friends about serious matters. Did the patrol duty at the Caledonia coal mines seem insufficiently military to him, or was he perhaps embarrassed and distressed that, as the army commander, he was perceived to be on the side of the unjust bosses?

In the same letter and in his best buttoned-up British military fashion, he then delivered another piece of news, that "on the 30th November a young son arrived."[2] Pauline, although seasick on the return voyage from England, had had a relatively uneventful pregnancy. She seems not to have felt the urge to pour into her journal her feelings about impending motherhood in the way that she had before Thérèse's birth. The baby, almost eleven pounds in weight, was named after his father and maternal grandfather: Georges Charles. Lord and Lady Byng were asked to be honorary godparents.

From all the points of the British Empire where the newly minted Camberley graduates had been posted, congratulations poured in on the arrival of Georges Vanier's son and heir. "What are you going to make him?" wrote one. "A soldier or a sailor?"[3] Georges told friends that he intended the child to be the Canadian amateur boxing champion. What name, however, was the infant to be called that would distinguish him from his father? Lord Byng suggested his own nickname, "Bungo," but Georges recoiled from the suggestion, claiming that there was only one Bungo. Someone came up with "Byngsie," and the name stuck.

As he settled down to his duties, Georges was aware that commanding a regiment in peacetime did not entail the strategizing and decision-making of wartime soldiering, let alone the tedium and squalor of the trenches and the horror of the battles themselves. Nor did peacetime military life offer the ideals of a great cause for which he had joined up over ten years earlier.

The daily drills and exercises seemed anticipatory, as if waiting to advance on the next conflict. In some cases, the routines even seemed regressive, as in the use of horses, which had proved futile in the last war. The story goes, however, that Georges welcomed the opportunity to sit astride a horse once again, as a means of exercise and relaxation. One day, out riding beyond the confines of the Citadel, he was thrown from the horse and his artificial leg broke. He had no choice but to crawl under a tree and await rescue. Eventually he was missed and was found sitting with stoic resignation in the shade of the tree.

A spirit of comradeship filled the ranks of the Royal 22nd. Most of the men had served with Georges in France, and his reputation was well known: a highly disciplined officer whose orders were to be strictly followed in every detail. There were certain lines that simply could not be crossed; foul language, even in the heat of battle, had pained him, and now, as commander, he outlawed it entirely. Other idiosyncratic examples have remained in Royal 22nd lore. In the years after the Great War, the regiment's budget was tight and meals were frugal. In an effort to maintain control over the rationing of food, it was said that every morning Colonel Vanier counted out the exact number of eggs to be served in the officers' mess so that no one would receive more than one for breakfast. And for himself, every morning he had his batman, or manservant, bring him two prunes in a fruit nappy – not one prune or three prunes, but two, and not in a plate or saucer or bowl, but a fruit nappy.

Incidents like this were typical of the meticulous way Georges went about his duties and the exactitude he demanded of the people working under him. And if he proved mistaken or unreasonable in an order, he was also known to apologize without reserve. Such an occurrence took place one day when he went into the officers' mess and saw one of the men putting shades on the candles in preparation for a banquet. He told the officer to take the shades off. Sometime later, after he had spoken with Pauline, who told him that candle shades were currently in vogue, he offered an apology to the officer for his hastiness. His obvious sincerity and simplicity on such occasions helped to relieve the frustration felt by those under him because of his tendency toward fussiness.

In the meantime, he gave his focus on detail a full workout in questions of protocol. A cross had been erected at the Citadel in memory of those who died at Vimy Ridge; should the cross be saluted in passing? Should colours be carried on church parade? What was the proper manner in which to give official toasts? Which institutions should the governor general visit in Quebec? Letters went back and forth between Georges and military authorities in England regarding the ceremonial bearskin caps that were proposed for the Royal 22nd: what size, shape, texture?

The regiment had also become a hub for Quebec high society. Tennis parties, with the regulation outfit of white flannels and navy blazers, were held in the summer (Georges had decided on his most useful position on the tennis court: at the baseline, where he could hit the high balls and leave the running to his partner). There were dinners in the officers' mess where invited guests were fed sumptuously (in contrast to the usual Spartan fare), and splendid military balls where officers in red dress uniform danced with women in dazzling ball gowns. An incident after one such regimental ball came to light many years later, when a Royal 22nd officer told a reporter that the only time he saw Georges Vanier ruffled was when he put on another officer's greatcoat by mistake, reached into the pocket for a handkerchief and pulled out a woman's silk stocking. "He wasn't the same for a month," the man said.[4]

He wrote to friends that he was enjoying his job more and more and would not exchange it for any other, but as the humdrum months stretched into a year, and then another year, there may have been a sense of irrelevance, or at least of insufficient challenge. In a document written for the Department of National Defence concerning the premature departure of soldiers from the army and the problem of recruiting in peacetime, he asked, "What is the soldier-type? He is a curious mixture: there is in him something of the sentimentalist, of the bohemian and of the adventurer. He likes to swing down the street to the strains of the band or of the drums; he likes to walk out, with his ladylove, in an attractive uniform!" But, he continued rhetorically, are a smart uniform and employment in tasks such as waxing floors, peeling vegetables, and whitewashing curb stones enough to keep a soldier in the army? He gave a rueful answer: people were enlisting because of financial hardship or temporary unemployment, but neither the pay nor the work was sufficient to keep them. "As a result the Permanent Force is endeavouring to compete ... with industry and commerce."[5]

He may also have been reminded of a wry letter from Lord Byng, written a few years earlier while the Vaniers were still in England, in which his good friend ridiculed certain ceremonial concerns. "Canadian officialdom is wracked with the most hideous problem of modern days. There is no Lieut. Governor, and the House of Commons in Nova Scotia has to be closed. The acting Lt. Gov. is the solicitor-general. He has no uniform. Now the question is: when he closes Parliament should he wear a hat? On this point the solidarity of the Empire is on the verge of breaking. On being consulted, I gave the Sphinx-like dictum: 'If he does not wear a hat on his head, he cannot take it off.'"[6]

Georges and Pauline were happy to renew their friendship with Lord Byng now that they were back in Canada. As commanding officer at the Citadel, Georges was an honourary aide-de-camp to the governor-general, and in this capacity he may have been aware of the political turmoil mounting in Ottawa in the spring of 1926. The Liberal prime minister, Mackenzie King, had been holding a shaky coalition government together ever since the federal election seven months earlier, even though the Conservatives under Arthur Meighan had received a majority of the votes. When a corruption charge against the Liberals threatened to bring down the government, King, on the last weekend in June, asked Lord Byng to dissolve Parliament rather than have the scandal of the corruption charge bring down the government.

Like all Canadians, the Vaniers awoke on 29 June to the news that the governor-general had refused to dissolve Parliament, and that King had then resigned as prime minister. The next day, Byng asked Arthur Meighan to form a government, but on 2 July, after three days of arguing whether the Meighan government was legal, Parliament decided by one vote that it was not. Byng had no choice but to allow Meighan to dissolve Parliament. A new election was set for 14 September and King launched an aggressive campaign, blaming the British Lord Byng for interfering in Canadian parliamentary affairs.

Georges and Pauline spent a brief period of time with Byng during the summer of 1926 at the Archers' country house. Georges later recorded one of their conversations in his personal notes. "The courageous course" for King, Byng told Georges, "was to fight it out and to stand or fall by the verdict of Parliament ... if dissolution can be obtained each time a prime minister fears an adverse vote in the House, it is the negation of Parliament's authority." What seemed to gall Byng even more than his adversary's denouncing him on the hustings was that King had reneged on his own principle: "Mr. King had always said in the past 'Let Parliament decide' and now when Parliament was to be given an opportunity to decide, he asked for a dissolution."

The old warhorse, who had first grumbled over having to lead Canadian soldiers into battle, and then had become deeply attached to Canada after the Vimy victory, now spoke sadly over having brought the nation to this crisis. "I have often asked myself is there anything I should have thought of that I did not think of? And frankly, I don't think there is. It is the hardest thing I have done for Canada." "And the best,"[7] said Georges, in part out of personal loyalty to a friend, but also out of admiration for Byng's honest stand on the principle of parliamentary democracy.

The Liberals, under the leadership of Mackenzie King, won the September election with a majority. Byng's last function as governor general was, ironically, the swearing-in of King and his ministers. Then, their five-year term having come to an end, the Byngs left Canada on 30 September 1926. As the ship pulled away from the Quebec shore into the St Lawrence River, Byng kept busy talking intently with an official, to prevent himself from breaking down. The strain of the whole ordeal had affected him deeply (chest pains, the first signs of a heart condition, began to afflict him in the months following the crisis), but it did not destroy his sense of humour. "I was drenched in a torrent of gush," he wrote to Georges, describing his encounter with Mackenzie King in London two months later, and then went on to describe his speech at the Canada Club dinner in honour of King: "I repeated my old Canada Club speech as if it was entirely new, and many of the uninitiated appeared to treat it as fresh from the oven of oratory."[8]

Georges later told Byng that history, he felt sure, would support his decision not to dissolve Parliament when King asked him to. Whether or not history has done so (the central question has been whether the governor general, in 1925, had the constitutional right to refuse the prime minister's request), Byng himself would have enjoyed, perhaps grimly, the moniker given decades later to the affair that blighted his last months in Canada: "the King/Byng Wing-Ding." Indeed, it was a title he could have made up himself.

* * *

In the fall of 1926, Lord Willingdon replaced Lord Byng as governor general. He had been the governor of Bombay and brought to Rideau Hall either an oriental elegance or a grandiose pomposity, depending on one's point of view. (An aide, mourning the disappearance of the warmth and informality of the Byng years, wrote that the Willingdons had been used to red-carpet welcomes and overhead fans pulled by coolies, and Lady Willingdon had been disappointed at not being greeted by a band.) Willingdon asked Georges, as the commanding officer of the Citadel, to be an aide-de-camp, which he agreed to, writing the governor general's speeches in French and making efforts to arrange his visits to Quebec. During this time the governor general's official Quebec residence, established by Lord Dufferin in the Citadel, was updated and refurnished (the Byngs had found it to be almost uninhabitable) so that there might be an ongoing vice-regal presence in Quebec. For Georges, the governor general's presence became a symbol of the Canadian unity that, in time, he would ardently promote.

In the late winter, the Vaniers secured the services of a second nanny, Isobel Thomson's niece, Agnes Young, who arrived from Scotland in time for the birth of their third child. The baby, born on 15 March 1927, was named Bernard de Salaberry. "Another recruit for the Royal 22nd, I hope!"[9] came the congratulations of a friend, unaware that Georges had begun to set his sights beyond the army.

The following June, the family rented a house in Pointe-au-Pic, a holiday resort on Murray Bay, north of Quebec City. One day shortly after they arrived, Pauline awoke early to the smell of smoke. She immediately roused Georges who, as he wrote later to the owner of the house, "rushed to the open window, and looking down saw smoke issuing from the direction of the living room window" – not adding that for a one-legged man, "rushing" was difficult. At the upper landing outside the bedroom, he saw smoke billowing up from the ground floor. He shouted to Pauline not to descend the main stairway, so she and the two nannies, carrying four-year-old Thérèse, two-year-old Byngsie, and three-month-old Bernard, escaped down the back stairs. Georges, meanwhile, ran down the front stairs into the smoke in the hope of extinguishing the fire – and was met with a burst of flame. He barely escaped through the front door before flames engulfed the house.

Some of Pauline's jewellery, as well as the rest of the family's belongings, was among the charred ruins. A more important casualty, however, was Pauline herself. She had been breastfeeding the baby, but after the fright, her milk stopped. The close call also traumatized her. Her fragile nerves had already been stretched by giving birth to three children in close succession, but because of her upbringing in Montreal society and her exuberant personality, she was still able to take on the role of hostess. A few days after the fire the Vaniers entertained Lord Willingdon at the Citadel, and, toward the end of July, the Prince of Wales and his brother, Prince George, who had come to Canada on the occasion of the fiftieth anniversary of Confederation.

In a pattern that was to continue for years, Pauline overextended herself on such occasions and the whirl of high energy was generally followed by bouts of exhaustion. Perhaps to give his wife a rest, Georges suggested a holiday in England, and the two of them left in mid-September. Isobel Thomson's letters from Quebec during this holiday show concern for Pauline's health. Among the nanny's chatty bits of news (the children have gone for walks and have been invited out to tea, Thérèse and Byngsie play with the baby, but Byngsie "is inclined to be rough"[10]), there are admonitions that Madame not get overtired.

It was no doubt a tonic to visit the Byngs at their home near the village of Thorpe-le-Soken, on the coast of Essex. The house, a Georgian manor near shooting and golf, Byng's two favourite pastimes, had been renovated with Canadian materials, and Lady Byng, who had brought cuttings and seeds and bulbs from Canada, had begun creating an enormous garden. On his return to England, Byng had been elevated to the title of viscount, an honour that amused him (in a letter he wrote that, in receiving this title, protocol had obliged him to appear before the "Garter King": "He began by asking me what name I wanted to take. I naturally said, 'What names have you this morning?' He thought this frivolous and the Garter nearly fell off his Arms. He then said I might keep my old one. To this I urged that that course was perfectly satisfactory as I could spell it, having as a boy written it frequently on the walls of a lavatory.")[11]

After the Vaniers returned to Canada, Byng wrote Georges that he would contact the War Office in London, "to see what they think about your being brought over, always remembering that you are not going to remain on soldiering."[12] The indication here is – perhaps on Byng's initiative, perhaps as a result of Georges's own restlessness – he had begun to outgrow the military life in its placid Quebec form, and he had discussed other possibilities with Byng. But Georges apparently did not seek the next life change that was held before him sometime after his return from England in late 1927. In fact, he seems to have been caught off guard when he received an offer from the Department of External Affairs to become Canada's representative on the League of Nations Permanent Advisory Commission for Naval, Military and Air Questions. The new job would take him to Geneva, Switzerland, where the League had been established as a result of the Paris Peace Conference of 1919. Sir Robert Borden had secured representation for Canada in the League of Nations as well as eligibility for membership in the League's governing council. In October of 1927, Canada had been voted in as a member of the council for a three-year term, and Senator Raoul Dandurand was to be the representative. It was possibly he who had suggested Georges for the military role. Eight years earlier, Georges had passed up the opportunity to be present at the Peace Conference; now he was being given a chance to participate in its aftermath.

He was, in fact, being handed a role to play at the centre of world events. "I didn't even know that Canada was entitled to representation on a military, naval and air commission," he said in an early 1928 speech, shortly before leaving for Geneva, "so you can imagine how great the surprise was." He confessed ignorance as to what the job entailed: "I have been asked by some of my friends what I am going to do in Geneva and I have replied that I don't know." He added that he had learned from newspapers that "the Commission to which I have been appointed does not sit permanently." Then, in the jocular, tone he adopted when speaking to mainly masculine audiences, he said, "This may be true, but I am not taking any chances and the whole family is embarking. I suggested to my wife that I go over first to size up the situation and the family could follow later. She replied that two or even more (and the more includes a young man eleven months old) could size up the situation much better than one."[13]

There is no evidence as to how Pauline actually felt at the time about the enormous move, her journal outpourings long past. Still suffering the after effects of the fire at Pointe-au-Pic, she was once again pregnant. Delicate and unsteady, she began the business of packing with little time to spare: Georges's presence was needed at a meeting in early March, 1928. They left Canada on 23 February, with fifty-two pieces of luggage, accompanied by the two nannies. For Pauline, whose pregnancy was progressing badly, it did not help that everyone but herself took seasick during the ship's crossing, and she was left on her own to be nursemaid to the whole family. The next several months were to be even more fraught, and compounding an increasingly nervous condition was the feeling that she was becoming a burden on the husband she cherished. "There's only one thing I want in this world, and that is to feel that I'm useful to you and, perhaps, necessary,"[14] she wrote to her husband in her 28 August letter of that year, as she lay ill in bed, eight months pregnant.

Georges's immediate energy was focused upon his new role as a diplomat on the international stage (he had been seconded to this position, remaining a member of the Royal 22nd regiment). The aims of the League of Nations were to prevent war by means of disarmament, and to settle disputes between countries through negotiation and diplomacy. The sticking-point was the so-called Article 10 of the League's charter, which called for "collective security." This meant that member nations should be prepared to defend other members if their peace was threatened by aggressive forces. Mackenzie King, like Borden before him, did not want Canada to make this commitment, nor did Dandurand. Historians have debated this isolationist stand – Canada considered itself "a fireproof house far from inflammable materials," Dandurand is said to have declared.

Whether or not Georges agreed with this position is not clear, nor is it known whether he acknowledged in so many words that Canada was a minor player in the League's deliberations. Lord Byng made a somewhat cranky assessment of the League of Nations in his letter of congratulations to Georges: "We all want peace, and consider that the League of Nations may be the best channel to reach it. But there is only one royal road to peace and that is friendship, real friendship. In my opinion friendship never will be obtained by vague talks on disarmament. Talks on disarmament lead to rivalry and rot." He finished his letter by pointing out that the words of the Bible might be best suited in the goal of peace among nations, "and it does not mention disarmament. The words 'love your enemies' seem to me to be better than 'reduce your cruisers.'"[15]

Regardless of how he may have taken Byng's words, disarmament was precisely the elusive goal to which Georges now pledged his best efforts, and he devoted himself to diplomacy as a means to achieve it. His eventual realization that he was a small cog in an ineffectual machine did not lessen his commitment. The problem of disarmament was, in fact, a major consideration as technology opened the possibility of increasingly powerful weapons. The challenge before the League of Nations was for nations to reduce arms as much as possible, keeping the minimum necessary for national security. The League had established a preparatory commission for military and naval disarmament that would eventually present proposals to the League's General Assembly at a major disarmament conference sometime in the future.

By the time Georges entered the picture, the preparatory commission had already met in four sessions. His arrival in Geneva in March of 1928 coincided with the fifth session. Canada's policies were straightforward: reduction of arms and of the number of soldiers, and the abolition of both conscription and the use of gas in wartime. The European countries, however, held vastly different views. For France, security in the face of recent German aggression was more important than disarmament. Germany was looking for increased military strength. Britain wanted to safeguard its naval power, and Russia wanted complete disarmament.

The Canadian representative on the commission was Walter Riddell, and Georges's principal role was in behind-the-scenes diplomacy: quietly meeting delegates from the various countries and reporting back to Riddell. The session ended nine days after it began, but this was only the start of interminable committee meetings. In giving Georges the task of representing the three-pronged naval, military, and air concerns, the Canadian government had given to one person what legitimately could have been the work of three.

In July of 1928 the committee on arbitration and security was established, and in August, meetings began for something with the unwieldy title of "Special Commission for the Preparation of a Draft Convention on the Supervision of the Private Manufacture and Publicity of the Manufacture of Arms and Ammunition and of Implements of War." From his office at 25 Quai de Mont Blanc, overlooking Lake Geneva, Georges noted in his report to the Canadian government that at the latter meeting, the Polish representative had expressed surprise that only a day after the August Kellogg Peace Pact had been signed renouncing war as a means of dispute among nations, the question was raised as to what would happen in time of war. In October, he was writing to Lt Col H.H. Matthews, Minister of National Defence, "When people in Geneva talk of the next war (curious place, I admit, to talk about war, but the words 'if it should come' are always added to 'war') the air and chemistry are two topics always coupled and never forgotten."[16] This fact had arisen from the realization that not only would a combination of air warfare and chemical warfare cause unprecedented destruction and suffering, but also that war would exploit machinery that had been developed for peaceful purposes.

As for the Kellogg Peace Pact itself, Georges wrote that it "is looked upon as a symptom – a good symptom – but not as a remedy... It is as if the nations got together and gave a cheer. But it isn't a cure – in fact that is the one thing it is not: a cure supposes treatment and the Pact offers no treatment of any kind. It says in effect 'we will not fight – we will settle all disputes by pacific means.' But what are the specific means proposed as a substitute for war? The Pact might have been a remedy if it had answered that question."[17]

Lord Byng did not let up on his critical attitude toward the League. In October he wrote to Georges: "I am sorry to say I am rather mystified at the work of the League. I read that there is a new disarmament conference every time I take up a paper, but I have not quite arrived at the point as to who is going to disarm and why – after seeing a good many accounts of disarmament conferences I now understand they are going to have a preparatory disarmament conference."[18] (Byng himself had been coaxed out of retirement to become the head of the venerable Scotland Yard, which he described as "a fearful and wonderful machine. It moves along creaking and groaning at every joint, getting tied up in its own cobwebs, and occasionally covering itself up under quilts of official goose-down.")[19]

In the meantime, important Vanier family matters had broken into international negotiations. On 10 September, Pauline felt her labour pains coming on rapidly. There was barely enough time for the taxi carrying her, and the baby's frantic father, to get to the hospital. With only a nurse in attendance (the doctor arrived too late for the birth), their fourth child came into the world. Frances Vanier wrote from Montreal: "Vive Jean François Antoine! Born in Geneva – he should bring peace to the world!"[20] The date and time of the birth coincided with a Canadian delegation dinner. Explaining his absence from the event, Georges wrote with obvious pride, "my wife presented me with a son, number three. Both are doing well: the baby is accused of greediness, because he wanted to be here for the big dinner. However, he only succeeded in preventing his father from being present."[21] Perhaps in deference to the two Scottish nannies, who stumbled over the soft *J* sound and the nasal intonation required to pronounce *Jean* properly, Georges – no doubt with a twinkle in his eye – dubbed the newborn "Jock." Immediately, the family and the nannies adopted this nick-name.

There was good reason for the infant's name to be easy for the Scottish tongue to pronounce: Nanny Thomson became, in effect, Jock's mother. With each new child, Pauline had become increasingly overwhelmed by the responsibility of motherhood. In only seven years of marriage she had experienced five pregnancies, four births, and five household moves, as well as a fire from which the family had barely escaped. Now, the anxiety that had plagued her off and on since her early teens had begun to resurface. The life of a diplomat demanded that a certain amount of entertaining be done – part of Georges's job, in fact, was to discreetly find out the positions on disarmament of the various countries that were involved, and dinner parties and other social gatherings were a necessary means of securing the kind of information needed. Pauline's anxiety seemed to help fuel her extroversion and her ability not only to function brilliantly in society, both as a hostess and as a guest, but also to put people at ease and take a genuine interest in them. But on the domestic front, exhaustion took over and, as it began to slide into depression, paralyzed her.

A portrait painted by the artist Philip de Laszlo during these years betrays nothing of her emotional turmoil, but rather romanticizes her, accentuating her tall, slender beauty, long arms, and expressive hands. Her strapless sea-foam-green dress and artfully draped shawl give the impression of a modern woman, the gold leaves in her dark hair suggesting a nymph or a goddess.[22] When the painting was finished, the artist wrote to Georges: "It is not often that one has the privilege to have a sitter so congenial and sympathetic."[23]

* * *

The year 1929 brought further disillusionment to Georges's world. A Montreal friend wrote admiringly, "You seem to keep in the centre of the world of events. Ability and good looks carry one a long way, and I should have added a charming wife ... I hope you have not become too respectable; I expect you are exactly the same underneath."[24] It is not known what Georges replied, but he might easily have responded that being at the centre of world events was not something to be desired when indecision was the main form of action and there was nothing positive that could give hope for the future. The emotional health of his "charming wife" was in jeopardy, and he felt powerless in the face of the forces that were pulling her down, and bewildered by the gap that seemed to be widening between them. As for himself, he had become a grey-haired, grey-suited functionary who attended long-winded meetings and wrote reports that went into filing cabinets. He was still "not too respectable underneath," but had also not achieved anything of discernable substance in his new career. The pencilled doodles and ink drawings on his meeting agendas, the hurried notes to himself on scraps of paper and backs of envelopes, the sketches of the conference tables and the placement of delegates all suggest frustration, boredom, and a sense of unease about the League's future.

After a four-hour session of the League's General Assembly in March 1929, he wrote a brief impression in his journal: "A ship without a rudder – suggestions rained down and intermingled in a confused fashion and they all collided without anyone trying to find a solution and without coming to a decision. Pitiful spectacle."[25] His notes about the following day's session are even more scornful: "Everyone revolved around the balloon (why not say bladder?) of the Soviets; everyone knew (the Germans and Turks especially) that the balloon contained nothing but poisoned air. But no one dared to touch it for fear of bursting it."[26] The atmosphere, he added, was one of fear bordering on panic.

The sixth session of the Preparatory Disarmament Commission began on 15 April 1929, and thirteen days later he was writing to Lt Col Matthews that "the dominant note was that of shame." The commission had not met since the previous year, and in the intervening time it was expected that Britain and France would iron out their differences and come to an agreement. They had failed to do so. He also sensed a feeling of uneasiness, which he put down to the ineptitude of the chairman of the commission, a Monsieur Loudon from the Netherlands: "it is fair to say that he is a complete failure. I feel sorry for the man because he is very keen about disarmament and is working hard to get the commission to function. Unfortunately he has no idea of procedure, with the result that the commission often turns about in circles without rhyme or reason: a great part of the discussion so far has been entirely 'out of order.' Speakers ramble on, imposing long speeches, altogether beside the point."[27] In his official report he wrote that three years of work had accomplished no agreement on limiting land armaments.

It may have been a relief when one of his great heroes from the war, Maréchal Foch, died and Georges took part in the grand state funeral in Paris; the obsequies memorialized a more glorious recent past and a man whose courage and leadership never failed to stir him. He described the lying in state and the funeral in loving detail to his mother, and later in an article that was published in *The Times*: "the great soldier" in his coffin dressed in his dark blue uniform pinned with many medals, "a look of strength" still on his face; the crush of people filing past the coffin which rested on a gun carriage beneath the Arc de Triomphe; the slow, moonlit funeral procession down the Champs-Elysées to Notre Dame Cathedral; and, finally, the movement of the cortège past the monuments of Paris to the coffin's final resting place in Les Invalides.[28] The whole experience was a stately and honourable contrast to the troubled scene playing itself out in Geneva.

In July, the Vanier family went to a holiday resort called St Lunaire on the coast of Brittany, where they were joined at Le Grand Hotel by the Archer grandparents. Georges noted in a letter to his mother that there was good golfing nearby, and so "father-in-law will be content for four or six weeks." He went on: "The children were – literally – wild with joy: they raced about the broad stretch of hard fine sand, carrying and waving all the beach para- phernalia – shrimping nets, pails, shovels; in Geneva they knew little real freedom of movement."[29]

Georges was forced to return to Geneva early, in order to represent Canada at a committee charged with the revision of the 1906 Red Cross Conven- tion concerning treatment of wounded soldiers and prisoners of war. The revision was not extensive, but experience during the 1914–18 war had indi- cated that the vocabulary of the articles needed to be more precise. Georges's greatest delight was in telling his mother that, as a Canadian government representative, he received a document called "The Powers" signed by King George V with the great seal attached: "Perhaps I may never be appointed a delegate with 'full powers' from the King to sign a convention in the name of the Government. It is a bit of luck that I was named."[30]

1929 ended better than it had begun. Within the next several months, Canada's three-year representation on the League of Nations would be over, and so would his work there, but his newly acquired skill at diplomacy had been noticed, as had Pauline's talent for diplomatic entertaining. He had been offered the post of first secretary at the newly established embassy in Washington, where Vincent Massey was ambassador. He turned down the offer, mainly because of his indecision as to whether to return to the army or remain in the diplomatic field. For the time being, he decided to leave the army option open, partly for pension purposes (although he was assured that his army pension would not be affected) and partly because he did not want to pass up the possibility of a military promotion. Lord Willingdon wrote with regret, hearing of Georges's decision, because "You and Pauline would have been ideal at Washington."[31] What was important was that his work had been noticed.

As well, the stock market crash in October seemed to have little effect on the finances of the Vanier family on Dorchester Street in Montreal, and Phil- ias Vanier, in his usual Christmas gift-giving routine, had sent fifty shares of Montreal Power. Georges described Christmas in Geneva to his mother:

"The tree was brought to the apartment at 8 pm after the young ones had gone to bed (I had read them the poem you taught me, 'T'was the night before Christmas'). We had sixteen electric bulbs of various colours on the tree, which was bright with tinsel and toys of all kinds. When the children came into the room they went first to the manger where they said a prayer and afterwards they were given Santa's many wonderful gifts. The children behaved well, much better than I used to, and managed to get through the Christmas period without indigestion."[32]

Best of all for Georges was the prospect of the upcoming Naval Conference in London, to which he had been chosen as one of Canada's delegates. He would be closer to where real decisions of consequence would be made ("the details of disarmament are unimportant compared with the aims, the ambitions, the aspirations, the interests and fears of the nations,"[33] he wrote to his mother.) He had arranged for Pauline, a two-fingered typist, to accompany him as his secretary. "What fun for Pauline!"[34] enthused Frances Vanier.

No one anticipated the degree to which "fun" would be in scarce supply during the next few months.

8

DIPLOMACY IN LONDON

The four Canadian delegates to the 1930 London Naval Conference stayed at the luxurious Mayfair Hotel, officially opened three years earlier by King George V and Queen Mary. The hotel stood near St James's Park, in the most fashionable part of London.

A photograph shows all four standing beside a wrought iron hand rail: Walter Hose, chief of Naval Staff and Col J.L. Ralston, minister for National Defence, in stovepipe hats straight out of a nineteenth-century novel; a youthful Lester Pearson, future prime minister of Canada, on his first diplomatic assignment, dressed in a jaunty trench coat; and a hatless Georges Vanier, who, alone of the delegates, does not look at the camera. His face is haggard, his shoulders droop forward, and the drawn look about his eyes suggest worry and insufficient sleep. Pearson recorded in his diary a first impression of this delegate: "rather quiet, serious, very polite, and without much sense of humor."[1] This last observation – that Georges lacked the sense of humour that was characteristic of him at his best – is a telling indication that all was not well in his life at this time.

The conference began in January at St James Palace. It was a follow-up to the 1922 Washington naval conference, which had brought about an agreement among the five major powers (the United States, Britain, France, Italy, and Japan) to build no new warships for a period of ten years. They had come together again to decide on how to limit the tonnage and size of weapons on future war vessels.

The meetings were long and contentious, punctuated by dazzling white-tie banquets where caviar, turtle soup, lobster bisque, and other exotic dishes were served on gold plates and accompanied by sherry, rare wines, and vintage port. But the days dragged on slowly, with political differences getting in the way of diplomacy. There seemed, also, to be a breakdown in procedure, and Georges described one scene that was worthy of a Marx Brothers movie: "in adjoining rooms two committees were meeting, one an

Export Committee and the other a Drafting Committee, and members went from one room to the other to consult one another; I suggested to Massigli (from the French delegation) that the doors be kept open and that an attempt be made by various members of both Committees to listen to what was being said in both rooms at the same time."²

In the end, the agreement on how to limit naval weapons was reached only among the United States, Britain, and Japan, and the General Treaty was signed on 27 April. Italy and France abstained, with Italy under Mussolini wanting parity in the matter of naval limitations, and France objecting because it had the Atlantic coast to defend as well as the Mediterranean. Georges wrote to a friend that "The result at the Naval Conference was a complete deadlock between France and Italy, producing irritation in both countries."³ No one yet suspected that another factor would soon loom over the decade ahead: the National Socialist party in Germany, still little more than a fringe movement. In three years' time its leader, Adolf Hitler, would come to power, joining Mussolini on the stage of world history. As a result, naval agreements and all other such treaties would eventually be rendered worthless.

In the meantime, Ralston, head of the Canada's delegation, wrote to Georges from his ship heading back home, to thank him for his efforts on behalf of the delegation, adding "neither of us forget that your charming and amiable wife was the perfect private secretary."⁴ Pauline's effervescent spontaneity and sense of humour never failed to attract male attention. Lester Pearson's first impression of her hints at a chaotic undercurrent, but still shows her ability to project an air of confidence and cosmopolitan sophistication even as her emotions were unravelling. After making her acquaintance, Pearson wrote in his diary that she was "very volatile, energetic, vivacious, tall and good-looking, and a rapid but interesting talker" who "knows many celebrities and is quite a woman of the world." It would have surprised Pauline, always aware of her inadequate schooling, to know that in her presence the Oxford-educated Pearson felt "like an imbecile – or like a colorless schoolgirl with no particular intelligence."⁵ Pearson also admitted later in his memoirs that he could not remember anything about Ralston's wife because Pauline Vanier had outshone all the other women.

It could be that Georges had brought Pauline to London as his secretary to give her respite from the demands of the household and children and the diplomatic milieu in Geneva. Life was dull in London, however, especially with her husband away at meetings all day and in some cases long into the night. There were occasional outings; the Canadians were treated to a West End play one evening, followed by dancing at an establishment with the somewhat racy name of the "Kit-Cat Club." They danced until one-thirty in the morning, and Pauline, who loved such high-energy fun, was momentarily in her glory.

It is not known what scenes played themselves out in the Vanier room at the Mayfair Hotel during the weeks that the Naval Conference droned on. It is possible, given their respective personalities, that there were crying spells coupled with exclamations of clinging devotion on her part and, on his, attempts at patient listening alternating with tight-lipped silence. Georges's own mind was too orderly for him to comprehend her inner tumult. Perhaps he felt constrained by the self-control that had been honed by years of military discipline and an innate sense of responsibility. But it was clear that the alternating torrents of exhilaration and neediness that his wife had expressed before their marriage nine years earlier had accelerated to the point where she needed professional help. Georges may have turned in desperation to Lord Byng because it was his old friend's doctor, a heart specialist by the name of Maurice Cassidy, who was consulted and who agreed to take Pauline on as a patient.

Georges returned to Geneva on 26 April for the meeting of the Committee on Arbitration and Security, leaving Pauline at the Mayfair Hotel for a three-week rest under Dr Cassidy's care. She wrote to him the same day: "My darling, I didn't say good-bye in the way I meant to and wanted to!!! And I'm so lonely, so blue and really could weep. Darling, you are a part of me. I somewhat feel lifeless without you. Oh my own you *do* know how much I love you. We are *old* married people now and we really can't live without one another for long."[6]

In the meantime, the Vanier children had been brought to London by their two nannies and Frances Vanier, who had come from Montreal to look after the Geneva household in the absence of Georges and Pauline. They stayed at the less expensive Leinster Court Hotel, where the children enjoyed exploring the rooms and playing in nearby Hyde Park, and where the dining room staff taught them how to make fancy shapes with the table napkins. Pauline saw them for only short periods of time, taking them on outings for tea and clothes-shopping and haircuts. She also went with them to the zoo one day but the trip was not a success: Pauline, who had danced into the small hours at the Kit-Cat Club a few weeks before, could not keep up. She felt no desire to sight-see or to visit museums. Her weight shrank to a skeletal one hundred and fifteen pounds, and although she was only thirty-two years of age, her dark, luxurious hair was already beginning to turn grey.

In the hotel room, alone, in bed, watching one sunny day after another roll by outside her window, she fretted about her faults: she was an emotional drain on Georges ("you are an angel to accept me with all my faults"[7] she wrote), she was selfish and egotistical and did not listen to him or understand him as well as she should; and even as she wrote, she realized she was writing only of herself and nothing else. She felt sad and lonely without him, but consoled herself with the thought that this time of rest was probably a good thing for him as well because she knew she was wearing him out. "*Mon petit, mon petit,* if you knew how much I loved you and how much I need you. I'm feeling absolutely helpless without you and there's a horrible emptiness around me." Even the chambermaid agreed with her about Georges's greatness, and she repeated for him the woman's awkward words of praise: "The Colonel is the most gentleman I've ever met in this hotel!"[8]

But as she lay in her hotel bed, disaffected and alone, anger began to surface. "Write me real letters, not summaries of your days,"[9] she wrote two days after he left. Then, six days after that, as if the anxiety and depression of the past three years had produced a certain clarity of thought, her courage rose up and she began to articulate the reasons for the emotional distance that lay between herself and her husband: "God knows how much I want to smash that steel armour you're imprisoning yourself in. I think I'd do anything to get rid of it. It's become such a habit for you to keep yourself imprisoned."

There was more: he was an angel and a hero, and he was the best husband in the world, but still, she felt that he did not consider her an equal partner in their marriage. "I know that you think me very much a child, but all the same, Georges, I'm your wife, and I understand things, perhaps better than you realize ... I know you're suffering, and I'm suffering because of that." With little left to lose, risking her husband's anger – or worse, his silent withdrawal into himself – she continued: "I don't want you to remain locked up. It isn't good for you or for me, Georges. If I'm suffering now, it's in large part because I've seen you without ever being able to know you. Georges, don't tell me I'm imagining all this, because I don't think I am. I remember too well our conversations and your letters before our marriage in which you let me really see you. Often – very often – I wanted to speak to you about it, but you never wanted to let me. Why?

Were you afraid of yourself or afraid of me? I know your horror of tears, you thought I'd become melodramatic." Her missive ends, "This letter may be difficult for you and perhaps it will also make you annoyed with me. I'm taking the risk because I can do no more. I've been suffocating too long."[10] At some point during this period, in a fit of rage, she destroyed all the letters Georges wrote to her during their engagement and the first year of their marriage (likewise, Georges's letters to her from Geneva during these few weeks of 1930 have not survived).[11]

After the letter had been posted, she again took to her bed. How would Georges receive it? She wrote again, trying to further explain herself: "I always feel such a need to confide in you, but I don't know how to go about it. I so badly want you to see me as a companion, but above all as a soulmate. You are one of those people who have difficulty revealing themselves, I know, but I want to share everything. Perhaps you're going to tell me that I'm asking for too much, that the best solution is action. It's true that action helps to control thoughts, desires and sensations, but it isn't necessary to control everything. In fact, it's impossible."[12]

She received George's reply by the end of the week, and she wrote back immediately, "Oh! I'm so happy! Your letter of Tuesday has just arrived, so full of tenderness and understanding. Oh! Life is beautiful with you, *cheri*." Once again, he was an angel and she, a spoiled and demanding child. She repeated, however, the request that had been eating at her: "I need you so badly to confide in me, just a little bit, *cheri*, just to show me that you have confidence in me. I feel so stupid sometimes! I don't know how to express things the way I want to, and that makes me feel like a kettle boiling over – I want to feel that I am absolutely necessary to you, mentally and physically." He had written that he did not want her to bother herself with his troubles, but she was not prepared to let go of the one thing that was an obstacle between them. "I want you to learn to have confidence. You will see that despite the way I appear, I'll understand ... and it will do me good to try and do something for you."[13]

Dr Cassidy, meanwhile, had determined that shutting herself up in a hotel room was not good for Pauline: far from resting, she was sinking into deeper neurosis. The best thing for her, he decided, was to return to Geneva to be with Georges. She began making plans; she would travel by train to Paris and rest there if necessary.

Something else, however, had also come up: a slight temperature, and then, a return of some abdominal problems that had been ailing her off and on. She assured Georges that it was nothing to worry about, that Dr Cassidy had ruled out appendicitis and diagnosed it as an intestinal infection aggravated by her weakened physical state. It turned out to be an ovarian tumour, and instead of returning to Geneva, she ended up in a surgical ward, where an operation took place on 21 May. Georges rushed back to London, where the news that the tumour was non-malignant brought some relief. In his personal notes he recorded his visit to her hospital room as she was regaining consciousness. He wrote with tenderness, mixed perhaps with wonder at the vulnerability of their lives. Her colour was good, he wrote, her hands waxen but not cold, her pulse and breathing normal. "Is it all over? ... Have they cut me up?" she asked him. She also asked for water on her tongue, and before lapsing into a morphine-induced sleep, kept murmuring, "Poor Georges, poor Georgie."[14]

In his reply to the letter in which Pauline laid herself bare – her self-described "*cri du coeur*" – Georges had indicated something important for her to hear: that he not only loved her, but he needed her. He may have realized then that she had exposed a crack in their marriage. This crack had the potential of widening to the point where they would move through life on parallel tracks, respecting each other, but each encased in private misery. Such a prospect may have stirred a new awakening in him. It is likely, too, that the sight of his wife in a hospital bed, helpless and in pain, her pet name for him on her lips, moved him beyond her tears or attempts at articulating her feelings.

This crisis in the late spring of 1930 probably marked a turning point in the Vanier marriage. Pauline had made it obvious that despite her emotional fragility, she matched her husband in intelligence and moral strength, if not in formal education. It may also have marked a step toward a new maturity in Pauline, in which her perception of Georges as a white knight and herself as a spoiled child became more balanced. However charged with uncertainties, their marriage was now the beginning of an equal partnership.

During Pauline's convalescence, Georges took the opportunity to pay several visits to Lord Byng. On one such visit, Byng raised the question of the Vaniers' financial situation. This was not an abstract question, nor did it come without some prompting. The family's financial decline – compounding the anxiety over Pauline's emotional state, her surgery, and his work in the midst of an increasingly dismal international scene – was a matter that Georges had kept bottled up. The stock market crash of the previous October had not seemed to touch the Vaniers in Montreal to any great extent; letters brought the insouciant news that Georges's parents might buy a new house, and in the meantime had done some renovations to their current home. And Georges's note of thanks to Philias Vanier's for his Christmas, 1929 gift of shares – "It is a tremendous help to all of us to receive this amount in addition to what we manage to earn during the year"[15] – gave little hint that there was trouble. But in fact, and without Pauline's knowledge, they had begun to sink into debt. Although Georges managed the family's finances, Pauline had her own source of funds in the form of shares from her father, and during the month of May, from her room in the Mayfair Hotel, we find her growing concern in a letter. "What will it cost in shillings?" she asked rhetorically of Dr Cassidy's care, and then she immediately alluded to shares that Georges had asked her for. "I hope everything is going well from a financial point of view, because really, what I've dispensed to you this year is incredible and I'm confused about it."[16]

Whether or not Georges gave Pauline the full picture of their finances at this stage, she became increasingly aware that all was not well and the matter weighed on her. She herself was responsible for some of the debt. Not only was there the matter of Dr Cassidy's care, but her surgery, performed by a Dr Richardson, and subsequent hospital stay, were unexpected expenses. She unburdened herself to Lord Byng when he visited her during her convalescence. Then, when Georges visited him at his country home soon afterward, their old friend found an opportunity to broach the delicate subject of finances. Georges later recorded the conversation in his notes. Byng began, "I know you have had a hard time lately. Can I help you? I would like to do something for you – and Pauline."

"May I think about it, Sir, and may I say how much I appreciate the thought," Georges replied. Throughout the day he reflected on the offer. He supposed his friend wanted to lend him money to pay for Pauline's medical expenses. Georges knew that he could manage, thanks to the generosity of his father and father-in-law. But Lord Byng wanted to help, so was it right to refuse his offer?

The next day at breakfast he told his host, "I have thought of what you said yesterday – really, I can manage very well ... on the other hand, I suppose one should pay these bills as soon as possible ... Richardson's account is paid."

"How much was it?" asked Lord Byng.

"The operation itself cost about 120 pounds – that is paid – but Cassidy's bill – he was very reasonable in his charges – is not paid yet and it amounts to one hundred guineas."

"Why don't you let me pay that?"

"Well Sir, it would be a great help and I could pay you back in a few months."

A moment of hesitation. Then Lord Byng said, "Oh Georges, it is a little *douceur* I would like to offer you. I have some pennies and would like to give you some of them."

Georges hesitated again. It was a humiliating moment: here he was, the son of a culture in which masculine pride derived from a man's ability to provide for his own family. "It is very nice of you, but ..." he began.

"Not nice at all – it gives me pleasure ... I have thought a great deal about this – I have wondered if we are great enough friends ... I would like to pay Cassidy's bill, Georges."[17]

Further protests came from Georges – he *could* afford to pay the medical bill, he must not act under false pretences, it would not be a hardship for him, perhaps he could accept only half the amount ... There may be no greater example of the intricacies in Georges's finely calibrated conscience, his well-tuned sense of justice and honesty, than in this tortured exchange. In the end, he accepted the full amount at Lord Byng's insistence. He, the war hero and army commander, the rising star on the Canadian diplomatic stage, had allowed himself to receive a handout.

He wrote that he accepted it as a "miracle of friendship," but because of his ongoing debts, the next few years would find Georges cap in hand at the doors of banks. Whether his money problems were the result of unwise financial choices on his part or of living beyond his means, or merely the kind of bad luck experienced by millions during the economic crisis of the 1930s, these setbacks had the effect of bringing his pride low.

Two days after Georges received the doctor's payment from Lord Byng, the two went out with Eva Sandford, Lady Byng's former lady in waiting, to cut thistles in one of the fields of the Byng estate. Georges noticed that Byng was moving slowly. He watched his friend with some concern, and suddenly, Byng fell to the ground. Georges and Eva rushed to his side and loosened his collar. He was unconscious; his breathing laboured. He was carried back to the house, and when he revived, he tried to cover over the incident by joking about having left his false teeth out in the field. The doctor, however, told Georges that his old friend and mentor had suffered a serious heart attack and if he were to have another, it would certainly kill him.

The next day, the two friends' conversation was subdued. Byng realized that the attack had brought him near death, and his response was philosophical: "each one of us is near death each day, sometimes several times in a day – some of these doctors have no knowledge of human nature. They mean well I suppose."

"A lot of people who mean well won't be in heaven," said Georges in a stern echo of his Jansenist Catholic background.

"That's what worries me, George – about Heaven and Hell. How can it be Heaven if there are people we love in Hell?"

"Yes, Sir," said Georges, backpedalling away from this particular conundrum.

"Theologians have worried about that for a long time." Neither man was trained in matters of the afterlife, or of theology, and they were probably both relieved to let the conversation end there.

As it happened, 28 July 1930 was the date of the Canadian federal election, and when the election results reached England – a majority government for the Conservatives under R.B. Bennett and a defeat for Mackenzie King – they provided fodder for serious talk of a different sort. The two friends expressed their satisfaction with the outcome, Byng hastening to add that he did not feel vindictive toward King because of the difficult position King had placed him in during his waning months in Ottawa, and Georges clarifying for himself his own political position: that although he considered himself a Liberal, he was not a knee-jerk partisan, and above all, his allegiance was to Byng because of his friend's integrity rather than to King, whose methods he did not trust.

Georges visited the Byng estate again in August, finding Lord Byng almost his old feisty self, chomping at the bit to return to Scotland Yard, but also unusually reflective. They reminisced about the Staff College and their war comrades (but, characteristically, not about their experiences of the war itself). Then Byng brought up the delicate subject of religion. Catholics and Protestants had for centuries been in a state of bitter divisiveness; the spirit of Christian ecumenism was still several decades away, and so friends of differing faiths tended to tacitly agree to leave the subject alone. Byng's niece had married a Catholic, however, and because of the mixed marriage, religious tensions and questions had likely arisen to some degree within the Byng family. In all their years of friendship, this was the moment, perhaps, that defined the closeness of the two men. "Do you consider yourself a good Catholic, George?" Lord Byng asked.

The question seemed to have come from nowhere. Georges hesitated, on guard. "I like to think I am."

"Would you think any the less of a person who became a Protestant?"

The conversation was now entering an ecclesiastical minefield, not worth risking a long-term friendship for, so Georges sidestepped the question – in fact, ignored it diplomatically and replied instead, "I do not think that it is altogether a question of being a *good* Catholic."

Lord Byng, likely fortified with wine or brandy (Georges recorded in his notes that the conversation took place just before they were heading off to bed), then launched into a brief history of the Reformation, which had been caused, he said, by "bad priests." Georges listened and remained silent. "If I thought I should be a better man as a Catholic than as a Protestant, I might become a Catholic but I don't think I should be any different to what I am," continued his host. "I was born a Protestant and I shall die a Protestant – I am an ad."

"And what is that, Sir?" asked Georges.

"One who does not believe in religious controversy."[18] That ended the discussion, at a point more or less where it began; Lord Byng had obliquely said his piece on whatever religious disputes were bothering him, and the friendship remained firm.

At the end of the summer, Georges and Pauline joined the rest of the family, including Pauline's parents, for a holiday at St Lunaire, on the Brittany coast, and Byng went back to Scotland Yard when he had sufficiently recovered. In early September the Vaniers all returned, with the Archers, to Geneva. Preparations were underway for the October meeting of the League of Nations General Assembly, at which Georges was to be a substitute delegate. Former prime minister Sir Robert Borden, still active at the age of seventy-six, had been named head of the Canadian delegation. Georges and Pauline hosted a dinner for the delegates on 11 September. Besides Borden, the guests included Irene Parlby, the Alberta cabinet minister and another Canadian delegate; General Hertzog, prime minister of South Africa; Sir Thomas Wilford, New Zealand delegate; Princess Gabrielle Radziwill, the League's liaison with women's organizations; and Judge Archer.

Organizing an evening for such a high-level group was an onerous task for a young woman who only three months earlier had undergone a serious operation and who was still in a nervous state. Georges, however, pronounced the evening a success: the men entertained each other with stories after the port had been served (the conversation of the women, who included two pioneering feminists – Irene Parlby and Gabrielle Radziwill – was unfortunately not recorded). More importantly for Pauline, her father had seen her in action as a diplomatic hostess, and he congratulated her on her achievement. Sir Robert Borden, however, noticed something else about Pauline. Writing a few months later to Georges, he noted, "During my stay in Geneva, the thought sometimes crossed my mind that she was overtaxing her strength."[19]

Indeed, Pauline was still far from well emotionally. She returned to England in early November and, again under the care of Dr Cassidy, entered a convalescent home. The diagnosis was a common one for the time: neurasthenia, a condition characterized by anxiety, depression, fatigue, and feelings of despondency and hopelessness. At the end of her first week there, the doctor wrote to Georges that she was somewhat depressed, but that at this stage of recovery, depression was normal. More cheerfully, he added, "No doubt she has told you that she is getting off with a General in the room next to hers, who has begun to send her works of poetry with marked passages in them!"[20]

The prescription was rest – and most particularly, a complete release from the pressures of managing a family and organizing diplomatic social functions. Dr Cassidy was aware that because of Pauline's extroverted personality and her spiritual outlook, she needed to reach out to others. Reading poetry in the refined company of a general was only one way of moving beyond herself. Another was visiting patients who were less well-off than she was. Among these, she became particularly interested in young coal miners who were suffering from lung disease, some of whom she kept in touch with until their deaths. These encounters, as well as her period of rest at the hospital, marked not only the beginning of her slow recovery, but also a return to the ideals she had expressed before her marriage in the desire that she and her husband might devote their lives to the service of others.

Pauline stayed in the convalescent hospital until Christmas. In her absence, Frances Vanier continued to help run the household and supervise the children. Their aunt's dimpled smile and fun-loving manner lifted some of the heaviness caused by the dull Geneva weather and by Pauline's depression. Georges, meanwhile, was nearing the end of his three-year commitment to the League of Nations. At the age of forty-two, he found himself once again at a crossroads. There was Pauline's health to consider; this would be the sixth move in their nine years of marriage. Both sets of parents in Montreal were becoming elderly, and growing up in Europe, the children were far removed from their extended family. He had rejected the Washington post, but the question of an appointment to Canada's High Commission in London was now in the air. Should he accept this position or move back to Canada?

Lord Byng was blunt with his advice. At the beginning of November he wrote, "don't think of refusing – you will be doing your country a great service ... I am inclined to think it would be unwise for you to go back into Law or other business after so long an absence."[21] And a few months later, his old mentor was still trying to persuade him: "I would like to see you in a job where your abilities, knowledge of men and matters, manner and Manners etc etc would have some scope – in fact, where you would have some ideal in life to chew upon. Geneva does not give it, the Royal 22nd does not give it."[22] He finished off his letter, as if the appointment was a fait accompli, "You and Pauline should make a huge success of London, and a huger success of French and English Canadianism in London."

In fact, by this time, the appointment *was* a fait accompli. Sometime in the early months of 1931, Georges received an offer to become the first secretary, or second in command, to the Canadian High Commission in London, and he accepted. A colleague of Georges's wrote, "If they had searched the Empire through and through, they could not possibly have made a more excellent selection."[23] It meant another uprooting and another new start, but the move would eventually prove to be productive and happy on several levels. Once again for Georges and Pauline Vanier, a new direction was opening up, even as the awkward peace attempts cobbled together at the League of Nations were beginning to fall apart.

9

HAPPY IN LONDON TOWN

"The whole of London is waiting for the Vaniers with open arms!" wrote Frances Vanier with characteristic ebullience in April 1931. The children, she added, "are happy in London town!"[1]

During the first months of 1931, the family was temporarily split up. The Vanier children, with Frances, Nanny Thomson, and Agnes Young, had debarked from Geneva for the Leinster Court Hotel in London to await Georges and Pauline and the finding of a new home. Georges had made a quick trip to Montreal, where Philias Vanier was in the process of settling his business affairs in the wake of the stock market crash (the crash had finally struck the Montreal Vaniers, and for the first time, the Christmas of 1930 had come and gone without the usual gift of dividends). Pauline, still recuperating and in need of "rest, recreation, exercise and air and a proper diet,"[2] stayed behind in Geneva.

The children, in their own small world with their nannies, had been told only in vague terms of their mother's illness, although they saw evidence of it themselves in her weeping and her inability to nurture them (on one occasion, she had Byngsie across her knee after some misdemeanour and was about to administer a spanking with a hairbrush, when she burst into tears instead; on other occasions, when he woke screaming from nightmares, it was Agnes, the nanny, rather than his mother who lay beside him and soothed him back to sleep). Jock, who had perhaps been the most deeply affected by his mother's emotional absence during the first two years of his life, was once heard screaming at her, "I hate you! I'm going to kill you!" Charles Archer, hearing the child's outburst, remarked (either facetiously or seriously) that they might have a future criminal on their hands in the person of this child.

While still recuperating, however, and as she became stronger, Pauline had spent brief periods of time with the children, teaching them short pieces of English poetry and supervising their writing lessons. She also introduced them to Shakespeare's comedies (describing her reading of *The Merchant of Venice*, she declared five-year-old Byngsie to be especially enthusiastic: "he is anxious to know 'if Antonio's boat will be back in time!'").[3]

By the time the children arrived in London, Thérèse, now eight years of age, had already begun her education with a governess. Georges was proud to report to his mother that she was speaking both French and English fluently. Embracing both the anglophone and the francophone heritage within their family would continue to be one of Georges's and Pauline's major objectives as parents. The four children had by now divided themselves into two groups: Thérèse, as the oldest and the only girl, and Byngsie, the oldest boy, tended to lord their authority over the two younger boys, rivalling each other in bossiness. Bernard and Jock became known in the family as "the little ones." Nanny Thomson, grey-haired, grandmotherly, and gentle in speech, proved to be a capable guardian of the rambunctious youngsters, combining just the right amount of humour and discipline.

By late spring 1931, the family was reunited in London, and Georges's appointment as first secretary to the Canadian High Commission was officially announced in May. The High Commission was situated on a plum piece of real estate, Trafalgar Square, in the heart of London. Formerly the home of a gentleman's club and renamed Canada House in 1923, the building had been opened in a lavish ceremony by the king and queen. Its mid-nineteenth century Greek Revival style featured Ionic columns, a classic pediment, and tall, stately windows; its gilded interior shimmered with glittering chandeliers, marble pillars, and elegant furniture. It was here that Georges was to have his office for most of the next decade, and where he laboured at often mundane and monotonous tasks with the same meticulous care as always.

The first thing he did after his appointment was to write to Prime Minister Bennett on behalf of his predecessor, Lucien Pacaud, who had also been the acting high commissioner for several months. Georges had learned that Pacaud was "standing in the ruins of an unfortunate marriage" and had left the diplomatic service with no financial prospects. Georges pleaded with Bennett to offer Pacaud a pension because "he has been a good servant of the country – he is broken now. You have the wonderful opportunity, Sir, of being magnanimous and helpful to one who was not of your party. It will be a great satisfaction to you and a relief to those who still believe that an ideal is not incompatible with party politics. You will have the wholehearted support of the opposition … Every Canadian would hate later on to see, in regrettable straits, one who for nearly a year was Canada's repre-

sentative and spokesman in London."⁴ It is not known whether Bennett
acceded to this eloquent and audacious request from the diplomatic neophyte.

His first official duty was to help organize a wheat conference. For the
decidedly urban Georges, whose knowledge of the grain industry was probably negligible, this task compelled him to venture into an unknown realm,
but not an illogical one. Since Canada was one of the major wheat exporters
in the world, it stood to reason that this agricultural product would be dealt
with at an international level. The conference took place in May 1931 at
Canada House. There were forty delegates from eleven countries. The object
of the conference was to explore how the world economic crisis had affected
wheat producers, who were being forced to sell at prices below the cost of
production. In the ripple effect that followed, farmers' standard of living
dropped, their purchasing power tumbled, and all business came close to a
halt. But the recommendations arising from this conference were too feeble
to succeed in the face of a complex worldwide problem. Thus nothing decisive was accomplished; a situation in which Georges had been finding himself
for several years.

Although no longer involved in the day-to-day proceedings of the League
of Nations, he observed from a distance its gradual unravelling. When it
was finally decided that the long-postponed disarmament conference would
be held in early 1932, he declared it to be seven or eight years too late. And
in a letter to his friend Harry Crerar, he painted a gloomy picture. Refer-
ring to the demands made on Germany at the Treaty of Versailles, and the
likelihood of Germany's reneging, he wrote, "It is possible ... Germany will
withdraw from the League, and that undoubtedly would be a most serious
matter."⁵ (His prediction proved correct. In 1933, eight months after the
Nazi Party's victory and two days before the General Assembly, Germany
would indeed withdraw from the League of Nations.)

In the meantime, the Vaniers went house-hunting in London. The challenge was to find a home suitable for a family of six, plus two nannies, with
room for diplomatic entertaining. They settled on 19 Cornwall Terrace, one of
a graceful series of white three-storey Regency townhouses circling Regent's
Park. From the upstairs windows, they looked down upon a lake and enjoyed
watching the swans and ducks and rowboats. Once again, they settled into
a domestic routine.

The Vaniers were not strangers to the English upper-class way of life, and
with what amounted to Georges's considerable promotion, they were moving closer to living that life themselves. But their finances, despite the increase

in his pay, could not keep pace with their increased social status. There were certain appearances to keep up, among them a servant-run household befitting the second-ranking Canadian diplomat in London. Some entertaining would come with the job, and Pauline was to remember in later life that she was cast as hostess more often than they could afford. Georges seems to have brought up the financial matter with Lord Byng, who wrote back, "I don't think you will find it too expensive so long as you leave the entertaining to Ferguson [the high commissioner], which you should do."[6] Georges either chose not to heed his old friend's advice, or he was given to understand that entertaining was indeed part of his job expectation. At any rate, he wrote to O.D. Skelton, the under-secretary of state for external affairs in Ottawa, asking for a house allowance and noting that officials of his level at the Canadian legations in Washington, Paris, and Tokyo had such an allowance. He also pointed out that his predecessor had lived in an apartment at the top of Canada House, but his own family was relatively large, and unsuited to such a small space. He added that "it was necessary to take a house sufficiently large and centrally located to be in a position to return the courtesies which government officials and others have been kind enough to extend to my wife and to me."[7]

But even with a housing allowance, debts continued to mount, and financial woes remained a leitmotif in the life of the Vanier family for the next several years. Georges watched with distress as the interest on his loans piled up daily. The family financial situation in Montreal meant that no help was available from that quarter either. In an undated letter from his mother, written probably in 1931 or 1932, she said she had been pressed by his father to give him a clear picture of the family's state and, in particular, to let him know that a request he had made for a thousand dollar loan was going to be difficult to meet. The tone of the letter, written in sentences that blend into each other in an anguished stream, reveals an elderly woman stunned to discover the hardship she has been reduced to after living a life of refined gentility.

The banks, his mother explained, refused to lend Georges's father more cash. Dividends did not come rolling in as they had in the past. "I am not exaggerating when I tell you we have never been so hard up trying to meet our obligations. I have cut all my expenses even to the help. I put them on 2/3 salary, I thought they would leave, but so far have decided to remain, as for pocket money Frances or I have none. We are doing the best we can. If I had any money I would certainly try and help Anthony who is trying to live on $100 a month." Anthony, who had followed his older brother into the legal profession, was now practising law in Montreal, where life was as hard as everywhere else; "the money he earns hardly pays office expenses these days, in fact they are in arrears for rent neither of the partners have money." It was impossible to sell any of their properties, rents were hard to collect, and so the domino effect of the hard times in Montreal meant that the thousand dollars Georges had asked for would be scraped together only in small bits, and only because it had been promised beforehand. "After that you will have to manage the best you can, he will not advance another cent, as we are tired and sick trying to make both ends meet, we have curtailed all our expenses, even to gasoline no more drives etc."

And then, finally, what must have been the hardest thing of all for her eldest son – who was in a sense her confidant and soul-mate – to read: "After having pinched and saved as I have it seems hard at my age we have been liberal with our children, that is your father has. As far as I go I have always had to fight for any money I received being more generous to you than to me."[8]

Georges was aware that his financial difficulties were part of the world-wide depression and that most people were worse off than his family was; the wheat conference had opened his eyes to the distress of the Canadian farmers. From his window overlooking Trafalgar Square he watched the hunger marches by the masses of unemployed workers. This did not lessen his own troubles, however, and as he was to tell Pauline a few years later, his financial worries were compounded by the fear that his health would break down and his young family be left in straitened circumstances.

By 1933 he had become so desperate that, although three years earlier he had been aghast at the notion of borrowing money from Lord Byng, he now approached his old friend of his own accord. Byng replied, "Of course I will try and help, but I must ask you to wait till we get to London so that I can go into my finances at the bank. I have been spending all the ready cash I have in giving employment down here to men on the dole, so I shall have to talk the matter over ... but I think we shall be able to manage it."[9]

* * *

Georges's role at the High Commission was as an assistant to the newly appointed high commissioner, Howard Ferguson, as well as his stand-in. At the time, there were thirty-eight staff members, most of them clerical

and secretarial workers. Although Ferguson never became a friend or mentor in the manner of Lord Byng, he and Georges worked well together. The
Canadian High Commission had existed since 1880, but Georges soon found
out that not only was his job ill-defined but the role of the High Commission itself was unclear. The various Canadian governmental agencies in
Britain – among them immigration, trade and commerce, and agriculture
– still operated independently, and communicated directly with Ottawa
rather than going through the High Commission. Four months after his
appointment, with Ferguson's strong encouragement, Georges wrote to the
Department of External Affairs recommending that there be coordination
among the Canadian agencies. He also suggested that the High Commission
be given overall authority so that "there would be only one interpreter in
Great Britain of all Canadian policy."[10] (As years passed, this coordination
gradually took place.)

Even though the overall mandate of the High Commission was unclear,
Georges's job as a Canadian representative was, in a sense, to present to
Britain the Canada of the twentieth century. To this end, he travelled the
country giving speeches on occasions such as the arrival of the first com-
mercial consignment of wheat on a new route from Port Churchill, the
unveiling of the Shorncliffe War Memorial, and the return of the British
Football Association from a tour of Canada. He represented the Canadian
government at the unveiling of war memorials in the north of France and
sat as Canada's representative on the Imperial War Graves Commission,
where he became friendly with the writer Rudyard Kipling, an unofficial
member of the commission.

The domestic life of the family hummed along meanwhile, with Pauline
becoming stronger, gaining weight, and continuing to curtail her activities.
There were a few outings for her, however: she went with Georges to the opening night of Georges Bernard Shaw's play *Too True to be Good*. "Bernard
Shaw sat in an upper box during the performance but disappeared immediately after, so that the cries of 'Author, Author' were sent up in vain,"
Georges wrote to Frances. They found the play mediocre: "only Shaw could
get away with it – there is a lot, a very lot, of speechifying and talking."[11]

A governess by the name of Madame Phister was engaged to continue
Thérèse's education in French, and she also taught the boys French a few
times each week. A small private boys' school called Egerton House, which
had about fifty students, was found a few minutes' walk from their home.
Byngsie went off first, at age six, pleased with himself in his new school

hat, blazer, and tie, and was followed in subsequent years by Bernard and Jock. Pauline, ever worried about finances, laid bare the family's straits to the headmaster, and letters went back and forth between him and Georges, negotiating the fees for tuition, lunch, sports, and the reductions for the second son and then the third son. Georges, a great fan of the boxing ring from his youth, was eager for his sons to learn the "manly art of box-ing"[12]; Byngsie took to the padded gloves with gusto, but the more sensitive Bernard, bewildered at having to hit another boy, balked at the sport.

At home, a collection of pets formed a menagerie of sorts – a black cocker spaniel named Niggs, two colourful budgies called Jack and Jill, a cat, and a number of goldfish. There were trips to the zoo, where the children rode on an elephant and a camel, and Shakespeare-in-the-Park, where they saw *The Tempest*. On Sunday mornings the family went to the Jesuit church on Farm Street, in the Mayfair district, and then home to read the comics and eat lunch in the dining room – a weekly treat for the children, who normally ate on the third floor with their nannies.

As Pauline's health improved and Georges's work took on the aspect of a normal business day, a regular family routine fell into place. Pauline taught the children prayers, and together with the Protestant nannies – in an ecu-menical gesture long before such activities were common – they said them every morning and night. At the end of the day, when Georges arrived home with the *Evening Standard* under his arm, he gave a short whistle, and the children tore down the stairs to greet him. They loved the fantasy stories he told about the exploits of a recurring character, who was either a boy or a dog – they were never sure – and they clustered around him as he fashioned stick-people from chestnuts, whittling limbs from matchsticks and attach-ing them to the larger nuts, and then making heads out of the smaller ones.

But the feat that made their father super-human (and that characterized his sense of humour), was his ability to jab a pin hard into his right leg with-out flinching. The children never heard him complain of the pain, discomfort, and fatigue he was suffering, and although they saw him walking with a cane and climbing stairs carefully, placing one foot after the other on each step like a small child, they never asked why he had an artificial leg: like his moustache, his stories, and the whistle that signalled his arrival home, it was simply part of who he was. Nor were the strict expectations he had exacted upon those under him in the army felt overtly by his children, on whom he lavished love and encouragement. Anger seldom broke through his iron self-control, and when irritation appeared, it took the visible form of gritted teeth and clenched fists, usually in rather inconsequential circumstances such as waiting for a meal to arrive in a restaurant. On rare occasions at work, he was known to make an abrupt about-turn and walk away, his body stiff, a signal to those around him to stay away.

The Archer grandparents visited the family every year and joined them on seaside holidays, but in 1932, Judge Archer, still active on the bench of the Quebec Superior Court, was diagnosed with cancer. Surgery was performed in London, followed by radium treatment. "Pauline and Mrs Archer are pretty well, considering the anxious time,"[13] Georges wrote to Frances.

Later that same year, Lord Byng, having just retired from Scotland Yard, was raised to the highest rank of the British army, that of field marshal. As always, he gave credit for his glory to the Canadian Corps and the victory at Vimy, writing to Georges, "I now feel, that if I deserved this culminating reward, that old force from the Dominion is the pedestal on which my credit stands."[14] The Vanier family stood by the gate of Buckingham Palace to watch their friend ride in to receive the field marshal's baton. "I loved seeing the little pack at the railings of Buck Pal," he wrote afterward to Pauline. "You all looked so jolly and happy. It seemed the best part of the show."[15]

Domestic contentment in London came to a temporary halt when Pauline learned, in April 1934, that her father's cancer had returned and he was dying. Georges accompanied her to Liverpool, where she embarked on a ship for Montreal. They had now been married nearly thirteen years, and perhaps because of the sad reason for her leaving, as well as his ongoing concern for her health, Georges felt Pauline's departure keenly. He stood on the quay and watched with a sense of desolation as "the ship became a black dot and disappeared over the horizon."[16] Back home, after the children had gone to bed, he wandered from one silent room to another, wanting her to be there. Their bedroom, now empty of feminine things, felt barren. He was doing what he could to make up for her absence; "morning and evening, the children kneel in front of me for prayer, in which *Maman* is never forgotten."[17]

He tried to make up for her departure in other ways as well, visiting one of the young hospitalized miners she had befriended while she herself was recuperating. His name was Billy Williams, and the whole family had become involved in the young man's life, Georges informing Pauline that seven-year-old Bernard had voluntarily bought a two-shilling pineapple for his father to take to him. And on the day before Williams' death from lung disease, Georges quoted the young miner's father as saying, with tears in his eyes,

"In case I should never meet your lady, I want you to tell her I shall never forget her kindness to my son."[18]

From nine-year-old Byngsie's chatty letters, Pauline learned the family's day-by-day proceedings ("It is 6 o'clock now and we are all in the sitting-room, with Daddy. Bernard and Jock are playing with the Meccano and Daddy is reading poems to Thérèse. The poem he is reading now is called 'Cyrano' by Rostand." "We had lunch in the dining room with Daddy. It was Sunday. Thérèse and I sat by Daddy as Bernard and Jock sat by him last Sunday."), complete with daily menus ("Lunch: soup, mutton, carrot, potato, onions, apple pie with cloves").[19] They were speaking French every day, he wrote, and he and Thérèse were racing each other in making their beds.

From Montreal, Frances Vanier wrote to assure her brother about how his wife was faring: "How well I found Pauline and how beautiful she was looking! And everyone in Montreal thought the same … Pauline doesn't look too tired and you are not to worry – she is one of the most magnificent soldiers in life that I have ever known."[20] In fact, it was a mark of Pauline's personality that when called upon to help someone in adversity, she had the ability to summon up courage and strength that often failed her in her efforts to help herself. She wrote that her father was facing death admirably, that he had spoken of the future with composure. She and her mother had gone to Notre Dame des Neiges cemetery to make arrangements for burial, and her mother had suffered through the ordeal without shedding a tear. As for herself, "I face facts and I can bear up, I assure you."[21] She felt alone, however, in her responsibility, as an only child, to both her parents, and admitted to Georges, "It would be so good to be able to take refuge in your arms."[22]

Charles Archer died in late June. Pauline continued to maintain her poise in spite of her grief; after the funeral, she arranged for a gravestone to be erected in the cemetery and then she helped her mother clear out the house, keeping some of her father's clothes for Georges. They stored the furniture and closed down the house. Pauline stayed in Montreal long enough to attend Frances Vanier's wedding to William Shepherd and returned to England in July. Her mother followed soon afterward, the plan being that Thérèse Archer would move to London to be closer to her daughter. Madame Archer found a small apartment in Mayfair and at sixty-four, embarked with vigour on her new – and, as it was to turn out, decades long – life of widowhood.

Pauline came back to the family with renewed vitality and sense of purpose. She would never be entirely free of the anxiety, nervousness, and depression that had driven her to near-despair a few years earlier. But perhaps because of the need to be an emotional support for her parents during the final weeks of her father's life, she discovered unknown resources in herself and realized that she could be strong in the face of suffering. She continued to rely on Georges, but there was also a new maturity that gave her confidence for the future.

* * *

The year 1935 was, in several ways, a watershed year for Georges and Pauline. After spending several months looking for a less extravagant house, they found one at 15 Oxford Square, a high, narrow row house, with smaller rooms and many stairs. They made the most of their reduced circumstances, assuring the children that although Regent's Park was no longer at their doorstep, they had moved closer to Hyde Park. Pauline reported to Georges's mother that the house was "cozier and more *sympathique.*"[23] It was also quieter at night, because their new home was on a square and not on a major thoroughfare. And as for a garden, Georges wrote to Frances that "with a few flowers in the dining room windowbox, one can feel [*sic*] oneself into believing that there is a real garden in front."[24] In fact, the move marked the beginning of an economic turnaround for the family. Complete financial freedom would still take another two years to accomplish, but with a greatly reduced rent, plus Pauline's inheritance from her father's estate, debts and accumulated interest began to fall away.

In June of 1935 came another death that Georges and Pauline had seen gradually approaching. The Byngs had spent the winter in California, where Lord Byng had suffered a mild stroke. Because of his weakened state, his wife had asked that no one meet him at the railway station on their return to London in early May, as the emotional greetings might be too much for him. Compounding the Vaniers' sorrow at the news of his decline, Lady Byng did not allow them to visit him afterwards. Intestinal complications soon developed, and he died on 6 June, shortly after surgery.

Georges wrote a tribute that was published in *The Times*, detailing Lord Byng's first encounter with Canadians on the French battlefield, where he had led them to victory at Vimy, and his love, as governor general, for Canada, where he had been welcomed by the returning soldiers, and where he was happier in the company of farmers, lumberjacks, and miners than in formal settings. More personally, he wrote to a friend, "We have lost a very dear friend, and the world for us will never be quite the same again."[25] Indeed, as a couple, Georges and Pauline would never again have a friendship of such magnitude and depth, combined with such a unique blend of sensitivity and humour, as their friendship with Julian Byng.

* * *

As the fall and winter of 1935 approached, those in the Canadian High Commission in London kept their eyes on Ottawa with more than usual interest. A federal election was looming, and when it was over, the Liberal Party emerged victorious and Mackenzie King once again became prime minister. Howard Ferguson, a Conservative political appointee, immediately resigned as high commissioner and was replaced by Vincent Massey, who had been the Canadian minister in Washington. It was the beginning of a new era at Canada House.

Massey, patrician in style and taste, had attended Oxford as a student and felt at home with the British aristocracy. Relations with Massey were respectful and cordial, but their differing interests meant that he and Georges never became friends. By this time, Georges's old comrade from his Naval Conference and Geneva days, Lester Pearson, now a rising young diplomat, was also a member of the staff at Canada House.

During these years, Georges's idiosyncratic office habits became legendary. It was rumoured that he did not allow a fire in his office, a chilly situation in a London building without central heating. His near-obsessive tidiness was such that he kept nothing on his desk except papers requiring immediate attention. Even his telephone stayed in a desk drawer. His window overlooked Trafalgar Square with its statue of Nelson and the pigeons settled at its base, and, to his left he could see the National Gallery. Across the square, he watched as homeless men and women filed into the crypt beneath the Church of St Martin-in-the-Fields, which was always kept warm for them. He noted with Canadian bemusement the speakers who stood in the centre of the square, declaiming passionately on behalf of various causes and then stopping abruptly for the English ritual of afternoon tea.

International affairs took a sombre turn when Italy, under Mussolini, invaded Abyssinia (now Ethiopia) in 1935. This act of aggression was followed by the amassment of German troops on the demilitarized Rhineland.

Fascism was now on the march in Europe. In Spain, Franco's forces, supported by Italy and Germany, began an armed insurrection in 1936. The same year, Georges was named one of the Canadian delegates to yet another Disarmament Conference in Geneva, where questions were bandied about as to whether sanctions should be put in place against Italy for its intrusion into Abyssinia. "If nothing is done about Abyssinia, it will be a severe, perhaps a mortal blow to the League,"[26] he wrote to his mother. Nothing, in fact, was done. From Geneva he expressed his disillusionment in general terms to Pauline: "Geneva makes me sad. First, you aren't here. But there's something else. I feel like I'm in a lax atmosphere where morale is missing. It's always a matter of politics, opportunity, expediency."[27]

But the threatening signs in continental Europe formed a distant background to a series of royal events that were beginning to unfold in Britain. King George V's Silver Jubilee celebration took place in May 1935, with great pomp and pageantry; it was followed not long after by the king's short illness and death in January 1936. Later in the year, there were the breathless few weeks leading up to the abdication of his eldest son and successor, King Edward VIII, in December. And then, the most resplendent of royal ceremonies, rich in historical and religious significance: the coronation of King George VI in Westminster Abbey on 12 May 1937. Georges Vanier was on the coronation committee as a representative of Canada, and the preparation was monumental. Every minute detail and every piece of protocol was carefully put into place, with practice after practice ensuring that the event would have the grandeur and solemnity it warranted. At Canada House, amid the tension and flurry and overwork, there was also amusement at the fussiness of it all. Lester Pearson later recounted in his memoirs, with lip-smacking detail, his experience of being chosen as a coronation usher and given the grand title "Gold Stick," for which he was obliged to deck himself out in knee breeches and a jacket festooned with gold buttons and yards of gold braid, complete with a sword, and to arrive at the Abbey at four-thirty in the morning, only to be placed behind a pillar where he could see nothing except makeshift lavatories. Georges and Pauline perhaps also smiled, when the clouds of awe momentarily dispersed, at the "dress regulations" on their coveted coronation invitation: "For Gentlemen: Full Dress Uniform or Full Velvet Court Dress. For Ladies: Full Court Dress as for a Court, but without trains. Feathers and veils must be worn."[28]

Wedged in between these larger-than-life royal dramas came one of the most significant moments of the 1930s for Canadians: the unveiling of the

Vimy Memorial in the north of France by the soon-to-abdicate King Edward VIII. The ceremony was attended by thousands of Canadian men who had fought in France twenty years earlier. The distinctive memorial, with its soaring pylons and sombre figures, had been created by the Canadian sculptor Walter Allward. Over the decades the Vimy Memorial has become a Canadian icon, along with the battle it commemorates, but Georges disliked it. "I do not like the association of monument and studio sculptures," he wrote several years later. "The figures at the top of the pylons worry one. They're too far away, they intrigue but do not satisfy ... Vimy Ridge in any event is an ideal spot for a monument, just a monument. This one lacks inspiration."[29]

As an official representative of Canada, Georges was intimately involved in all these royal events, arranging for the official visitors and navigating military and political protocol with scrupulous attention, completing his duties as perfectly as possible. But the exhausting work was taking its toll, and, uncharacteristically, Georges complained in letters to Pauline about the round of visitors who not only ate up his time but – even worse – were boring. "The series of visits continues, it's maddening and is preventing me from doing my work," he wrote.[30] In her August "anniversary" letter of 1936, Pauline wrote in encouragement, "This year has been, I think, one of the most difficult for you, from all points of view, and you have suffered through it admirably."[31]

Compounding the stress were certain tensions that had arisen within Canada House. Vincent Massey and Mackenzie King had serious differences, not only in terms of personal style (Massey the aristocrat versus King the populist) but more broadly in their attempts to thrash out the evolving relationship between the Canadian and British governments and their attitudes to the worsening situation in Europe. Georges may have found himself caught in the middle. There are subtle indications that Massey favoured Pearson: he had tried to get Pearson named as "counsellor," which would have ranked him above Georges. Also, Massey had chosen Pearson as a delegate for the 1936 Disarmament Conference, but was over-ruled by King, who admired Georges's abilities and personal qualities. (Whatever power struggles took place within Canada House at the time, it is a tribute to both Georges Vanier and Lester Pearson that nothing ever hampered their friendship.)

By early 1937, the strain on his nerves and his physical health became such that Georges realized he needed some time away. At the beginning of March, he went for a three-week stay to a health farm called Champneys Tring, in Hertfordshire. "I had begun the habit, through fatigue, of eating too much and drinking too much,"[32] he wrote to Pauline on his first day, adding that this unhealthy regimen had been in danger of spiralling out of control. At the health farm there was a regular routine: rising at seven-thirty in the morning and retiring at ten o'clock at night, and in between there were fasts – "four oranges a day and a mixture of honey and lemon" – as well as massages and salt-water treatments. And, blessedly, there were no meetings to attend. Canada House and his various responsibilities seemed far away. He reported to Pauline that the women outnumbered the men, but the women went about in multi-coloured bathrobes that covered them up. Besides, he assured her, they were sufficiently advanced in age as to "not give the men bad ideas."[33] The rural calm and the physical treatments revived him, and towards the end of the three weeks he wrote, "My stay here has saved my life, I'm not joking."[34]

* * *

On the Vanier home front, family developments had also been taking place. By the end of 1935, as Byngsie reached his tenth birthday, serious thought was given to his further education and, in the tradition of the British elite, Georges and Pauline decided to send him to boarding school. They chose the Jesuit-run St John's, near the town of Windsor, that would prepare him for an upper-level Jesuit school known as Beaumont. On 19 December, Georges wrote to the headmaster at Byngsie's school to tell him that his son would be transferring. The headmaster did not take kindly to the news. "I quite understood that your boys would remain with me up to Public School age, unless you left the country, or I should not have made the very large reductions for the two younger boys," the headmaster wrote in reply to Georges's letter. "I was definitely told by Madame Vanier on several occasions that you were very badly hit and found it very difficult even to send the boys to a day school," he went on. "I felt sorry for you and did my utmost to help. We have made every effort to get Byngsie on as fast as possible, so that he might be able to earn a scholarship when it was time for him to leave." He added that sending their son away to a school with stiff fees "puts quite a different complexion on the matter. Do you intend to do this in the case of the two younger boys?"[35]

We do not have the benefit of Georges's reply; he wrote to the headmaster, asking to see him in person, and they met a week later. What was Georges's response, when the two met face to face, to the headmaster's understandably angry reaction? Had Pauline, in her anxious and impulsive way, exaggerated their financial difficulty? Did Georges offer to make up for any miscommunication in the form of back-pay for the three boys? Was there, indeed, a reasonable explanation – had St John's, perhaps, offered a substantial reduction in fees for Byngsie? The misunderstanding no doubt caused Georges, who valued honesty and integrity above all virtues, acute embarrassment. What seems clear, however, is that whatever his explanation, the headmaster was sufficiently mollified to write, three months later, "Byngsie has worked very well and made excellent progress. He ought easily to get a scholarship at Beaumont."[36]

And so, like generations of brave little schoolboys before him, Byngsie went off on his first taste of life away from home, leaving behind a proud and stoic father and a weeping mother. St John's School had been designed by John Bentley, the architect of Westminster Cathedral in London, and it housed about sixty boys. It was also (probably to Byngsie's relief) surrounded by large fields for cricket, soccer, and rugby.

In early June of 1937, Margaret and Philias Vanier celebrated their fiftieth wedding anniversary in Montreal. Their fortunes had turned around again, and despite both having had a succession of illnesses, Georges's mother pronounced herself "as thrilled as a schoolgirl."[37] Their children presented them with masses of American Beauty roses, and they renewed their wedding vows on 1 June. The only family members missing from the celebration were their eldest son and his family in London. At the end of July, however, Georges, Pauline, and the four children boarded a ship for Montreal, the children now meeting their cousins and Vanier grandparents for the first time.

In September the family returned to London. For the autumn school term, Thérèse, now fourteen, left for a convent boarding school in Mayfield, Sussex. Bernard and Jock joined their brother at St John's. The two boys' final reports from Egerton School declared that Bernard "has worked very well and made excellent progress, he has also improved at cricket." For Jock, "a rather slow starter" who "finds difficulty in expressing himself clearly," the report was somewhat less glowing: a boisterous and fidgety child, he was declared to be "erratic and untidy" and lacking in concentration. The best that could be said was that he "has worked fairly well."[38] Jock was small for his age and had less stamina than the other two boys, and in letters that also contained cartoon clippings and contributions to the boys' stamp collections, his parents continued to reveal their concern about him. "Be sure to muffle up well these days, because the weather is very changeable,"

Georges wrote to Jock in one letter, "and remember what I told you about wrapping up immediately after playing games. No standing about in the cold, young man."[39]

Isobel Thomson and Agnes Young, the two intrepid nannies, left the household as well (the family would stay in touch with them for the rest of their lives) and now, for the first time since their early marriage, Georges and Pauline were alone together. Several months earlier, while he was at the health farm, Georges had written, "This rest is reviving me and preparing me for action. I have a feeling we're entering an interesting period. We'll see."[40]

As the calendar turned over into 1938, "interesting" would prove to be a vast understatement: the events about to happen would permanently alter, in several ways, the Vaniers' world.

Georges Vanier at four years of age. Library and Archives Canada/Georges
P. Vanier Fonds/Acc. No. 1971-311 Box 5820

Georges around 1902. Library and Archives Canada/Georges P.
Vanier Fonds/Acc. No. 1971-311 Box 5820

Officers of the 22nd battalion, 1916. Georges is fourth from the left in the
middle row. Library and Archives Canada/Georges P. Vanier Fonds/Acc. No. 1971-311
Box CO520

Georges, still recuperating from his leg amputation, June 1919. Library and Archives Canada/Georges P. Vanier Fonds/Acc. No. 1971-311 Box 5820

Back in Montreal, June 1920.
Library and Archives Canada/Georges P.
Vanier Fonds/Acc. No. 1971-311 Box 5820

A gathering on the grounds of Rideau Hall, 1922. Pauline is seated, third from the right. Georges is standing, second from the right.

Library and Archives Canada/Georges P. Vanier Fonds/Acc. No. 1971-311 Box 5820

The Vaniers in costume for a fancy-dress ball, Quebec City, mid-1920s.

Georges with O.D. Skelton, undersecretary for external affairs, London, mid-1930s. Library and Archives Canada/Georges P. Vanier Fonds/Acc. No. 1971-311 Box 5820

Pauline Vanier on the occasion of the coronation of King George VI, May 1937. Library and Archives Canada/Georges P. Vanier Fonds/Acc. No. 1971-311 Box C0520

Georges and Pauline greeting Canadian army commander General Andrew McNaughton, Paris, January 1940.

Library and Archives Canada/Georges P. Vanier Fonds/Acc. No. 1971-311 Box 5820

Pauline speaking on behalf of Charles de Gaulle's Free French and the war effort in Trois Rivières, 22 October 1942. Library and Archives Canada/Georges P. Vanier Fonds/Acc. No. 1971-311 Box CO520

Portrait of Georges Vanier, London, 12 November 1943. Library and Archives Canada/Credit: Yousuf Karsh/Georges P. Vanier Fonds/Accession 1971-311, Negative 9021

The Vaniers with General Leclerc, Algiers, 1944. Library and Archives Canada/ Georges P. Vanier Fonds/Acc. No. 1971-311 Box 5820.

10

COUNTDOWN TO WAR

In March 1938, Pauline Vanier turned forty. Tall and slender, with the carriage of a queen and the wide open smile of a child, she radiated a mature beauty. Her hair, now nearly white, made a striking contrast with her dark eyebrows and still-youthful face. She had never gone in for the bobbed styles of her contemporaries, preferring to keep her hair long, gathering it at the back and pinning it up. She admired fashionable clothes, but simple lines better suited her statuesque figure, and she tended to favour classic suits and dresses in black, grey, and white.

She also captivated people with her combination of chatty friendliness and worldly sophistication, and by her willingness to laugh at herself after she put her foot in her mouth with an indiscreet comment or an unfortunate combination of words (such as when she told a distinguished gentleman guest that he must take advantage of the housemaid). Because she had been thrown into the international milieu of Geneva, she was able to move more or less seamlessly into the world of London society and the more rarefied arenas of diplomatic circles. She made up for her lack of a proper education with a formidable memory, a natural intelligence, and an ability to listen intently to serious conversations and pick up bits of information and opinion to use on future occasions.

She shone as both hostess and guest, putting people immediately at ease by taking a genuine interest in them. The Vaniers had long ago broken through the barrier separating the British upper crust from the hoi polloi because of their friendship with Lord Byng and the invitation they had received years earlier to dine with the king and queen. Georges's contribution to entertaining was to supply the wine; he left the rest to his wife. Although his knowledge of world affairs, courtly manners, and overall *savoir faire* made him a good conversationalist in small groups, he had far less physical stamina than his wife, and standing at social receptions proved excruciating for him because of his prosthetic leg. He had a deplorable memory for names, so the couple devised a system in which, whether as hosts or as guests, Pauline would address others first, saying their names loudly enough for her husband to catch on to who they were.

A 1937 letter from Dr Cassidy to Georges reveals the beginning of an eye weakness that would plague Pauline for the rest of her life. Quoting the specialist she had visited, Dr Cassidy diagnosed the problem as "some opacities in the jelly between the lens and the retina" and "some areas of degeneration in the retina of the left eye," but otherwise there was nothing to be immediately alarmed about. As for a prescription, "I have advised her not to strain her eyes too much on small detail, but I gather that she does not do a great deal of reading or fine needlework."[1]

Indeed, the traditional feminine art of fine needlework had never been one of Pauline's chosen pursuits. By the mid-thirties, having regained her physical energy, she had once again, acting on Dr Cassidy's advice, begun to visit hospitals. And something else besides her various social activities had begun to claim her attention: a quest for spiritual depth in her life and a desire to meld this with a life of service to others.

Ever since moving to London in 1931, the Vaniers had been attending the celebrated Jesuit church on Farm Street. The Jesuits in England had come a long way in the four centuries since members of their religious order were accused of treason and then hanged, drawn, and quartered under Elizabeth I. Their fortunes had risen and fallen according to the religious and political tenor of each succeeding period. The Jesuits really began to come into their own in the aftermath of the Catholic Emancipation Act of 1829, which paved the way in abolishing the discriminatory laws against Roman Catholics in Britain. The London street where the Jesuits built their church had, at one time, been the stable yard of a farm. In the mid-nineteenth century it was still a back street, but it was closer to the heart of London than any other Catholic church had dared to come. Built to seat a thousand people, the church combined clean neo-Gothic lines and an ornately Victorian interior, complete with soaring nave and gilded high altar.

By the 1930s, the little back street with the modest name had become part of the fashionable Mayfair district of London. Farm Street Church was one of the best known Catholic churches in Britain, partly because of the erudition and fine preaching of the priests, and also because of the beauty of its liturgies with their splendid brocade vestments and outstanding choir. Among its worshippers were gentry and literati (the Jesuit poet Gerard Manley Hopkins had been posted there as a young priest, and the novelist Evelyn Waugh had become a Catholic there in 1930). Although the Jesuits frequently became spiritual guides to the well-off, they themselves lived modestly (Waugh noted in his diary that in the priests' quarters next to the church, the furniture was shabby and mismatched; he also modelled the humble priest in his novel *Brideshead Revisited* on the rector of Farm Street church).

Around the turn of the twentieth century, some theologians began seeking ways for Catholicism to forgo the siege mentality it had lived under since the Reformation. They wanted the Church to begin examining its relationship to the modern age, especially in the light of recent scientific findings and other scholarship. Among them was a Jesuit by the name of George Tyrrell, who lived at Farm Street. He criticized the Church for being resistant to change, and pleaded for a flexible approach in its teachings as well as a re-evaluation of how those teachings were to be interpreted in the light of changing times. The movement became known as "modernism," and the Vatican came down like a thunderbolt on these new ideas. Tyrrell was expelled from the Jesuits and from the Catholic Church, and although most of his fellow English Jesuits reacted negatively to the harsh treatment meted out to him, they themselves fell in line, and ultramontanism – the subjection of thought and action to the authority of the Pope and the Vatican – remained the order of the day. But the shadow of the modernist crackdown cast a pall on the Jesuits' lives and work.

Theological wrangling, however, was the furthest thing from Pauline's mind when, in late 1934 or early 1935, she set out for Farm Street to seek spiritual help. It was a quest that, in a sense, renewed the fervour of her youth. There were several possible reasons for this. There was still a lingering grief over her father's death. As well, she had begun to emerge from the paralysis of her emotional breakdown and likely felt the freedom to explore her inner life now that the children were older and away at school. She probably also sensed the kindly influence of her mother, who was now living in London and to whom she had always been close. In addition, shortly after moving to London, Pauline had become close friends with two other women who were looking for deeper meaning in their lives: Edith Drysdale, who was Lord Byng's private secretary at Scotland Yard and later the wife of his deputy, Trevor Bigham; and Ruth Kane, an American married to a film producer. These two eventually became surrogate aunts to the Vanier children, who addressed them as "Drysie" and "Aunt Ruth." Whatever the immediate reasons, Pauline began a daily routine of Mass and regular guidance from a partially blind Jesuit by the name of Roger Clutton.

At some point, Father Clutton suggested that she visit a Carmelite monastery in the town of Hatfield, north of London, where he knew the prioress, Mother Mary of the Cross. Pauline was to develop a lifelong association with the Carmelites. They were a cloistered order of nuns who, because they lived behind medieval-looking iron grills, seemed from afar to be rather remote and fearsome, but in fact proved to be friendly and approachable. They counted among their spiritual forebears the luminaries St Teresa of Avila and St Thérèse of Lisieux, and although they worked at simple jobs like gardening and making vestments and communion wafers, their lives were otherwise spent in meditation and silent contemplation. They took as one of their mottos the simple injunction of the prophet Isaiah, "In silence and in hope shall your strength be." Mother Mary of the Cross was seven years older than Pauline and so was probably in her mid to late forties when Pauline first met her. Originally from Ireland, she was known to have a temper as well as a ready smile and a robust sense of humour. Pauline was to seek guidance from her until the nun's death in 1952.

Although Georges referred to his wife as "the best of women and of mothers,"[2] it is likely that Pauline never learned to be maternal in the sense of a nurturing, assuring presence. Her anxiety came to the surface in her dealings with the children during their growing years. She seems not to have learned the art of gentle persuasion, instead tending to lay expectations rather heavily upon them. But it is probable that her simple goodness and deepening spiritual life, overlaid with her ability to laugh at the ridiculous side of things, permeated the household. Letters from Georges to her indicate that he held her in awe. "I realize that few men have had the happiness to find in life a woman whose physical beauty is matched by beauty of the soul and the heart," he wrote in 1936, adding that "if [the children] are becoming good and strong in spirit it will be your work. You have brought them up admirably, by your advice, by your direction, by your example."[3]

Life was not perfect between them; Georges continued to be closed-in, non-demonstrative, and fastidious to a fault, and his lifelong hesitation in making decisions caused his wife considerable irritation. "I was very unjust toward you,"[4] he wrote contritely in the summer of 1935 when the family was on holiday in the seaside town of Rottingdean, "and I'm reproaching myself more than you think for having made you put up with the uncertainty. It was very bad." (This was probably one of the occasions when his indecision regarding summer holidays meant that the family was left with less than acceptable accommodation at a more than acceptable cost). He

also felt acute embarrassment over the way he had handled the family's financial affairs in the early years of the decade: "I'm not proud ... of myself,
mon petit, when I think of my failure in steering our barque ... I am profoundly humiliated before you by my lack of success."[5]

As a husband, Georges treated Pauline with old-world gallantry, always
remembering her birthday and their anniversary, giving her flowers as a gesture of gratitude on the birthday of each of the children, and rising from his
seat every time she entered the room. But it was in the most intimate part
of their life together that he was most grateful and in which his vulnerability as a man is revealed most clearly. It had been obvious from the time of
his marriage proposal that, easily as he might downplay his wartime injury,
the question loomed large for him as to whether, with only the stump of a
right leg, he could be romantically and sexually attractive to a woman.

Pauline never wavered in that regard. "You are the best, the most tender
of women," he wrote in response to her 28 August 1935 letter. "In marrying me you gave me back my physical pride; since then I have never felt the
least sense of inferiority or diminishment – it's thanks to you – and to say
that I am grateful to you *is to say nothing!* I owe you all my success (which
is relative, it's true) ... I am profoundly moved when I consider that never
have you seemed to feel that anything was lacking in being married to a
man who, after all, is incomplete. There is only one explanation – your
beautiful and generous nature makes you capable of a love greater than
that of other women."[6] And the following year, for their fifteenth wedding
anniversary, he wrote, "In marrying me you restored my confidence in myself. You gave me a clear indication, and it was obvious you meant it, that
you didn't in the least consider me physically diminished. When you agreed
to marry me, bursting with open-hearted sincerity, you confirmed me in my
dignity, in my pride, and perhaps also in my vanity as a man ... I thank you
for your love, your help, your example, for the gift of your whole being."[7]

He was also proud of the way she attracted other men. From Geneva, he
wrote in 1936 that others were telling him that she was the most important
element in their alliance. A delegate from India, who had heard people speak
about Pauline, said to him, "She should have come the other half of you,"
to which he responded, buttons bursting, "And more."[8]

He still puzzled over the lighthearted way she approached her religious
faith, seeking spiritual depth and retreating to a monastery to pray, and yet
still enjoying the glamour of parties and other social functions without any

feeling of guilt. Georges himself had come a long way from the ultramontane atmosphere of the Catholic Church in Montreal, where people were encouraged to take part in rote forms of piety and discouraged from thinking for themselves. His exposure to ideas and views other than his own had given him a sophisticated view of the world. When it came to his own practice, however, the view of religious faith as gloomy and difficult made him approach life with a rather heavy spirit and an amorphous sense of guilt. He could not understand that religion might be viewed in any light other than a series of moral obligations. Pauline's passionate insistence on freedom of the spirit confounded him.

Although there was never any doubt about his wife's love for him alone, there was one group of men he may have wondered about: Catholic priests. Until the end of her life, Pauline was to seek out priests for spiritual solace. For now, the unassuming Father Clutton remained her rock, but she also came under the influence of another Jesuit, named Robert Steuart, who gave talks that were known as "Wednesday Conferences" every week at Farm Street. It is likely that Pauline began attending these conferences and that something in Father Steuart's message made her want to hear more. She found out that he gave religious retreats of two or three days' duration in various locations near London, and began attending some of them. She soon became an avid devotee.

At the time, Father Steuart was one of the most celebrated preachers and writers in England. He came from a family of Scottish gentry, and as a young man he had spent a short time in the army, spending money extravagantly, drinking excessively, and taking up with wild and rebellious friends. His activities enraged his father, whose refusal to allow him to come home was instrumental in his decision to become a Jesuit. As a young priest, he combined worldly elegance and religious zeal, fretting about his increasing baldness and using potions to stay the loss of hair (even in middle age he wore his fringe somewhat long in a vain attempt to give the illusion of having more hair than he actually did). At the same time, he tried to overcome his natural indolence and vanity and become more dedicated and selfless. He was also naturally shy, a condition that led to his appearing outwardly brusque.

At some point during his early years as a Jesuit, Father Steuart declared himself unable to meditate and pray, and unusually for a priest, he sought help from a nun (in most cases it was the other way around), who led him away from mental fussiness into the deeper, wordless form of prayer known as contemplation. It may have been this nun's influence that made his conferences and retreats especially attractive to women. At any rate, after spending the war years as an army chaplain in France, he spent the rest of his life as a preacher and a writer. He had been a friend of the ex-communicated Jesuit George Tyrrell, and indeed he himself was described as having some of Tyrrell's spirit.[9] This suggests that perhaps he had developed an ability to express spiritual matters in original ways rather than in formulas, allowing him to zero in on the heart of what was important.

Father Steuart leaned, like the Carmelites, toward the gentle passages of the Bible that offered wisdom in few words ("Be still and know that I am God," "God is Love"), and preferred simple maxims such as the saying of the medieval mystic Julian of Norwich that "Love is His meaning." He did not minimize suffering or the condition known as the "dark night of the soul," but rather encouraged abandonment of the ego and surrender of oneself in the face of such afflictions. He also gave robustly practical advice, such as get enough sleep, take enough nourishment, and seek medical help when needed. He enjoyed good food and wine himself, and did not go in for preaching harsh asceticism.

* * *

It is not clear how it came to be known in the Vanier household that Father Steuart would be preaching the service at the church of St Ignatius, Stamford Hill, on Good Friday, 15 April 1938. One version has it that Georges saw the notice in a newspaper and remarked to Pauline, "Did you know your Father Steuart is preaching at a church quite close to us?"[10] and then, feeling trapped, reluctantly agreed to go and hear the priest. The other account has him saying with some irritation, having been cajoled by his wife once too often, "All right, then, I'll go and hear your Father Steuart!"[11] The interesting common element in the two versions is Georges's use of the personal possessive pronoun, "your," coupled with an expression of resistance. Had Georges heard this priest's name on his wife's lips one too many times? If so, it would not have been the first time that a wife's devotion to a priest had come between her and her husband. Regardless of what lay behind his reluctance, it was clear that Pauline wanted to hear Father Steuart preach on Good Friday, and so Georges agreed to tag along.

Stamford Hill, in the north London borough of Hackney, was a less fashionable area of the city than Mayfair, and St Ignatius Church, built in the early years of the twentieth century, did not have the aristocratic cachet or the Gothic aura of Farm Street. The interior was unadorned and surprisingly modern – a black and white tiled floor, plain white pillars, a deep sanctuary with two rows of choir stalls. The gilded words on the black gates of the communion rail, "Laudate Dominum Omnes Gentes" ("Praise the Lord, all peoples"), were the only signs of ostentation. A pulpit stood about three-quarters of the way up the nave, with a wooden canopy built to carry the preacher's voice. The church had rows of chairs rather than pews, and on Good Friday, it appeared even more plain than usual. As was required for the last two weeks of Lent, purple cloths covered the Stations of the Cross, the statues and the paintings. All floral decorations had been removed.

As people streamed into the church, Father Steuart, still handsome and fine-featured at the age of sixty-four, was likely pacing back and forth behind the altar, as he usually did before preaching. At noon, he strode inside, wearing a loose short white shift known as a "surplice" over his black cassock, and a purple stole around his neck. The fair-skinned dome of his head shone as he mounted the steps to the pulpit.

The church was always packed on Good Friday, with people standing in the side aisles. The most sombre service of the Christian calendar, commemorating the death of Jesus, the Good Friday liturgy of the 1930s lasted three hours, following the period from noon when, according to the gospels, Jesus was nailed to the cross, until three o'clock when he died. The service consisted of a meditative sermon called "The Seven Last Words of Jesus on the Cross," with hymns sung at intervals. As was his custom, Father Steuart took off his watch and laid it on the ledge of the pulpit in front of him. He began to speak, using no notes.

The "Seven Last Words" were discourses on the final utterances of Jesus as recorded in the four gospels. What exactly struck Georges as he sat in discomfort on his rigid chair during the three hours is not known. It may have been simply Father Steuart's presence, pouring his whole being into his sermon, or it could have been one of the dramatic series of words spoken by the dying Jesus – "I thirst," or "My God, my God, why have you forsaken me?" – that touched him. Perhaps the priest brought in one of his own favourite biblical passages, "With an everlasting love I have loved you; therefore have I drawn you," from the Book of Jeremiah. In some way, a realization of the mysterious connection between suffering and love brought him the recognition of a profound truth: that the divine resides in places of the heart, and not in a narrow moral code.

When the Vaniers emerged from St Ignatius church with stiff bodies after three hours of sitting, Georges's view of the Christian way of life had taken an about-turn. Outwardly, he would remain the same intelligent and con-scientious diplomat, with the same dry and teasing sense of humour, the same devotion to his children and quiet friendliness and sincerity that struck everyone who met him. But the door of moral and spiritual rigidity that had gradually become unlocked during his seventeen-year marriage to Pauline now stood open to the essential Christian message of love, mercy, and forgiveness.

A month later, Pauline went for a five-day retreat given by Father Steuart at a retreat house in the village of Grayshott, in a lush green corner of Sur-rey. The retreat house was a large mansion set among cedar and pine trees; it was situated beside a small church where the graves of Canadian soldiers from the army camp of Aldershot lay in three rows. A letter Georges wrote to her there contains his only written reference to the man responsible for the change in his spiritual outlook: "Indeed, Father Steuart must possess robust health in order to display such huge vitality. The conferences must exact an outlay of physical as well as emotional energy, judging from Good Friday."[12]

In Pauline's annual letter the following August, she indicated that a final barrier in their intimate life together had now been removed, and both laid the reason for it at the door of Father Steuart's Good Friday discourses. "If I've always admired and loved you tenderly, never before this year have I felt myself to be in this communion of soul and of heart that I now feel to be with you,"[13] she wrote. Georges replied, "Yes, *mon cheri*, this year there is something new, more beautiful and greater in our love. This change is due to you, to your example, to your prayers and I thank you for it with all my heart."[14] Georges never spoke of this experience to anyone but Pauline, and it was only after his death that his children learned of it.

* * *

The first months of 1938 had brought no signs of hope in Europe, and many indications that the situation was worsening. The Nazis invaded Austria in March, and by now there was open talk of the possibility of war. On

London streets, there were clashes between the communists and Oswald Mosley's British Union of Fascists. Hitler's ranting speeches could be heard on British radio, and air raids and anti-gas measures were quietly being planned. Men were encouraged to enlist in army units.

In April, disquieting family news came from Montreal. Georges's brother Anthony, now thirty-seven, sent a letter for Georges's fiftieth birthday in which he revealed that he was about to have surgery the next day because "a large tumour [is] growing behind my stomach and between the kidneys, this naturally has been pressing down on certain nerves about my back." He went on to add matter-of-factly, "He will find either that it is cancer or only a benign (what an expression to give it!) tumour, in which latter case he will operate to remove it."[15] A cablegram from Frances a week later indicated that the surgery had been unsuccessful; the tumour was growing rapidly and could not be removed. Georges's mother wrote throughout the summer to keep him updated on Anthony's condition. She was pleased to report that both she and Georges's father were "very well and strong"[16] so that she could focus attention on helping to nurse her invalid son. Her letters gave full details of Anthony's suffering and the attempts to relieve it – the sleepless nights, the X-ray treatments, the codeine. She spent every afternoon with him, exhausting herself in the summer heat.

On the international front, observers in Britain held their breath during the spring and summer months as German forces moved toward Sudetanland, an area of Czechoslovakia that was home to large numbers of ethnic Germans. Prime Minister Neville Chamberlain maintained a policy of appeasement toward Germany, hoping to reach a peace agreement with Hitler. As the summer progressed, however, Hitler's ranting became more belligerent. Headlines spoke of increased numbers of troops being amassed in Germany while Britain held on to the desire for peace. On 30 August, Georges wrote to Pauline, who was on holiday with the children in the French resort of Varengeville, near Dieppe, "The European political outlook isn't bright. Ten days from now matters will adjust themselves (or probably will be adjusted), but no one knows how … I'm still optimistic."[17] The next day he wrote, "The political situation remains the same, but I don't think there's going to be a war. There will be some difficult moments to go through, but common sense will prevail."[18]

In early September, events began to move rapidly. But for Georges, whose concern had been heightened by his brother's worsening condition, personal news broke in first. Early in the morning of 7 September, he received a cablegram from Frances saying that as a result of two gall bladder attacks, their mother was seriously ill. A few hours later another cablegram arrived: their mother was dying. And then less than two hours after that, the dreaded news: "Mother died quietly 6:40 this morning." Margaret Vanier was seventy-four years old. Georges cabled back: "Shocked beyond words and distressed I was not with dearest Mother when God took her."[19]

On 15 September, Chamberlain flew to Germany to seek a meeting with Hitler; he returned the next day, having secured a date to discuss peace. The tension grew, compounded, for Georges, by a biting sorrow that intensified on 17 September with a cablegram from his sister Eva that "Anthony much less well advisable come out immediately."[20] He cabled back: "In view international situation cannot possibly leave Pauline children till danger period is over ... Am distressed not able leave immediately but know family will appreciate my predicament."[21] Then came another shock from Montreal for Georges, who was still reeling from his mother's death: his father, Philias Vanier, died of heart failure on 21 September, exactly two weeks after his wife. Georges could do nothing but grieve alone while Britain hung between peace and war.

The next day, Chamberlain flew to Munich, where an agreement was signed allowing Hitler to take over the Sudetanland and no other territory. The prime minister returned to Britain on 30 September, and stood in the wind, his collar starched and stiff, waving the signed agreement in the air. There was a collective sigh of relief. In Ottawa, Mackenzie King applauded Chamberlain's success. At Canada House, views varied: Massey was pleased, convinced that the basic decency of the German people would prevail over Hitler's aggressiveness; Pearson was darkly pessimistic. For Georges, still mourning his parents' deaths and worried about his brother, the agreement allowed some breathing space. The danger was over, war was averted, and he could take the first ship back to Canada.

He left the next day, 1 October, on the *Empress of Britain*. In Montreal, he spent his days visiting his parents' graves and sitting by Anthony's bedside for long hours. He found Anthony weak, but courageous and interested in everything that was going on. Ever the optimist, he wrote to Pauline that he was convinced Anthony would be healed through prayer. The more realistic side of him knew that a miracle was not going to happen. But how long would his brother linger? The doctor could not say, and so Georges, unable to stay beyond the end of November, returned to England.

Anthony died on 8 December, leaving a wife and two young children. Two weeks later Georges wrote to Frances, "I haven't had the heart to write to you about Anthony. I know how you feel, and you know how I feel, so I took refuge in silence."[22] There was a bittersweet consolation, however, in knowing that the last piece of news Anthony received before lapsing into unconsciousness was about the brother he had hero-worshiped. Georges had received a promotion.

Rumours had been in the wind for six years: Canada was expanding its diplomatic presence, especially in Europe, and Georges was an obvious choice to assume a more responsible position. But where? Holland, Belgium, and France had all been mooted. On 5 December, the official announcement came: Georges Vanier was named "Envoy Extraordinary and Minister Plenipotentiary" to France. Although the Canadian legation in Paris had not reached the level of embassy, this was tantamount to an ambassadorship. On 14 December, O.D. Skelton, the under-secretary for external affairs, wrote, "The confidence we all have in the work you will do in France is strengthened by the fact that you will have Madame Vanier to support, inspire and criticize you as occasion requires."[23]

Much as they had loved living in London, this promotion was the culmination of Georges's ambition to attain a position in which his leadership ability and his experience in the world of international diplomacy would shine. And France – the home of his paternal forebears, which still held evocations of romance, myth, and heroism, on whose soil he had fought for freedom, and whose pastoral countryside was dotted with the graves of his fellow Canadian soldiers.

In little more than a year, his ancestral homeland would once again be under siege, and he along with it.

11

BEGINNING OF WAR

If Georges Vanier had any inkling that in moving to Paris he was entering the lion's den, he did not show it. In a speech to the Canada Club, given at the Savoy Hotel in London, he implied that the only thing that would have held him back from accepting the Paris posting would have been resistance from Pauline. "I owe much to her inspiration, much to her advice and criticism in which for my good she is not always sparing. Without her by my side, I would not like to face the task in Paris."[1] As he stepped into his new role, his silver-grey hair, his military bearing, and his height of just over six feet gave him a distinguished appearance. His gaze was clear and direct, giving the impression of a quiet confidence. To those who welcomed him, his loss of a leg on French soil while fighting for freedom made him an instant hero.

Having left the children in their English boarding schools to finish out the school year, Georges and Pauline moved into a one-floor apartment, with tall windows and ornate wrought iron ledges, at 55 avenue Foch, one of the grand boulevards leading down to the Arc de Triomphe. At some point after his experience of Father Steuart's Good Friday sermon the previous year, Georges had begun to accompany Pauline to daily Mass, and they continued this routine in Paris, beginning each day at the church of St Honoré d'Eylau at Place Victor Hugo, a short walk from their home. They also set aside a half hour each day for private prayer and meditation. For this quiet period, Georges found a small white church tucked into rue Cortembert, a long and narrow street of townhouses with geranium-filled window boxes and iron balconies. The church was open day and night, and had a tranquil, neo-Gothic simplicity. The busy sounds of the nearby Place du Trocadéro were a reminder that he was not removing himself from the world by spending this time in solitude, but paradoxically, immersing himself more deeply in it.

To Pauline, Paris was the centre of all that was chic and cultured. She was attracted by the glittering society of aristocrats and intellectuals that awaited her there as Canada's chatelaine. But she also felt ambivalent about being swallowed up by a life of vanity and superficiality, faced with social obligations when she longed for the peace of a Carmelite monastery. Thirteen-year-old Byngsie commiserated with her: "I'm sorry you have so much social stuff, which is really so pointless and yet it has to be."[2] In London, she had been sustained by Father Clutton's calm direction and advice, Father Steuart's conferences, and her occasional visits to the Carmelites where she consulted Mother Mary of the Cross. What would be her spiritual mainstay in Paris? Father Clutton sent the following advice: "Be assured you are all right ... Don't mind your vanities – laugh at yourself."[3]

The first weeks in Paris were taken up with diplomatic formalities. The Canadian legation, which had a staff of twelve, stood on rue François I, overlooking the Seine. Most of Georges's initial duties consisted of protocol visits to the French prime minister and the various ambassadors, and Pauline followed suit, introducing herself to the ambassadors' wives. To the "poor children, abandoned by their father"[4] back in England, Georges wrote chatty letters, and Thérèse replied with news of her roles in dramatic productions, the boys by regaling their parents with cricket scores and rugby triumphs. London friends kept an eye on the children.

The children joined their parents in Paris for the Easter holiday, at the end of which Georges and Pauline waved them good-bye at the Gare du Nord. There was a sense of adventure travelling on their own back to England, and Byngsie wrote to his parents of the thrill he felt when the boat pitched and rolled on the choppy waters of the English Channel. In less than two months, however, Georges and Pauline themselves were back in England. Byngsie, whose weekly letters unfailingly cheered them, lay dangerously ill.

The phone call came on 11 June from the school's rector. Their son's appendix had burst, leading to a pelvic abscess. Emergency surgery had been performed, but a residual abscess formed, which burst through the scar tissue. Antibiotics were not yet in use, and sulfa drugs were the only means of fighting infection. Georges and Pauline sat by helplessly as the question hung in the air whether the abscess would poison Byngsie's system or pass through the drainage the doctors had put in. On 21 June the abscess broke and was discharged through the drainage, and the boy's life was spared.

Their son's illness had temporarily blotted out the world's problems, but back in Paris the danger of the international situation struck the Vanier couple with full force. A scant two months after their arrival in January, German troops had marched into the remainder of Czechoslovakia in direct violation of the Munich agreement. Chamberlain soon realized that Hitler had no intention of keeping the peace, and on behalf of the British government he announced that if Hitler invaded Poland, Britain would become militarily involved. It was the end of appeasement. Georges sent a dispatch to External Affairs stating that "If the British guarantee to Poland puts an end to German expansion through the threat of force, it also puts an end to the policy of non-interference and carries with it the definite risk of precipitating war."[5] This was a straightforward assessment of the situation, and he was equally blunt in a letter to Pauline. "I think the international atmosphere is less polluted *for the time being*, but the same problem still exists: there is an abscess that has to be drained sooner or later."[6]

The "sooner or later" attitude drove the whole of life in Paris during the summer of 1939. It was decided that Pauline, her mother, and all the children, including the convalescing Byngsie, would spend their holiday again in Varengeville on the Normandy coast, away from the possible targets of London and Paris. The Canadian legation began preparing a register of Canadians living in France. Evacuation plans were put in place. By the end of August, Georges was reporting that the army had taken over industrial firms that produced arms and other military equipment. The number of trains taking people away from Paris was increased, and those without urgent business in the city were pressed to leave. All staff members of the legation received gas masks and instructions on how to use them.

At the Hôtel de la Terrasse in Varengeville, the days were long and sunny and the beach perfect for swimming. The presence of the movie star Bette Davis at the same hotel added glamour to their stay, and the Vanier children scrambled to get her autograph. If there was worry emanating from Paris, it did not cloud their fun. But the idyllic and innocent summer was drawing to a close, and the long annual seaside holidays the Vanier family always enjoyed were now nearing their end.

On 26 August, Georges wrote to External Affairs, "It looks like war."[7] On 1 September, Hitler's troops stormed into Poland, and two days later both Britain and France declared war on Germany. On 10 September, Canada, asserting itself as a sovereign nation, also declared war. With uncertainty hanging over them, Georges and Pauline decided that for the time being the family should remain in France together, and that Pauline, her mother, and the children should move to the safety of the countryside. Georges would join them whenever possible. Through a distant cousin of Pauline's, they managed to find refuge with a faded aristocrat by the name of Marquis de Cortavel, who was pleased to have paying guests so that his chateau would not be taken over by the army. Georges's chauffeur, Joseph, drove the family to the chateau, which was situated in a village called Baillou near the town of Mondoubleau, southwest of Paris. There, with little more than their holiday clothes, they settled in for a long wait. Thérèse, who at sixteen had finished school and was now ready for university, took turns with her mother teaching religion to the village children, spending the rest of her time knitting and writing letters to her friends back in England. The boys went to the local school.

The marquis's son had recently been killed fighting with the Italian army, and the atmosphere in the chateau was dreary. He was glad that his property was being put to use and also glad of the income it brought, but he was not happy with the presence of the Vaniers. The boys, who only a few months earlier had worked off their youthful energy playing cricket and rugby, grew restless as weeks became months and life remained at a standstill. They were blamed every time a piece of crockery was broken or any other mishap occurred. Thérèse wrote to her father ("My darling Pops") with caricature drawings of the marquis, whom she labelled "Corty," and "Poor old Peckhand [the gardener, Monsieur Pecquard, who resented the Vaniers' presence] wheeling the barrow."[8] For Georges, who spent the weekends at the chateau, a happy note brightened the strained conditions: the boys were not only speaking French, including the local slang, at school, they were sometimes speaking French to each other as well.

It was the period of the so-called "phony war," with armies amassing and nothing happening except in Poland, where advancing troops had cleared the way for a vicious "cleansing" of non-Germanic people, mostly Jews and those of Slavic origin. The strain of their living conditions wore on Pauline's nerves, and she wrote of her irritability and her spiritual darkness to Mother Mary of the Cross, who counselled her to "get fresh strength in the sanctuary of your soul" in her daily meditation. She sometimes returned to Paris with Georges, ostensibly to work at the legation, which was helping Canadians find accommodation or passage back to Canada, but probably also to get away from the oppressiveness of life at the chateau. Life in Paris was not much better. The streets were lit with a gloomy "blue light" at night, and mostly deserted during the day. In the early spring of 1940, she accompanied Georges to the Maginot Line, a series of casements and fortifications built along the border with Germany. The view of heavy German troops ranged on the other side did nothing to calm her anxiety.

By April 1940 people began to trickle back to Paris, including the Vaniers, who had worn out their welcome at the chateau. The springtime air was subdued by a heavy military presence, and life was cautious and tense. The war in western Europe, declared eight months earlier, was at a standstill. And then – endless columns of German troops marched into Norway, and after that, facing little resistance, Denmark. In Britain, Chamberlain encountered opposition for the way British forces had failed to hold the Germans back, and on 10 May he resigned. Winston Churchill became prime minister with a shaky British government.

The next day, 11 May, the German army charged into Belgium, and four days later air bombardments began to hail down upon Holland, followed by panzer tanks and masses of marching German foot soldiers. Parisian springtime came and went. The city was in chaos. Refugees streamed in from Holland and Belgium and countries to the east, and Parisians again packed up their cars and boarded trains to exit the city. On France's borders the news was all bad – the Italians to the south, the Germans to the north and east. Toward the end of May, German troops reached the English Channel, taking over the ports in northern France. The ineffectual British and French armies became trapped at Dunkirk.

Once Belgium and Holland had fallen, all Canadian women and children were urged to leave France as soon as possible. Georges and Pauline had wanted the family to stay together but now there was no choice. Pauline, the four children, and Madame Archer, left at once in the legation car toward the port of Bordeaux, with Joseph at the wheel, a collection of overnight bags crammed around them, and Pauline's stylish mother dressed in her Persian lamb coat in spite of the spring warmth. The roads heading south out of Paris were filled with cars piled high with luggage and furniture, people on bicycles, cartloads of farm animals, and, on foot, desperate refugees from Belgium and northern France whose homes had been razed. The procession crawled, while air raid warnings screeched around them. The family moved from one house to another, eventually arriving at the town of Chitenay in the Loire valley, at the home of a distant cousin of Pauline's. There, they waited. Hope still lingered that French forces would stop the enemy advance.

Georges was to say later that his most difficult decision during this period was the question of when he should close up the legation and leave Paris. In the decades to come, analysts would sift through the complex combination of reasons for France's rapid decline during the next few weeks. The army was ill-prepared to defend against the German "blitzkrieg," or lightning war, in which air bombardments were followed by the overpowering strength of tanks; France's military strategy failed; the living memory of the devastation during the war twenty years earlier resulted in a lack of will to fight. The government ministers disagreed as to which approach to take in the face of German aggression, and in March the government had collapsed. The new prime minister, Paul Reynaud, was unable to form a unified government, and the military command was equally divided. The only well-organized activity in France was the relentless advance of the German military machine.

Yet in early May of 1940, even as the north and east of France were overrun by enemy tanks and German soldiers were taking control of one port after another along the Atlantic coast, it seemed unthinkable that they would ever reach Paris. For Georges, the realization came on 16 May, when the French Foreign Ministry told embassies and legations to burn all their secret documents. He burned the Canadian documents in the basement furnace of the legation, describing later the drama that ensued at the Foreign Ministry itself, where documents were thrown from windows into a huge bonfire in the courtyard of the Quai d'Orsay. The next day, Reynaud fired the head of the French army, General Gamelin, and replaced him with seventy-three-year-old General Maxime Weygand, and he brought Marshal Henri Pétain, who was eighty-four and a hero of the earlier war, into the cabinet. As a precaution, the French government decided on the city of Tours as a possible centre to relocate. The Canadian legation followed suit, preparing a makeshift location in Pernay, a town about seven kilometres from Tours, and office equipment, records, and other important files were sent there.

Georges wrote later that he and the staff lived these days "like soldiers who sleep with their heads on their haversacks,"[9] their luggage standing in the hall, ready to be picked up at a moment's notice. But even in the midst of this uncertainty there was business to attend to. Frantic requests poured in from people who had lost contact with family members in France. Desperate refugees swarmed outside the legation seeking admittance to Canada. Because of the new laws enacted against them in Germany, Jews were in a particularly precarious position. The Canadian immigration office in Paris had closed with the outbreak of war, and Georges, having no authority in such matters, cautioned them that all he could do was plead their cause to Ottawa. On 24 May, he cabled to Mackenzie King, "There is a wonderful opportunity for Canada ... to relieve by immediate grant of money million and more refugees of many nationalities pouring into France destitute. If consideration is given to this suggestion no delay should be lost in making announcement because this is day of greatest need." Two days later he sent another cable: "Now estimated that 3,000,000 refugees with 1,000,000 more on the road. This condition is distressing. France in addition to fighting for her life is doing everything possible to succor them."[10] King, and some members of his war cabinet, were not unsympathetic to Georges's pleas. But the government's inaction – based on mistrust of "foreigners" (and in some cases, anti-semitism), the unwieldy bureaucracy of the Immigration Branch (which was under the jurisdiction of the Department of Mines and Resources and carried on its European immigration work through its office in London), and a tightly controlled immigration policy – would, in years to come, prove to be a black mark on Canada's wartime record.

For Georges, the situation was impossible on all sides: a French government incapable of governing, a French army in disarray, refugees clamouring for his help, and an intransigent Canadian government out of touch with the immense scale of the unfolding human disaster. And storming through France, bearing down on all sides, were the marching columns and panzer tanks of the enemy.

On 9 June he met with General Weygand, who made it clear that there was little hope; the German troops fought with a ferocity that seemed endless, while the French army was already close to exhaustion. The Germans had almost reached the Somme River, a hundred kilometres away. The next day, 10 June, the radio broadcast the news that the French government was moving south from Paris to Tours. The final exodus now began, and vehicles clogged all roads leading south. Cars were abandoned when their gasoline ran out, and people continued on foot. Georges sent most of the legation staff away immediately. He cabled External Affairs that the diplomatic corps had been invited to leave Paris. One of his final duties was to hand over to the American ambassador, who was staying on, the task of protecting Canadian property and the interests of Canadian nationals still in France. As he completed his final work, smoke from the German advance settled over the city like a pall, carrying with it the smell of the explosive cordite, and Georges "experienced the smell of the battlefield again after twenty-five years."[11] Streets were crowded with police and busloads of soldiers, awaiting orders that never seemed to come. That night Paris, the "city of lights," had its first blackout.

Shortly before midnight, he affixed a notice to the door of the legation announcing that "All Canadian Government services have been evacuated from Paris."[12] He then turned the key in the lock and walked to the waiting car. The drive from Paris to Pernay, normally less than three hours, took seventeen. "We became one in a line of cars and carts that was between 30 and 40 miles long," he wrote later. "Bumper to bumper, we crawled and crept, yard by yard and stop by stop, over the 60 miles of that nerve-wracking journey."[13] Making matters more difficult, the vehicles snaked along in total darkness; drivers had been instructed to extinguish their lights because German planes and the shriek of bombs could be heard in the distance, piercing the night air.

At Pernay, the Canadian legation was established in a small chateau by the Loire, but four days later, in the early morning of 14 June, Georges was wakened with the news that the Germans troops had taken over Paris and their tanks were now nearing Tours. He sent the chauffeur, Joseph, with a hasty note to Pauline, who was waiting at Chitenay: "The French government wants us to leave this area for the Bordeaux region as soon as possible. You must leave before 8:30 this morning. I've instructed Joseph on the route to take. I'll meet you there."[14] The next day, he and the legation staff drove to Margaux, near Bordeaux. Here the family was reunited, before moving on to the nearby village of Cantenac, near the port of Le Verdon-sur-Mer. In the village *mairie*, mats and blankets were arranged on the floor, and they climbed over one other to settle in for the next two nights.

On 17 June, Paul Reynaud resigned as prime minister of France. Marshal Pétain replaced him and almost immediately began to make overtures for peace with Hitler. Enemy occupation was now nearly a reality. That same day, Georges got word from the British embassy that a destroyer would take the fleeing British and Canadians to Le Verdon-sur-Mer, where a cargo boat was waiting for them. In all, twenty-nine people – all the Vaniers (except Georges), the legation staff, and assorted others who had been stranded in France – boarded the boat.

The trip took several days. Their boat, owned by the Royal Mail Steam Packet Company, had come from Argentina carrying tins of meat, but all there was for the rescued passengers to eat was a small ration of salmon-paste sandwiches. What was far worse, the sea was full of magnetic mines and German U-boats. German planes flew low, and the air was rife with the nearby sounds of explosions as the boat steamed out of the Bay of Biscay. At one point, it took to the Atlantic Ocean in an effort to manoeuvre around the U-boats. The Vanier children alternated between terror and excitement. Madame Archer's presence helped to sooth Pauline's taut nerves (like her daughter she had the ability, when faced with others' adversities, to forget her own). At night, her Persian lamb coat served as a makeshift pillow for the boys. At last the boat reached Milford Haven in Wales, and the exhausted family went on by train to London. They stayed with their friends the Bighams and, with Pauline's nerves near the breaking point, waited on tenterhooks for word of Georges.

Georges was now alone, the only Canadian officially in France. With him remained the British ambassador and the South African minister who "became, during those dark days, like brothers."[15] (Joseph the chauffeur had disappeared, looking for his wife further south.) When he learned on 21 June that Pétain had signed an armistice, the terms entirely dictated by Hitler, fear mingled with sadness. Up to this point, he had always felt admiration for the eighty-four-year-old war hero. Georges's love for France had always been tinged with a sense of the sacred, and his quasi-religious feeling remained the same (he told General Weygand that he had "unquenchable faith in her resurrection"). But a new situation had arisen – "the status of France, vis-à-vis the Allies, was changed"[16] – and he now stood on enemy territory, his life in danger.

Early on the morning of 23 June, as a light rain fell, he left with the other two diplomats for the fishing village of Arcachon, south of Bordeaux. The vessel waiting for them was a small sardine boat that was spectacularly misnamed *Le Cygne* (The Swan). The fishy smell was overpowering, and the waves high. "We were slewed to the top of a wave and catapulted into its trough,"[17] he later wrote. He lay overcome with seasickness and drenched with the rain that was now pelting the boat. Four hours later, the bedraggled diplomats were picked up by a Canadian destroyer, HMCS *Fraser* (which would be sunk by a German mine four days later), and then transferred to the British cruiser *Galatea*. "That cruiser turned its nose toward England, and like a horse that sniffs its stable, just went hell for leather. It just didn't give a damn for waves, nor mines, nor torpedoes, nor planes,"[18] he wrote later, savouring the memory of his escape, but typically not mentioning what others observed: that climbing the swaying rope ladder onto the cruiser with an artificial leg was a heroic feat in itself. Eighteen hours after they had stepped off French soil, they reached the English port of Plymouth.

* * *

In London, Georges's old friend from Canada House, Lester Pearson, was given the task of meeting the beleaguered Canadian minister to France at Paddington Station on 25 June. The train was late, and Pearson took the opportunity to write a letter to his wife while waiting in the car. Because of this happy circumstance, we have a glimpse of one episode that occurred during the frantic days after the Vanier family's safe arrival when Georges's fate was still unknown. On one of those days Vincent Massey, the Canadian high commissioner, and his wife invited all those who had escaped from France to the Dorchester Hotel for dinner. The gathering that evening in the hotel's gilded dining room was thick with tension and overwrought emotion. Pauline was still in a state of nervous exhaustion, and beside herself with worry about Georges. The scene, as Pearson described it, unravelled as polite conversation broke down and sparks began to fly between her and Mrs Massey. "Mrs Massey started it by insisting as soon as she met Pauline that the latter must be off to Canada *at once*." Pauline, who had never established a warm relationship with Mrs Massey, bristled at the order. Bitterness toward the French was running high in London because France had capitulated, leaving Britain standing alone against the enemy, and Mrs Massey, reflecting this feeling, began to speak disparagingly of the French. At that point, "a real row" erupted. Pauline "burst into tears and launched a counterattack." Mrs Massey then, "more or less hysterical," turned to Pearson, telling him to come to the Masseys' defence. Pearson responded that he "despised beyond words the French government and some of their military leaders" but "wouldn't say one word against the French people." Mrs Massey hissed in Pearson's ear, "'Disloyal!'" A tone of civility soon returned to the gathering and "we all became calm or relatively calm and friendly again." But as she was leaving, Mrs Massey, speaking, in Pearson's opinion, "with simple, incredible stupidity," said to Pauline, 'When you are safely back in Canada will you think of us being bombed to pieces over here.'" [19]

Pearson's overall assessment was that, since all the women among the new arrivals would be soon returning to Canada, "it's just as well that Mesdames Massey and Vanier will be far apart." He ended the letter, "I should have been at the office an hour ago. I hope Mrs Massey doesn't think

it 'disloyal' of me to spend so much time meeting a Vanier!"[20] (The episode
found its way into Vincent Massey's diary as well, but he gallantly left his
wife out of the fracas, saying merely that he himself had "inadvertently
aroused Pauline Vanier's morbidly pro-French sensibilities and for a few
moments she was very difficult."[21]) Georges's train arrived as Pearson was
finishing his letter, and having been mercifully spared the dinnertime drama,
he sent a bloodless cable to Ottawa stating "Arrived London this morning
after good trip."[22] Two days later, in a radio broadcast from London to
Canada, using the effusive and romantic language he was prone to whenever emotion took hold, he said, "Once more France has bared her breast
to the invaders' cruel blows, once more she has shed her best blood in the
world's struggle for freedom ... I have seen the misery of the refugees, broken by the horrors to which they were subjected. Never before has an army
had to contend with such heart-breaking conditions."[23]

The South African minister, Colin Bain-Marais, with whom he had escaped
from France, offered a more realistic assessment of the fall of France. "France
failed because she built the Maginot Line and then rested on her oars ...
Inertia bred of the feeling of security, overconfidence, easy living, a lack of
men of vision, and German intrigue and propaganda did the rest. England,
her ally, could have done more. At vital points France manned her lines with
inferior troops. This fact the Germans knew well. The strength of a chain
is determined by its weakest link."[24]

Madame Archer and the Vanier children sailed for Canada in the first
week of July. Thérèse was put in charge of the money, and Georges instructed
the boys to brush their teeth, visit a dentist, take care when swimming in a
lake, and obey their aunts and uncles. He and Pauline, who refused to leave
London without her husband, waved them away from Euston Station.

The wartime odyssey of the Vanier family had just begun. Like that of
many others, it would be marked by separation and absence.

12

THE FIGHTING FRENCH

As Britain stood on the brink, facing the enemy ranged on the coast across the Channel, the Canadian minister to France tried to create a small centre of normalcy in the midst of uncertainty and fear. Georges set up a makeshift office in the Sun Life building beside Canada House in London, and with a diplomat's practical instinct, he sent a cable to Ottawa, asking "that a substantial indemnity be granted without delay to all personnel to purchase clothes and other indispensable articles,"[1] since they had all arrived with few possessions. He and Pauline stayed at the home of their friend Ruth Kane on Grosvenor Square.

Georges's position was an awkward one. According to the terms of the recently signed armistice with Germany, France was now divided into two – the northern and western part, which was occupied by Germany, and the south-eastern section, where a subservient government headed by Pétain had been set up in the town of Vichy. Georges was still technically Canada's minister to France but as he wrote to a friend, "my plans are a bit uncertain in view of the fact that the Germans have pushed me out of France."[2] Ottawa, too, seemed unsure of what he should be doing. The capitulation of France to the German forces had happened so rapidly that the Canadian government had not yet decided what its new diplomatic position should be. For the time being, he remained technically the minister to France, but without a definable job. Meanwhile, France's minister to Canada remained in Ottawa, with full diplomatic accreditation.

As for Pauline, with Georges at her side once again, her nerves gradually settled down. Soon after their arrival in London, she discovered that the Red Cross was looking for French-speaking people to visit the thousands of wounded French soldiers who had been evacuated with the British from Dunkirk. It was a job tailor-made for her. She wrote to the children about her encounters with the soldiers, their surprise that she spoke French, the tragedies of the maimed and dying men, and the worries about the soldiers' families in France. "It is quite hard work," she wrote, "but so very interesting that I simply love it and I do feel that I am able to help these poor men as I speak their language and know their country."[3] Georges added in another letter that one of the soldiers said to her, "I know you are not English because you talk a great deal – just as we do!"[4]

Throughout the summer of 1940, Georges offered various proposals as to how he might be directly involved: mediating between Britain and France, returning to France as Canadian minister, or joining the Canadian army in England. On 17 July, he asked External Affairs for the Canadian government to instruct him to return to France, adding that "The French government were convinced that Canada was in a better position than any other to act as helpful intermediary between the United Kingdom and France."[5] From the point of view of External Affairs, the matter was unclear – what was the status of a country that had signed an armistice with the enemy, and indeed, was the seat of the French government in enemy territory? For the time being these questions remained unanswered.

As the summer drew to a close, German bombing raids, which had been carried out on the airfields of southern England, now made London their target in successive waves of terror that became known as the Blitz. Georges wrote casually to the children, "Recently, as you will have read in the papers, they have begun to drop a few bombs in and near London. We are expecting that this will go on for some time, but we trust it won't affect even our sleep very much. For example, last night we were wakened out of sound sleep, went down to the basement where we waited until the all clear was sounded and then within five minutes we were both asleep again, and slept without a break until morning. It is just a matter of getting used to a new routine!"[6]

In fact, it was a routine of avoiding death. German bombers screamed over the streets with swarming escorts of fighter planes, the concentrated noise rattling buildings and nerves. Every morning, when the Vaniers walked out onto the streets, they found craters and piles of rubble where buildings had been the day before. Yet Pauline, possibly because of Georges's calm presence, assured her mother that the sound of the bombs held nothing of the terror that she had experienced during her last days in France. They were both astounded by the courage, kindliness, and humour they saw all around them. Georges described the sight of a fireman at the top of a hundred-foot ladder, directing a hose toward a burning roof while a wailing air raid warning sounded. Pauline quoted a cleaning woman at Farm Street church, who said, "I am going to have to speak to this Mr Hitler; every time I get it all clean, he comes and makes a mess of everything," and an easygoing policeman who led them into a public shelter while the siren blared, reassuring them that: "You will be cosy and comfy here."[7]

Through it all, life carried on for everyone, in a somewhat altered fashion. Several years later, Georges recalled his visit to a tailor to be fitted for a new suit. When he arrived at the shop, the tailor said casually, "I am afraid, Sir, that a time-bomb has just landed behind the shop. As all the fitting rooms have glass windows, I suggest that it might be better to put off the appointment until after the bomb has exploded."[8]

Early in the summer of 1940, the Vaniers had become aware of the presence in London of a little-known fifty-year-old French general by the name of Charles de Gaulle. The extremely tall general cut an odd but striking figure, with an elongated head, large nose and ears, and sloping eyes that lent a dour expression to his face. De Gaulle's military career had not been particularly brilliant; he had spent most of the First World War either wounded or in prisoner-of-war camps, where escape attempts had been hampered by his great height. But he had been openly critical of the 1938 Munich agreement between Hitler and Chamberlain, claiming that it left France in a vulnerable state, and on 5 June he was appointed under-secretary of state for war.

The day after the pro-armistice Pétain became the French leader, de Gaulle left France alone for London. The next day, 18 June, he broadcast through the BBC an appeal to all French soldiers and citizens to join him in a new resistance force that he called the "Free French." As the weeks progressed, a number of army officers under assumed names landed clandestinely from France to join him, bringing with them swashbuckling tales of escape. Pauline wrote to her mother, "Someone you know well has come, but I can't tell you who, because it's important to be careful in the case of possible reprisals in France."[9] The person she referred to was Philippe de Hauteclocque, a thirty-eight-year-old distant relative who had taken the assumed name "François Leclerc," and who would eventually pass into history simply as "General Leclerc." A captain in the French army, the slightly built Leclerc had been captured by the Germans and had gone through a series of spectacular escapes before landing in London. His wife and eight children had remained in occupied France.

Although Georges already had his ear to the ground for a way he could stay in London and help in the struggle, it was probably the appearance of

Leclerc, and the inside information he provided, that gave him a new line in his pleas with the Canadian government. De Gaulle, he learned, had set his sights on the French colonies in Africa as possible locales for an alternative French government from which he could launch his Free French resistance troops. Leclerc was sent to the French Cameroons as governor and military commander in a first step toward realizing this plan. Georges became convinced that Canada should be aligned with the Free French.

De Gaulle was unknown in official circles, however, and it would take some time for the Canadian government to come around to this way of thinking. On 28 August, Georges received a cablegram from External Affairs urging him to return to Canada. "Minister of National Defence will wish to have you consider while here possibility taking on temporarily some military duty in Quebec," the cable read, adding, "In the circumstances it would probably be well for Madame Vanier to come to Canada now also."[10] Georges wanted desperately to stay on in London, close to where de Gaulle's fledgling movement was gaining momentum, hoping against obvious opposition that he might become Canada's representative to the Free French. He replied, "In view of developments in French African Possessions ... might it not be wise to delay departure for Canada. Your reference to my wife is appreciated indicating you understand we work as team."[11] Georges's latter assertion is striking: nine years earlier, a weeping Pauline had begged her husband to stop regarding her as a child, and now he made it clear that she was indispensable to his front line work. He had come to realize over the previous decade that his own quiet and meticulous style was insufficient for diplomacy; it also required her overt friendliness and ability to draw people out.

For the time being, however, he was sidelined. In mid-September 1940, the Vaniers returned to Canada while Pierre Dupuy, Georges's first secretary, was left in London as Canadian chargé d'affaires to the Pétain government. They were reunited with their children in Montreal, where Thérèse was enrolled in a secretarial course and the boys attended Loyola College, their father's old school. Georges met with Mackenzie King in Ottawa, and the prime minister found him looking much older than when they had last met and sensed in him "a certain sorrow which he seemed to be carrying."[12] In Canada, the Vaniers found big changes: a massive arms production program was underway, and munitions factories were employing women in what had once been men's jobs. And previously unemployed men now lined up to enlist.

Politically, Mackenzie King had turned to the United States for solidarity in the defence of Canada's two coastlines, and Georges was immediately appointed to a newly created Joint Defence Board between the two countries. The Vaniers were shocked to find that in Quebec, attitudes among their acquaintances ranged from indifference to the war and the bombing of Britain to outright support for Pétain's Vichy government. (Although Vichy lost no time in declaring anti-Jewish decrees, which de Gaulle publicly condemned in October 1940, Quebec's intelligentsia, political leaders, and Catholic hierarchy continued to favour the conservatism and return to "traditional values" that the Pétain government appeared to represent.)

But the most striking of the discoveries in the few weeks after their return to Canada was that Pauline, at the age of forty-two, was once again pregnant. She wrote to Mother Mary of the Cross about her "shock" and her spirit's "numbness" and her ongoing worry about her maternal failings. The nun replied with encouraging words: "Let not your failures trouble you – your children are ever sure of your loving goodness to them."[13] An added worry was fourteen-year-old Bernard, who was stricken with rheumatic fever in the spring of 1941 and taken by stretcher to the hospital, where he spent several weeks recovering.

Michel Paul was born on 29 July 1941 and given the nickname "Mickey" by his father. Two weeks later, Georges was promoted to the rank of brigadier and named "District Officer Commanding" of the military district of Quebec, and he and Pauline and baby Michel moved to Quebec City, where they lived on rue St Louis. Before taking up the position, he accompanied Mackenzie King on a flight to England to inspect the Canadian troops. It was King's first time in an airplane, and he remarked that "it gave me a feeling of greater reverence for God and greater regard for man and his achievements ... I enjoyed having Vanier on the opposite side knowing his sympathy and spiritual perceptions. I don't get the same companionship out of the intellectual type, with the conventional attitude of some University men whose philosophy is more materialistic."[14]

Back in Quebec, Georges's main job was to change attitudes and, in particular, to recruit more Quebecers for the armed forces. He set to work all over the province, especially rural areas, establishing public relations campaigns, training more French-speaking officers, and publishing French training manuals. He appealed to mayors, aldermen, and community groups, using the passionate rhetoric of patriotism and self-sacrifice ("The only frontier now is between civilized countries and uncivilized countries, and that frontier is wherever men fight and die for the cause of liberty and justice!"[15])

Always aware of his financial situation (and perhaps more so now that there was a new child in the family), he had taken a cut in pay from $8,720 as minister to $7,580, and he asked that his pension be based on the earlier salary. "This, I hope, will protect my wife and family in the event of untimely demise (to which I am not looking forward)."[16]

Pauline too became involved in the effort, speaking to women's groups about the family's harrowing escape from France and the devastation and terror they experienced firsthand in England. During this period, a twenty-four-year-old French woman who had worked as Charles de Gaulle's secretary in London appeared in Quebec. Her name was Elisabeth de Miribel, the daughter of a proud military family who had shocked her Pétainiste parents by her passionate adherence to the Free French movement. In Quebec, her job was to rally support for de Gaulle, an uphill task made at least somewhat easier by her association with the Vaniers. To Elisabeth, they seemed a golden couple, strikingly handsome in appearance and generous in spirit. She described herself, alone in Canada and estranged from her family, as an adopted Vanier daughter.

All this time Georges retained the empty title of Minister to France, but by May he could no longer live with it. He sent a letter of resignation to Mackenzie King on 17 May 1941:

> There can be no doubt now of Marshal Pétain's intention to collaborate with Hitler. I have felt always that the Marshal's hand would be forced whenever it suited our enemy's convenience ...
>
> So long as His Majesty's governments in Canada and in the United Kingdom believed that some useful purpose could be served by maintaining relations with the Vichy Government, so long as that government's collaboration with Germany was not too overt or shameless, I felt it my duty to retain the title of Canadian Minister to France. You will appreciate, I know, that to do so now would not be consistent with a sense of honour, of decency, or of patriotism ...
>
> In the above circumstances I trust that you will find it possible to relieve me of my title of Canadian minister to France ... I pray that before long Free Frenchmen throughout the world will set up a gov-

ernment which will conform to the glorious traditions of freedom which are part of France's natural heritage, and that you may then consider me not unworthy of being accredited to it: this is my fondest hope.[17]

King did not acknowledge Georges's letter in writing, but invited him to lunch at his Ottawa residence six days later, noting in his diary that Georges's "whole view is that France has come to be very corrupt; that other nations will point the finger of shame at her in years to come ... [He] feels certain that Germany will ultimately do what she pleases with France and use her to her own ends meanwhile."[18] King's diary entry does not state his own point of view, but his admiration for Georges was such that his own opinion was likely inclined in the same direction. It would still be more than a year, however, before Georges's position on the Free French became the official Canadian one.

* * *

In the meantime, two of the Vanier children were developing plans of their own. Thérèse, having grown to the statuesque height of her mother, turned nineteen in February 1942, and having completed her secretarial course, had grown impatient with the indifference to world events of her contemporaries in Quebec. The Mechanized Transport Corps was recruiting young Canadian women to become motor mechanics and drivers for the armed forces in England, and this was what she wanted to do. Georges could not have been more proud. Pauline, perhaps remembering the young woman who against her mother's wishes had shed her debutante lifestyle to work in a hospital for wounded soldiers during the earlier war, gave her blessing as well. On 11 April, Georges sent a telegram to Byngsie in Montreal: "Thérèse leaving tomorrow and will telephone you and Bernard tonight nine o'clock to say goodbye please both be near telephone."[19] The next day, she sailed from Lévis for England.

The Vaniers' third son, Jock, had also been growing restive, although a school journal he kept for five weeks in November and December of 1941 gives little hint of what was actually going through his mind. Barely thirteen years old, he wrote his journal entries with the droll humour reminiscent of his father, dryly noting the misbehaviour of his classmates and the ineffectual corrections of the teachers. Many of the classes at Loyola were taught by young Jesuits-in-training, fresh from studying the finer points of theology and ill-prepared for the rowdy antics of teenaged boys.

The journal begins on 17 November. "We've got a new notice board today, bigger and better than the old one. Maroon with a Loyola crest on top. Hope it is kept filled with news, cartoons and local gossip." It moves on to 20 November when it is noted that "Our honourable teacher muttered 119 "Ahs" and "Ehs" this afternoon in 50 minutes"; the next day, "The dean warned us about our conduct in Elocution class." Five days later, the entry is longer: "The Elocution class this afternoon was a marked improvement over the last one as far as noise and conduct, but as far as learning anything it was just as bad. G. Driscoll telephoned nearly everybody explaining he was the commander of the Loyola Air Cadets and that if we didn't stop missing our drills there would be trouble. We weren't scared (much). The real purpose was to get clothes for the poor. Maybe he wanted the pants he scared us out of." As for the actual schoolwork, his entry for 5 December reads: "Greek Trans. and Chemistry this afternoon. The outlook is not bright." Five days later he notes that "We had an elocution exam but we won't go into details about the fifty boys who were exchanging answers." And as the Christmas holiday approached, "Class was started by the reading of the very descriptive story of the 'Halifax fire' in 1917 … Tony de Souza and G. Cleary were playing cards. D.E.D. sj [the teacher] took them – the cards. Vic Ryan came in 1 hour late. Mr D.E.D. sj then read 'Christmas Carol' by Dickens. During which T. Colmeneres played on his mouth organ."[20]

It may have been during these few weeks – while the bored youngster was jotting his journal entries, perhaps contributing to the lower element in the school and helping to drive his hapless teachers to distraction – that he also wrote a letter to the Royal Naval College in Dartmouth, England, to seek admission there. With the onset of adolescence churning inside him, perhaps he was longing to be back in the shelter of an English school. For more than a year, from the summer of 1939 to the fall of 1940, he had received no ongoing formal education. Up to now he had stood in the shadow of his two older brothers, who outshone him academically. Had his father's eloquent pleas for war support, especially among generous and courageous young men, struck a chord with him? Did he have an inarticulate sense that his time had come?

The incident that followed probably took place during the Christmas holiday, when the family was together in Quebec City. According to Pauline's recollection in later years, Jock wrote a note to his father to ask if he could see him at his office about an important matter, and Georges, mystified by his son's request, agreed. When father and son met in Georges's office, Jock asked for permission to enroll immediately at the Naval College in England. His father gave his ready assent, but Pauline, who with a profound sense of trust had let her nearly adult daughter go, was horrified at the thought of sending her son, only thirteen and small for his age, into the deadly Atlantic. Little more than a year earlier, a ship called the *City of Benares*, carrying British children to Canada, had been sunk in spite of large signs that read "Children" in both English and German. Georges tried to mollify her with his conviction that their son's desire to leap from the life of an indolent schoolboy into that of a navy cadet indicated a release of energy that could not be ignored. His unwavering trust in the rightness of Jock's unusual request calmed her somewhat, but her worry remained. Later she was to acknowledge that the Naval College turned the restless teenager into a disciplined young man, but the mother of 1942 knew only of the mines and torpedoes in the sea and the bombs still threatening England.

Even with Georges's ability to pull strings, Jock's departure took several weeks. There were entrance exams for the cadetship at the college, then an exit visa that required a special order in council because of his young age. Throughout the early spring of 1942, messages went back and forth to the Department of National Defence: should Jock travel by passenger ship, or would passage in a troop convoy or a destroyer be the safest way to reach England? Finally, all was settled and in late May Jock, accompanied by his father, left Quebec City by train for Halifax, where he boarded a troop ship. En route on the train, Georges wrote to Pauline that "Jock isn't too nervous – a bit tired and strained, but less so than I would have thought. It's fortunate that I'm going with him. He would have found this stretch the hardest. Once in Halifax, the adventure and action will take over. He is full of initiative and courage, sensible and generous – a beautiful nature that has found its voice. You were admirable in making the sacrifice."[21] Jock arrived safely in England, but hardly had he settled in than the Naval College was evacuated from the coast to the relative safety of the city of Chester.

During the spring of 1942, it was suggested that Georges be named a senator and be brought into the War Cabinet as a Quebec representative. Despite Mackenzie King's assertion in his diary that he would "probably act on it,"[22] no action was taken. Some months later, the prime minister recorded a meeting between the two and noted that Georges "had been perturbed about what people might think of his having been passed over." King went on to hint at the reason: "The truth is the Department of Defence and others feel Vanier has been ineffective in his work in Quebec." Fortunately for Georges, who had spent an uphill year trying to rally Quebec recruits for the Allied cause in the face of ongoing Pétainiste support, King "was careful, however, not to say anything of this to him."[23]

But it was not long before further developments happened. On 9 November, Georges heard that an extraordinary breakthrough had taken place: Canada formally ceased to recognize Vichy as the legitimate French government of France. This new situation now paved the way for him to come forward, and two days later he wrote to Norman Robertson, the undersecretary of state for External Affairs that "It is a reasonable assumption that very soon, a matter of hours or days, a French government will be set up in North Africa ... I know it is not necessary to remind you once more that the former Minister to France hopes and prays that he will be allowed to continue the work begun in 1939."[24]

Before the month was over, Georges was named the Canadian minister to the Allied countries whose governments were exiled in London and, to his joy, the military representative to de Gaulle's Free French, who had become known as the French National Committee in London. Another Vanier was to be on the wartime move across the Atlantic. His physical defences betrayed him, however; he had hardly accepted the appointment that he had spent two years waiting for than he landed in the Royal Victoria Hospital in Montreal, laid low by pneumonia.

Christmas of 1942 was bleak for the splintered family, and in a note to Byngsie (now known outside the family by his birth name, "George") and Bernard, Georges exhorted them to "look after your Mummy and be thoughtful with her during these holy days,"[25] noting that their family was at least intact, unlike some others that the war had touched. He was mindful that his influence over his two oldest sons might be lessened by his absence, and he expressed gratitude to various male friends who had offered to keep an eye on them. In a letter to his friend Robertson Fleet, he drew a picture of his sons' differing temperaments. "George is dynamic, direct, and later will not suffer fools gladly. To put it mildly also, he does not suffer from an inferiority complex, but the knocks of life will put that right. Bernard ... is introspective and ruminative; not so sure of himself, and shy. Both, judging from their school reports, have fairly good brains. If at any time you would like to have a very good argument about philosophy, remember that it is

George's favourite subject, although Heaven knows what the quality of his knowledge is."[26]

During his recuperation, which lasted several weeks, Georges was promoted to the rank of major-general. By the end of March, 1943, he was well enough to take up his new position in London. He left for New York, where he had a meeting with Jacques Maritain, a philosopher whose writing on democracy he admired and who belonged to a group called L'Ecole Libre of New York, a movement of more than a hundred European intellectuals living in the United States who were supporting de Gaulle. On 4 April he flew to London.

Georges knew from the beginning of his appointment that he did not want to take on this new task without Pauline's help. His letter on the day of his departure is an echo of the sentiments expressed by Pauline before their marriage twenty-two years earlier: "As in the past, I want our destiny to be together, not only in thought but also in daily action,"[27] he wrote. It is not known exactly what discussion took place between them before his departure, but what is certain is that Pauline's decision to split up the family even further by joining her husband was one that sundered her emotionally and would continue to haunt her for the rest of her life. It was true that the two older boys were by now well into their teens and boarding at Loyola College in Montreal, but Bernard, weakened by his bout with rheumatic fever, had been distressed at Jock's leave-taking; besides being the closest in age as brothers, the two had been best friends. She sensed in him a particular need for her. But above all there was Michel, not yet two years old, to consider. The decision was excruciating.

From the moment Georges arrived in England, his letters contained pleas for her to join him as soon as possible: she could serve with the Red Cross; help with the complex diplomatic work in which he found himself; perhaps accompany him to North Africa, where de Gaulle was to set up his government; and, finally, looking far ahead, return to France with him. When arrangements were finally made for her to leave by plane, he instructed her – as if fearing that her anxiety over taking her first airplane ride might do her in – to take the tranquilizers the doctor had prescribed, and not to drink coffee or tea before boarding. Leaving Michel and his nanny in Montreal with Madame Archer who, as always, rose to the occasion, Pauline took a train to Baltimore and boarded a plane for London on 21 June.

Georges had set up an office at 14 Berkeley Street, and the couple rented a flat in Arlington House, on a cul-de-sac, a short walk across Piccadilly.

External Affairs had given him directives: he was accredited as Canada's representative to the six governments exiled in London – Holland, Norway, Greece, Yugoslavia, Poland, and Czechoslovakia – and was to find out information concerning their countries' war status, acknowledging that these governments were far removed from what was actually happening and would exercise little authority once the war was over. There were also instructions to find out matters concerning de Gaulle's government and such post-war questions as the organization of relief, the trial of war criminals, and the influence of communism. Already, now that the Americans had entered the war and the Russians had defeated the German army at Stalingrad, a new world order was anticipated.

For Pauline, one positive result of the move back to England was the chance to see Thérèse and Jock again after a year's separation. Thérèse had joined the Canadian Women's Army Corps and had learned "all the secrets by which one may disable permanently even strong men!" her proud father wrote to Byngsie, adding "Fair warning to disrespectful brothers!"[28] Jock was happy to tell his parents that not only had he gained twelve pounds, he was at the top of his class in mathematics, history, and English. Pauline reported to her mother that she could now see that he had made the right move in returning to England (although in the same letter she wrote that he asked her, when on leave, "Mummy, do you love me?" – an indication that a child still resided inside the smart cadet's uniform.) She was lonely for Michel ("how I wish I could hold him ... and hear his first words, which are now probably becoming sentences"); she wept over snapshots of her toddler son that Madame Archer sent her and then tried to console herself by regarding her decision as the choice of a greater good ("the sacrifice is so small compared with the sufferings of so many others.")[29]

Pauline was shocked at the devastation of London after the Blitz, which had bombarded the city right into the spring of 1941. The area around St Paul's Cathedral "gives the impression of a dead city, like Pompeii, it is quite weird and eerie,"[30] she wrote. She went to work immediately, visiting the exiled royalty and diplomats of the countries Georges had become accredited to. She also met Madame de Gaulle, who impressed her with her simplicity and moral courage. She wrote to Byngsie about one occasion, a dinner for the king of Norway, when the septuagenarian monarch "made me a sign to come and sit next to him; I was rather taken aback but of course obeyed this royal command. He kept me for a long time, at least half an hour and told me the most interesting things; amongst others, all about his last days in Norway when the Huns tried to kill him by bombing him wherever he was."[31] Typical of Pauline's effect on men, this experience of being singled out by those of high rank was to be repeated during the remaining years of the war.

Although by temperament she enjoyed such gatherings, she was disappointed that much of her activity entailed entertaining and going to receptions and other social affairs, far from the more gritty and immediate war relief work she had expected. It hardly seemed worth the struggle she had made in deciding to leave Michel with her mother – especially since she was also having to deal from afar with domestic issues such as Michel's vaccinations and the nanny's request for a raise. From time to time, she went to see the Carmelite nuns, who had lost most of their income but nonetheless managed to sustain themselves by keeping chickens and a large vegetable garden (as well as a cow, paid for by the Vaniers and called "Georgie"), even having enough left over to contribute to the war effort.

The news on the war front was promising on the whole: the German army had been forced to retreat from Russia the previous winter, and the Allies had successfully invaded Italy. The Allied attempt to land in France at Dieppe a year earlier had failed, with disastrous results for Canadian troops, but another plan was underway and hopes were high. In the North African desert, Allied forces had routed Rommel's German army. De Gaulle had arrived in Algiers to establish his headquarters and had set up a provisional government known as the French Committee of National Liberation. The Germans now occupied the whole of France in retaliation for their loss in North Africa and administered it with the vicious Nazi machine. By this time de Gaulle's committee was recognized by all the Allies except the United States as the legitimate government of France. And the most promising portent of all, as far as France was concerned, the "Free French" – those who had fled Vichy and Occupied France – had been joined in common cause by those still inside the country who were determined to overthrow the enemy. Together, they became known as the "Fighting French" and, sometime later, the "French Resistance."

In early October 1943, Georges was appointed the Canadian representative to the French Committee of National Liberation in Algiers. It was the news he had been hoping for. His plane took off for Algiers in the broad sunshine and crisp air of a late December day, as Pauline, Thérèse, and Jock waved

him away. The plane developed a leak and was grounded for two days in
Cornwall before descending into Algiers. When it finally landed, the Mediterranean Sea, which the Vaniers were to later describe variously as aquamarine,
jade green, and sapphire blue, sparkled in the distance, and the desert sun
beamed on copper-red rocks and stretches of sand. It was now the new year
of 1944, and as Germany's defeat was certain and hopes soared for a quick
end to the war, the members of the Vanier family were more scattered than
ever – over three continents.

13

TOWARD VICTORY

Algiers in January 1944 was lush with vegetation: roses and brilliant wild-flowers, citrus trees laden with ripe fruit, and in the surrounding area, endless vineyards on terraced hills. The city was also dirty, noisy, smelly, and over-crowded. Although red wine was plentiful, as were such delicacies as dates, figs, olives, and oranges picked right off the tree, most stores stood nearly empty. The city also lacked paper, phones, and other practical and mundane necessities of the diplomat's life, and if a car broke down, there was no hope of getting it fixed.

Georges Vanier had received these warnings in advance about the exotic city's condition, and was prepared for such annoyances. But he had not been given notice that the building requisitioned for him as both office and living quarters was a large Moorish-style villa festooned with archways and semi-tropical shrubs and plants. The villa stood, like a Hollywood set, at the end of a long avenue of eucalyptus trees. For a man who valued austerity in war-time almost as highly as he valued self-sacrifice, his palatial home appeared shamefully luxurious, and he remained disdainful of it throughout his months in Algeria. It was located in Cheragas, a village seven kilometres from Algiers, and the upstairs terraces overlooked a magnificent view of the Mediterranean. The villa was soon to become known as La Maison de la Résistance in Algeria, thereby shedding some of its pre-war glamour and taking on the rough-hewn edge of heroism.

Georges's job, as usual, was to gather information for Ottawa on Charles de Gaulle's fledgling committee. De Gaulle's credibility had improved since his arrival in London as an unknown general nearly three years earlier. But his governing body in Algiers had not been established with ease. Power among the Allies had shifted with the entry of the United States into the war in December 1941. From the outset, Roosevelt's vision of France had clashed with de Gaulle's. The American president saw France as a defeated nation, and he had wanted to ignore de Gaulle and nudge Pétain into a position where the Vichy government would become part of the Allied struggle against Germany. De Gaulle, however, regarded the Pétain government as a usurper and betrayer of the true France. France, in his eyes, was still a great nation, and he regarded himself as equal in stature to Roosevelt and Churchill. De Gaulle's personality did not help his cause – he was temperamental and difficult to get along with, and he often acted with overbearing arrogance and rudeness.

Roosevelt preferred to work with another French general, Henri Giraud, the high commissioner of North Africa. A power struggle ensued between the two generals, and a compromise was reached by having de Gaulle and Giraud named as co-presidents of the French Committee of National Liberation. Perhaps neither general realized that they did not matter to Roosevelt except for their usefulness in rallying French forces to the Allied side. (The American president, amused at the imperious antics of the two generals, with their military stick-men poses, referred to them as "the bride" and "the groom.") In the jockeying for leadership that followed, de Gaulle outsmarted Giraud and became the sole head of the committee.

Roosevelt continued to mistrust de Gaulle, however, accusing him of having networks of spies, and refusing to recognize him as leader of the legitimate French government. Questions remained about de Gaulle among the other Allies as well – was he a dictator in the making? Was the military uniform he insisted on wearing a sign that he was taking on a military role as well as a political one? De Gaulle himself was frustrated that the Allies did not recognize his sense of destiny – that it was he who was called to lead the French back to freedom. But as plans for the invasion of France intensified, de Gaulle and the Fighting French were frozen out.

Georges kept close to what was happening through his connection with the British minister to de Gaulle's government, Duff Cooper, who had arrived in Algiers with his wife, the socialite Lady Diana. He also kept in close touch with Harold Macmillan, the British government's representative to the Allied Headquarters. He quoted Macmillan as saying that de Gaulle had "a touch of genius"[1] and was actually at his best when he was contrary and irascible. When Georges himself met de Gaulle he found the general weary, and he wrote, "He certainly did not strike me as an embryo dictator." And yet he had "a strange feeling" in the general's presence, which he was told came from de Gaulle's conviction that "he always sensed at a distance the real state of France and the feeling of its people."[2]

Pauline arrived in Algiers in early February 1944, fed up with sashaying around London with exiled royals while Londoners themselves were suffering the effects of their burned-out city. She was ready for more meaningful action. Algiers did not provide it. She found it to be just a military station, with colonels and field marshals and generals coming and going, and Pauline had them all for lunch, tea, or dinner, and often as overnight guests, since other accommodation was almost impossible to find. Bevies of ambassadors, lesser diplomats, and journalists came as well, and, on one occasion, the movie actor Douglas Fairbanks, who was serving as a naval officer. She wrote to her children of their difficulties with cooks – one had put his fist through a pane of glass in a fit of drunken rage; another had been bitten by a dog – and as a result, "Madame l'Ambassadrice is housemaid, bottle washer, etc."[3] Despite the menial tasks and meaningless conversations, her success as an outpost hostess eventually reached the ears of Lester Pearson in Washington, where he had been assigned, who wrote to Georges about the praises "which I hear about you and your mission, and, more particularly, about your wife."[4]

Pauline herself remained conflicted about whether she was doing anything useful, and wrote to Jock that "there are times when I would like to chuck it all overboard and go to work in one of the hospitals where they are in need of help, but I suppose that wouldn't be doing my duty."[5] Her favourite visitors during her first few weeks were two air force pilots, one a Canadian and the other a New Zealander, both wounded in a plane crash. The pair liked to sit in the Vaniers' villa reading the newspapers and making themselves at home. "What a contrast these two boys are to the others," she wrote. She reported one of the pilots as pointing to a member of the never-ending stream of diplomatic hangers-on and saying, "What does he know about war, that guy?" Pauline herself added, "Yes, what do any of us know about war really?"[6] Another highlight was the brief visit of some prisoners-of-war on their way back to Canada, looking dazed and pale, some of them wounded, some missing limbs. One of the airmen in the group told Pauline she looked like an ad for Lux soap, a compliment she recorded for her children with a laugh. "Of course they none of them have seen any women for many a day, so even an old thing like me seems to give them pleasure."[7]

She described for her children the sights of Algeria: the villages strewn along the coastline, the dazzling white houses, the Arab men walking with bare feet on the dusty roads, their postures erect with dignity. After a short trip to Morocco she told them of the meals eaten sitting on divans before a low table where one course followed closely upon another. "We ate with our right hand, in the first three fingers only, one doesn't use forks or knives; you pick the meat out with your fingers. Then came six chickens cooked in a sauce with almonds floating about; then a pastia which is a meat tart sweetened, then a couscous which is semolina meat, then sweet meats, dates, oranges, almonds, nuts and finally thé à la menthe, which is delicious and very necessary after such a meal."[8] On one occasion, as they passed some Arab men, "they looked at us with a certain scorn, a look which seemed to mean, 'You may think that you're grand because you drive about in cars, but we are the people that really belong here, not you!'" She added, "How they must hate the whites who have installed themselves in these lands, using them more or less as slaves – to do what? Make money!"[9]

Through the excitement, the exoticism, and the ennui, she was also torn with anxiety about her children, the two in England and especially the three left in Canada. This was wartime, when extraordinary measures were called for, and there was no possible way for the family to be together. She realized this, and yet – "I sometimes wonder if I shouldn't go back to be near you and Mickey!" she wrote to Bernard. "And yet I don't know what to do about Daddy who also needs me. I am torn between all of you." She pleaded for news of three-year-old Michel: "Please tell me about Mickey, how you think he is developing. Does he give you the impression of being excessively sensitive? Does he suffer not having a Mummy to run to?"[10]

As if the war and her decision to separate herself from her children were not enough to worry about, she also berated herself in letters to Mother Mary of the Cross for wining and dining in Algiers, and for being vain about her appearance, while a few miles across the sea others were engaged in a vicious war. The nun replied with brusque good humour, telling her to not worry about drinking wine, and adding, "Your positive vocation in life is to be a well-dressed, well-groomed woman. For the love of God (said with a smile and a wink!!), do not be turning yourself into an old frump!!"[11]

What probably made the spring and summer of 1944 in Algiers most worthwhile for Pauline was the appearance of the French resistance. The resistance movement within France itself had grown steadily during the previous four years, as increasing numbers of French citizens became disillusioned with the Vichy government. De Gaulle's radio broadcasts from abroad, appealing to their spirit of idealism and courage, spurred them on: here was someone who embodied the true France, and who would lead them in overthrowing the tyrant. The Nazi screws had become tighter, food production was geared toward the German war effort, and communists, freemasons, and particularly Jews were increasingly harassed and then rounded up and deported.[12] Then came the occupation of the whole of France and the conscription, in 1943, of young men and women to work in factories and forced labour camps in Germany. Many of these young people instead fled to the south of France, where they joined the clandestine movement called the Maquis, named for the scrub brush in that region of the country. The resisters, an amorphous group acting in one way or another in all parts of France, not at all unified in motive or method, had one thing in common: the desire to free their country of the Nazi yoke, with Charles de Gaulle as their leader. Those who found their way to Algiers, particularly the few Catholics among them, eventually wound up at the Vaniers' villa.

The Vaniers already knew – and gradually discovered more graphically first-hand – that the French Catholic bishops had embraced the Pétain government for a number of reasons: they feared the menace of communism more than the ideology of Nazism; they thought that under Pétain's leadership the Catholic Church would regain the prestige it had lost after the French Revolution; and they believed that Catholic doctrine required obedience to legitimate authority, which had been brought about by Pétain's signing of the armistice. De Gaulle, a practising Catholic, was regarded as a faithless revolutionary who was bent on overthrowing the legitimate government and whose followers were Godless communists. Some bishops had forbidden priests from saying Mass for members of the resistance. The Vatican had recognized the Pétain government almost immediately and maintained the presence of the papal nuncio (the Vatican's ambassador) at Vichy during the whole of the occupation. Likewise, an ambassador of the Vichy government remained stationed at the Vatican.

In the balmy luxury of their Moorish villa, with the scent of almond blossom in the air, the Vaniers heard stories from the other side. A young bearded priest, dressed in grey trousers and a brown sport jacket, his body taut with frayed nerves, denounced the French bishops angrily, adding that the "lower clergy" were much more in tune with the resistance than were their ecclesiastical superiors. A Jesuit priest, and others who wrote for the underground paper *Cahiers de Témoignage Chrétien*, which had provided the spiritual impetus for Christian resistance, also visited them. The Vaniers heard horrifying stories of executions and murders (on one occasion, after shots had been fired from a window of an apartment building, Nazis locked the building's doors and set it on fire with all the inhabitants inside). Increasingly, resisters told them of relatives back in France who had been rounded up by the Gestapo, their whereabouts unknown. In a May 1944 letter, Pauline wrote that the tales coming out of France were "so dreadful that one can hardly credit them. But coming from people such as these we know that they are alas! only too true. The horrors that are being done on the continent are ghastly. The Germans are trying to wipe out the populations ... In France they are now doing what they have done all along in Poland."[13] They heard about the cruel measures taken against members of the resistance by the Milice, the French troops that had been formed under the auspices of the Nazi SS and who now effectively created a police state.

For relief, the Vaniers enjoyed watching the antics of a family of swallows that lived under the roof of one of their terraces. As the spring wore on, all visitors – especially those who appeared for tea on Sunday afternoons – were treated to the sight of the baby birds first opening their beaks, then trying their wings over the side of the nest, turning their heads inwards and their tails out, and finally, taking tentative flight: the natural growth and progression of life, in contrast to the unnatural brutality taking place not far away.

Georges was raised to the rank of ambassador in May 1944. Although this moment of pride was followed by a telegram of warm congratulations from Mackenzie King, his energies were engaged in a more immediate and momentous mission: plans for an Allied invasion on a western front. General Leclerc, whom the Vaniers had last seen in London and who had been dispatched to Africa in 1940, appeared one day in late March. He had fought against the Germans in North Africa, and in a singular feat, he had led troops on foot from Lake Chad to Tripoli, where they joined the British and American forces in liberating Italy. He was said to be second only to de Gaulle in French heroic popularity. There was talk inside the French Committee that Leclerc should lead a French force as part of the Allied invasion of France.

But as plans for the D-day invasion gained momentum, de Gaulle's committee was still frozen out by the American and British military leaders. De Gaulle's intransigence and prickly personality, his rudeness toward Churchill and other decision-makers, and his sense of himself as the embodiment of the true France had continued to work against his own interests. Georges also heard from the American representative to the committee that de Gaulle and his entourage were unreliable – that the general himself might agree to something one day but then the next day the committee would decide the opposite. In the meantime, de Gaulle's committee declared itself, without any international support or recognition, the Provisional Government of the French Republic. For his part, having been told by Mackenzie King that the Canadian government was inclined toward recognizing the provisional government but was waiting for the Americans to do so (Roosevelt still stood firm against de Gaulle), Georges Vanier could only keep on trying to make his voice heard in Ottawa. "Ever since I came to Algiers I have been endeavoring to prove to the Department that the only reasonable course for us to follow was to acknowledge the Committee as the future and later 'de facto' administrator in France after Liberation."[14]

Realizing the symbolic importance of having French involvement in the D-day invasion, Georges Vanier and Duff Cooper combined their diplomatic skills in trying to have a Leclerc-led French division included in the Allied push into France. Told that it would be impossible to transport a French division from North Africa to Britain to participate in the invasion, Georges wrote to Ottawa, "The absence of an important body of French troops in the northern area will be to the French people a crowning humiliation which will be neither understood nor forgotten irrespective of all reasons or excuses which may be put forward. I submit that the Canadian government would render a great service to France by making every effort to obtain the inclusion of at least one French division in the north."[15] In the end, a compromise was reached; a partial French division was sent to Britain, and it was decided that Leclerc's troops would not be part of the first wave of the invasion of Normandy but would join later on, when they would be fresh, to take over Paris.

The news of the long-awaited D-day, 6 June 1944, was received in Algiers in a conflict of moods. It was now clearly the beginning of the end of the European war but, as Pauline wrote, there was still tragedy and horror ahead, as the Allies bombed and fought their way across Normandy. "After the first day of the excitement of hearing about our landing in France we seem to be very flat and rather sombre," she wrote. "The fighting is dreadful and is going to get inevitably worse."[16] In the months ahead, there would be more people killed or displaced by bombs, and more white cemetery headstones marking rows of young men's graves.

In the meantime, they heard that Byngsie had graduated summa cum laude from Loyola College and, like his father before him, had been chosen valedictorian. With modesty mixed with bursting pride, Georges wondered "how on earth we had managed to produce such a prodigy ... I have come to the conclusion that he must get his brains from Pauline and his looks from me!"[17] Bernard, who with his brother had won most of Loyola's academic awards the year before, was again laid up with a recurrence of rheumatic fever and had missed his exams. Georges was acutely aware that his older sons were growing into manhood without his direct guidance. He wrote to both sons, exhorting them to apply for Rhodes scholarships. Looking ahead to Byngsie's future, he suggested that his son consider spending six months at Oxford and six at a French university, "where you would try to develop your French so that later in life you might be able to make a real use of it. I believe that with your name the good which you will be able to do in life will be multiplied a hundred fold if you have a thorough knowledge of French, such a knowledge which will enable you to speak ex tempore in public."[18] For the time being, however, Byngsie was opting for the army and was already in military training in Brockville, Ontario.

As for Michel, Georges wrote to Madame Archer, "I want to tell you again of our profound gratitude for the material care that you're giving to Mickey, especially in the current situation, when conditions are so difficult ... I hope that you will continue to note down your daily impressions. Pauline and I count on this very much – it lets us see what we can't observe for ourselves in his development."[19]

The heat intensified as summer of 1944 progressed. The arrival of mosquitoes made it necessary to take daily doses of quinine to ward off malaria. Pauline wrote of the locusts that now carpeted the walkways, destroying the flowers ("billions of them and these little black hopping monsters are everywhere ... eating the leaves on the shrubbery, crawling up the trees"[20]), and of the appointment of a personage solemnly known as the locust liaison officer. She began to get herself physically fit by doing ten minutes of exercise every morning, followed by a cold bath, in anticipation of getting back into France.

Georges made two trips to Italy during these weeks. On the first visit, he congratulated the Royal 22nd for helping to break through the German hold in that country by means of door-to-door, hand-to hand combat that was reminiscent of Courcelette in the earlier war. He wrote to his old commander Tremblay that even the mud they had to slog through reminded him of Flanders. On his second trip, in July, he joined the Royal 22nd in an audience with Pope Pius XII and then had his own private audience. The Pope wanted to know what Georges thought about the religious situation in France, specifically, about the status of the Catholic clergy vis-à-vis the resistance movement. Word had obviously reached the Pope that anger against certain bishops and priests who supported Pétain had reached a point where it could not be ignored by the Vatican. As diplomatically as he could, Georges suggested that – without naming names, a task that would come later – it was thought within France that certain bishops should be removed. The Pope, as fitted both his position and his personality, kept his own opinions to himself. Georges noted later, however, that shortly after his audience with the Pope, the French bishops openly allowed priests to minister to members of the resistance.

The Allies made faster progress eastward in France than anyone anticipated. Leclerc's division joined the fighting in Alençon, one hundred and seventy kilometres west of Paris. On 23 August, in driving rain and with tanks that slid all over the slippery roads, Leclerc reached Rambouillet, on the outskirts of Paris. The next day, they marched into Paris in two columns. Cyclists, catching sight of them, spread the word that liberation had come. A radio broadcast called for church bells to ring, and the German commander of the city, Dietrich von Choltitz, phoned his superior in Germany and held up the receiver, through an open window, to the sound of bells from all over Paris. The "Marseillaise," forbidden during the occupation, was sung everywhere on the streets. People jeered and spat at the car carrying Choltitz to the prefecture of police, where he surrendered to Leclerc, but eventually history would thank him for disobeying his final orders from Hitler: that every German in Paris was to fight to the last man and that the city itself was to be set on fire and left in ruins.

The same day, Pauline wrote to the children:

PARIS IS LIBERATED! We heard it yesterday noon and I don't mind telling you that all day yesterday we all behaved like lunatics. Last night just by chance we had five men of the resistance to dinner; two of them had got away from prison camps in Germany a year ago and had worked in the resistance afterwards, until one of them was caught by the Gestapo, was put into the prison of Fresnes in Paris, but was got out by his colleagues. I don't think that I need tell you what sort of evening we had. It was quite delirious. I kissed them all (shame on you, Mummy), even a Jesuit Father (more shame, Mummy). This morning we hear that Leclerc's division has entered Paris, that Roumania has capitulated, that Marseille has been liberated, that Grenoble has been taken, that we are marching on Lyon, that Lisieux is taken, that we are nearing Le Havre, that another column is going up towards Lille. Oh me! It is nearly too much emotion all at once.[21]

More soberly, Georges wrote to Byngsie, "Uncle Philippe [Leclerc] is entering the history of France. As long as France remains France, school children will learn that it was to General Leclerc that the German commander made his surrender."[22]

Charles de Gaulle, having given Leclerc the spotlight that was his due, made his way to the Arc de Triomphe the next day and walked down the Champs-Élysées to the Place de la Concorde, crowds roaring the whole way. The liberation of the city had not happened tidily, with guns suddenly silent; sniper fire had continued here and there. As de Gaulle was getting into an open car and beginning the drive to Notre Dame Cathedral, shots rang out and a skirmish ensued. The towering hero stoically ignored it and continued the victorious ride through the streets. At the cathedral, de Gaulle walked alone up the long centre aisle of the nave: a striking symbol of a victory against tyranny that had been won with little help from the Catholic hierarchy. Cardinal Suhard of Paris had been told to stay away (only weeks earlier, Suhard had presided at the funeral, with full state honours, of the assassinated Philippe Henriot, Vichy's minister of information, even though hostages had been executed in retaliation for Henriot's killing). Again, inside the cathedral, shots rang out and people flattened themselves on the floor, but the tall figure of de Gaulle remained upright as the short service, a sung *Magnificat* (the scriptural prayer which praises God for exalting the humble and humiliating the mighty), took place.

On 2 September, Georges and Pauline Vanier left the palatial splendour of their Mediterranean villa for the last time and boarded a plane to London, en route to the newly liberated Paris. In London, they were briefly reunited with Thérèse and Jock, who was now six feet tall and who noted, with the candour and unerring eye of a sixteen-year-old, that he found "Ma a little fatter and Daddy a little thinner – he kept showing off his figure, obviously very proud of himself!"[23]

An unexpected restriction temporarily dampened the Vaniers' exhilaration: for safety reasons, and also because of the necessity to keep airplanes available for military personnel, only those in uniform were allowed to travel to Paris. Pauline was clearly a civilian, but a solution was soon found courtesy of Basil Price, the director of the British Red Cross. She wrote breezily to her mother, "I had an extremely hard time getting a uniform from the Red Cross, for whom I'm going to be the something-or-other for the Paris region."[24] He gave her the title of convener of Red Cross activities in Paris, and so, clad in an official uniform, she was allowed to board a plane to Paris. The unexpected result of this subterfuge was that before long, Pauline would actually find herself doing what she had hoped to do all along: to be of service for those suffering the effects of war.

On 7 September, at eleven o'clock in the morning, in a Royal Canadian Air Force plane escorted by two Spitfires, the Vaniers left London for France. When the coast of Normandy came into view, they both fell silent. Georges later wrote that he was overwhelmed by the realization that Guillaume Vanier had left this very shoreline for Canada three centuries earlier. The green, rolling land beneath them was punctuated with bomb craters and destroyed towns. At quarter to twelve, they saw the Eiffel Tower in the distance, and at noon they touched down on the Bourget air field.

Paris was run down but, unlike London, basically unscarred. The stately buildings and grand boulevards were still intact. On the streets, the only vehicles were bicycles and military cars. The few pedestrians looked weary. Signs of war were everywhere in the form of burnt cars, bullet holes in walls, broken windows, and fallen lampposts. Contrary to the accounts of others, Pauline found the Parisian women to be smartly dressed, although wearing ugly hats, and she wrote to Frances Shepherd that "I am pleased that I am in uniform so that I can't compete with their elegance."[25]

Thérèse joined them three days later, posted as a liaison officer of the Canadian Military Mission, wondering whether this was due to her father's influence ("The less kind are no doubt saying that Daddy 'pulled strings,'" she wrote to Byngsie. "And I must say it looks darn suspicious."[26]) She had just received the highest grade ever given in the CWACs and had been voted by the other cadets as the officer under whom they would most like to serve. Jock too had earned high praise from his instructors as "a very promising young officer, extremely cheerful, yet serious when in a position of responsibility" who also seemed "to be a natural leader with considerable influence."[27] The success of her children prompted Pauline to write, "What a family! Our Lord has certainly been good to us all. And He will certainly expect a great deal from you all after endowing you so plentifully and so richly … You will always remember that you will have to give, you who have received so much."[28]

Georges and Pauline settled into a furnished flat in the Hôtel Vendôme that had a sitting room with red plush furniture, a dining room that sat six comfortably, and an extra room that Pauline used as a study. Thérèse, who worked in an office next to Georges's, joined them for one meal a day, giving them a sense of family once again. Their food, American army rations, was simple and monotonous, unlike that of the higher classes who continued eating in style, as they had during the occupation, through access to the black market. But it was plentiful, in contrast to that of working class people, who suffered from hunger and malnutrition due to high inflation and the Nazi policy of sending French-grown food to Germany. "There is going to be a lot of work to do and I am pleased of it as I am longing to get my teeth into something really worthwhile," Pauline wrote to Frances Shepherd. "We know the people that we don't want to see and the ones that we do want to see, which makes things easy." She added that they were avoiding "the smart set – that I promise you!"[29]

Almost immediately she began sending pleas to Canada for food and clothing. Meanwhile, there were tours to see first-hand what more than four years of occupation and war had wrought. At Dieppe, Georges – a stickler for protocol and its symbolic importance – lost his temper when he discovered that an American car and chauffeur had been provided for them. "What wonderful headlines for the Canadian press: 'Canadian ambassador cannot find a Canadian car and Canadian chauffeur to go to Dieppe where there is a Canadian army fighting in France,'" he wrote in his personal notes. "One bright suggestion ... was that the American chauffeur might put on a Canadian uniform. This would have made a better headline: 'Impossible to find a Canadian chauffeur to fill a Canadian uniform.' Finally, we got started after a little rise in the blood pressure."[30] When they eventually made their appearance, they were greeted by a large crowd in the town square. Flowers and champagne were pressed upon them, and they were moved to tears by the playing of "The Last Post" at the war memorial and their walk among Canadian soldiers' graves. The scene was repeated in one ruined town after another. At the city of Caen, people emerged from the caves where they had been living since their homes had been flattened to greet the Canadian ambassador and his wife.

Pauline and Thérèse were taken to a factory that had been the resistance headquarters, where a group of resistance members shouted, "Vive le Canada!" The leader "said a few words of welcome, but broke down in the middle and couldn't go on, everybody was weeping," Pauline wrote. "I tried to say a few words too, standing on a table, but I was so *émue* that I hardly managed to do so ... These men and women have all done something heroic. They hid some of our airmen who bailed out, some were in the Service de Renseignements, they took all sorts of risks. The *adjoint du maire* ... helped 200 airmen to get away amongst many other things that he did."[31]

In Lyon, the centre of the resistance, they were met by the mayor and Cardinal Gerlier, and by people who Pauline noted were mostly "of humble state, men and women with rough hands,"[32] an observation that mirrored the gradual recognition that the resistance had been supported most by the lower classes. Georges noticed that the cardinal seemed "extremely depressed and I should think disappointed that he did not take a firmer stand during the occupation."[33] He also took note that a woman whose son had been arrested and killed by the Gestapo was seated side by side with a man known to have been a collaborator – a sign of the strange state of affairs following the liberation.

The *épuration*, or purge, had begun immediately. All the Vichy ministers were dismissed and replaced with resistance members. Thousands of officials were arrested. Revenge was fierce, and many executions took place without trial or recourse to the law. Women who had cavorted with German officers were stripped naked and their heads were shaved. Some people, hiding their own culpability, turned in neighbours, and many of the Miliciens, who had captured and imprisoned people on behalf of the Nazis, now did the same in the name of the resistance. *Collaboration* was the catch-all word for "guilt," but it was a slippery term, applied to everyone from those who openly embraced Nazi ideology and betrayed fellow citizens to those who simply tried to accommodate themselves to the regime for their own survival.[34] When it came to the Catholic leaders, the call for a purge was especially loud among Catholics themselves. "We are certainly living on a volcano,"[35] Pauline wrote.

Georges Bidault, who had been the head of the Conseil Nationale de Résistance, the co-ordinating body of the resistance and was now the foreign minister, spoke to Georges Vanier about certain bishops he wanted purged. The intellectual Charles Flory and the philosopher Jacques Maritain, who had returned from the United States to France with his wife, spoke of the matter as well. So did the "magnificently resistant" writer François Mauriac (who, Pauline wrote, "is certainly not a communist, but has very leftist tendencies and as you know, so do we, Daddy and I."[36]) The blacklist contained the names of about eight churchmen, including Cardinal Suhard and Cardinal Gerlier.

On 13 December, Georges met with the French Cardinal Tisserant, who had spent the occupation years in Rome and who, Georges heard, had been anti-Pétain from the start. Perhaps predictably, however, Tisserant disagreed with the request for changes among the bishops, telling Georges that the agitation was mainly in Paris and among small groups of Jesuits and others. "He admitted quite frankly that the episcopate as a whole had not been strong," Georges reported to Ottawa, "but there was a great distinction to be made between weakness and collaboration. He admitted, of course, that there were a few bishops who had been more than weak, but their cases seemed to be settling themselves."[37]

And, in fact, these cases did settle themselves: of the prelates deemed most pro-Vichy, one had already died and three others were pressured from within their dioceses to resign. Most of the bishops, once their initial enthusiasm for Vichy had waned and they realized the extent of the regime's injustice, straddled the fence between resistance and accommodation. One of their number, Gabriel Piguet of Clermont-Ferrand, had been arrested and deported to the Dachau concentration camp and would not be released until the camp was liberated in 1945. The turning point for some others had come in the summer of 1942, when the harassment of Jews escalated into massive numbers of deportations. Five of the bishops, including Cardinal Gerlier, protested the deportations. Several of them helped to find and protect hiding places for fleeing Jews. But in keeping a collective silence, the bishops were mirroring the silence of the Vatican itself in the face of the war's brutalities.

In the end the Vatican did not replace any of the bishops and made only one concession in the aftermath of Vichy: to recall the papal nuncio, not for culpability (he had, in fact, warned the Vatican about the deported Jews' suspected destination), but for diplomatic reasons. It was not until more than fifty years later, in 1997, that the French bishops' successors, one of them a Jewish convert (Cardinal Jean-Marie Lustiger of Paris) whose mother had died at the hands of the Nazis, would make a formal apology for the Catholic leaders' insufficient actions during the Vichy era. And it would be left for history to recognize the "lower ranks" – priests, nuns, and lay people – who hid Jews, especially children, in seminaries, schools, hospitals, and private homes, at their own peril. And for some, at the cost of their own lives.

* * *

The task of governing post-occupied France was not smooth: some areas were still under enemy occupation, and fierce fighting continued as the Allies systematically drove the German army eastward. Communication lines to various parts of the country were down. In some places, resistance groups were operating independently as governing bodies. The question over who was and who was not a collaborator still ran at high fever, and in the ensuing confusion summary justice continued to be carried out. On Georges Vanier's advice, Canada finally recognized de Gaulle's committee as the Provisional Government of the French Republic, and eventually Britain and the United States did as well. The Allies were closing in from all sides on Germany, and the war that had torn Europe apart was nearing its end. Already, the Vaniers' post-war work had begun.

But unspeakable sights were still to be discovered. The Vaniers already caught a glimpse of what was ahead; in a letter to the children shortly after the return to Paris, Pauline wrote about the suspected fate of their embassy's pre-war chauffeur, who was Jewish: "We heard yesterday that poor Joseph was arrested last June by the Gestapo and taken to Drancy, which was one of their worst camps in France. He hasn't been heard from since July and his poor wife is nearly frantic. I don't wonder and I am afraid that it looks very bad."[38]

14

END OF WAR, BEGINNING OF POST-WAR

By the spring of 1945, the Parisian *beau monde* was beginning to make a sparkling comeback, but the Vaniers took little part in the fashionable *soirées*. Their social contacts were rather more downscale and prosaic: resistance friends such as Elizabeth de Miribel came regularly to their hotel suite to take baths (the hotel had hot water between certain hours of the day), and for the diplomatic circle they held simplified "cocktail receptions" rather than dinners. They also mingled from time to time with the Allied Command's "big mukamuks,"[1] as Pauline called the military's top brass.

Sometimes Pauline found herself a dinner companion to the highest of the brass. The day after Winston Churchill and Charles de Gaulle rode up the Champs-Élysées to thunderous cheers, she was seated next to the British prime minister at both lunch and dinner. British ambassador Duff Cooper assured her that after a glass of wine, Churchill would lose his glowering bulldog scowl and become sociable. By the end of the dinner she had become so friendly with him that she asked for his cigar box as a souvenir for her sons. On another occasion she sat next to Field Marshal Montgomery, whom she found "absolutely charming and I completely fell for him."[2]

The Red Cross job she had fallen into was made to order for her. She became a one-woman social work agency with, in the words of a Canadian journalist, "an encyclopedic knowledge of what this country needs in food, clothing, sustenance."[3] Normally, her days were divided between writing begging letters to Canada and England and visiting Canadian troops on leave. Jock, on holiday in Paris, wrote to his brothers, "I can't tell you how busy poor Mummy is, her Red Cross job is a full time one in itself, but on top of it people are continually coming in to see her and she gets all sorts of letters asking her for things and begging her favours."[4] Indeed, hundreds of letters descended on her desk with pleas for help. The extent of the country's privation was staggering, and it required the non-glamorous work of trying to relieve the distress of a disenfranchised people. French children were subsisting with very little milk, eggs, or fruit and many were severely anaemic. Lack of fuel and proper clothing remained a problem. As shipments arrived, Pauline supervised the distribution of clothing, shoes, blankets, baby items, and food.

Every influx of help was matched with further requests: for vitamins, hospital supplies, pharmaceutical products, and medical aid for returning prisoners of war. The distress did not end with the needs of French citizens; poignant letters arrived from distraught Canadian families asking about missing relatives and from grieving parents who begged for information about the location and condition of their soldier sons' graves. Attempts were made to answer every letter, either by Pauline herself or by her secretary, a young resistance member.

Pauline took a particular interest in the plight of children, and acted as a liaison between the Canadian Committee of the Save the Children Fund and the Comité Français de Secours aux Enfants. As well, she acted as the Paris conduit for money and supplies sent by the Comité des Français Libres du Canada. She also became the honorary president of "Amis des enfants de Paris," an organization that helped orphaned and mentally disturbed children by setting them up in a village outside of Paris, where they were given an education in a healthy environment.

Letters of gratitude also arrived on Pauline's desk. From the Vosges region in eastern France, an aid worker wrote of conditions after the Germans had retreated in October 1944, having turned people out of their homes and deported all the men between the ages of sixteen and forty-five. "We spoke to many people who are still sleeping on straw in cellars, and who had had no change of clothes for three months," the worker wrote. "Sometimes they had a blanket, sometimes not. Most of them have lost everything: furniture, linen and clothes, kitchen utensils and even their animals. Some families have managed to save a cow. Apart from their physical misery, many of them have also lost members of the family, sometimes killed in battle, sometimes killed by mines." The worker offered the example of a family where the mother and three children had been killed by a mine explosion and ten more children, all suffering from rickets, were living in two rooms with their father. "I wish you could have seen the gratitude of all these people when they saw the clothes, and all the wonderful things which came from Canada … It made the work seem really worthwhile, but we could have distributed ten times the amount in the tiny district which we covered. It was heartbreaking to have to turn people away because we had nothing left."⁵ Others wrote of ongoing plights: children with no shoes and so unable to go to school, people with only a cardigan sweater to wear against the winter's cold.

There was still more to be discovered. In mid-April 1945, as the Allies pushed on into Germany, stories began to emerge about the horrors that they found in concentration camps, giving the world a new knowledge of the Nazis' legacy. Up to now, rumours had swirled in only vague and general terms about the camps' appalling conditions and the inhumane treatment the inmates were subjected to. But on 19 April, the full scale of the barbarity behind the barbed wire fences began to emerge when photographs appeared in European and North American newspapers of emaciated men in the forced labour camp of Ohrdruf, and of naked skeletal bodies stacked one on top of another. At Nordhausen, more than two thousand unburied bodies were found. On 20 April, Georges wrote in his notes that reports had been received from Buchenwald, which had been liberated nine days earlier, indicating that three Canadians had been executed there in mid-September 1944.

One of the three was Frank Pickersgill of Winnipeg (brother of Jack Pickersgill, assistant to Mackenzie King), a thirty-year-old journalist who had studied in Paris and had been interviewed by Georges for diplomatic work just before the fall of France in 1940. Pickersgill had been interned by the occupying Germans as an enemy alien and had later escaped by means of a hacksaw hidden inside a loaf of bread and subsequently made his way back to England, where he joined the Canadian army. The other two were John Kenneth Macalister of Guelph, Ontario, a Rhodes Scholar and lawyer, also thirty, whose poor eyesight had prevented him from being accepted into the French army; and twenty-one-year-old Guy Sabourin of Montreal, about whom little was known except that he, like the other two, had been an agent of the Special Operations Executive. The aim of this spy organization was to arrange for special agents to enter enemy territory and train internal resisters in methods of sabotage. Pickersgill and Macalister had been parachuted into the Loire region of France, behind enemy lines, in the early months of 1944 and had been arrested at a checkpoint soon afterward. They were taken to the Gestapo headquarters in Paris and eventually arrived at Buchenwald in late August 1944. Wanting to find out for himself the fate of the Canadians, Georges decided to visit Buchenwald.

He flew to Weimar, Germany, on 22 April, with eight American congress-men, who were also on a fact-finding mission. It was a cold, clear day, and on the five-mile drive from the airport to the concentration camp, which stood at the end of a long avenue of beautiful pine and chestnut trees, Georges thought of the German poets Goethe and Schiller, who had called this area home. At the entrance to the camp he saw the sign, ZOO GARTEN BUCHENWALD declaring the place to be a zoological garden. Inside, they found that sixty thousand people inhabited buildings intended to house eight thousand political prisoners.

An Austrian ex-prisoner at the camp was able to confirm that the three Canadians had indeed been executed. The worker remembered that the trio were always in good humour, not suspecting that they would be killed, but in fact hopeful (thanks to a radio they had found, as well as Allied bombs they had heard nearby) that the camp would soon be liberated. Pickersgill was heard placing a bet that they would all be home by Christmas. (Later reports revealed that these three, along with other Allied agents – thirty-seven in all – had been tortured before they were executed. Some were hanged, their hands and feet manacled, and the others were shot.)

The visitors returned to Paris two days later, shattered by what they had seen. Georges's personal notes do not reveal the depth of his experience once inside the camp, but on 1 May he recorded his impressions of Buchenwald for a radio broadcast in Canada. "You know this camp already from the accounts and the photographs you have seen in the press, but perhaps you could not bring yourself to believe what you read and saw. To many of you listening in Canada I am known. May I ask you to take my word that these things, however ghastly, are true … How deaf we were then to the stories of cruelty and the cries of pain which came to our ears, grim forerunners of the mass torture and murder which were to follow."

He went on to describe in detail what he saw: blackened bodies inside the cremation ovens, noise-making machines that drowned the screams of the torture victims, naked bodies "piled like so much cord wood." In im-provised hospitals the group saw "hundreds of men, some with running sores, their bodies so devoid of flesh that they could not lie for long in one position. Some who were able to stand were little more than skin and bone. One marvelled how the knee and ankle joints held together." They also saw several hundred children, most of them identified as Polish Jews; "some had been in prison camps for years. Those of ten and over worked as slave labourers on munitions. Not one so far as I know, had any idea of where his parents were; in view of the barbarous treatment inflicted on Poles and Jews by the Germans, it is probable that all are dead."

Perhaps the most chilling sight of all was a lampshade made from tattooed human skin – "and this I saw," he insisted, as if afraid that his listeners might consider his testimony too fantastic to be believed. "Our world of today," he said, "which has had an opportunity of viewing this atrocity against mankind, must pause and take account. In this camp of Buchenwald is written a record of infamy which time can neither atone nor efface."[6]

As one camp after another became liberated and thousands of French inmates were returned to their homeland, a Paris repatriation centre was installed in a hotel on Boulevard Raspail. There they received medical treatment, and those near death from starvation were put on milk diets. Pauline went to the centre every afternoon and once again, she was writing begging letters to the Canadian Red Cross. "I saw a few that had just got back by plane," she wrote. "Most of them were in a frightful physical condition, so thin and weak that they could hardly walk; their shaven heads and their diaphanous faces are pathetic."[7] And to her mother she wrote that the spectacle of the deportees from the camps continually haunted her. "This is truly the bursting out of evil in all its horror."[8] On the lighter side, she enjoyed visiting with Canadian soldiers on leave, not telling them she was the ambassador's wife and letting them guess who she was (one insisted he had seen her as a waitress in Montreal).

A litany of personal losses flowed into their lives during the months following the liberation: besides Frank Pickersgill, whom they had both known briefly, they heard of one acquaintance after another who had lost fathers and children in the camps. The beautiful young daughter of one friend had died at Ravensbrück after months of forced labour and starvation; Georges's secretary learned that her mother had also died at Ravensbrück and her father had succumbed at Buchenwald while her two brothers were still unaccounted for. And the embassy's chauffeur, Joseph, who had probably been sent east on a cattle car from the infamous transit camp of Drancy, was now numbered among the perished millions.

With these revelations still fresh, it is little wonder that on 9 May 1945, the French celebrated the Allied victory in Europe in somewhat muted fashion. Crowds gathered along the Champs-Élysées, sirens and car horns sounded, loudspeakers blared the "Marseillaise," but Georges noted that "the people were not jubilant. They were good natured and courteous; they were happy of course, but with an undercurrent of seriousness." The feeling he picked up was that they realized "they could not justifiably rejoice to the same extent as the British, the Americans and the Russians in the final victory."[9] (In England, by contrast, Jock described how he celebrated V-E Day while at a friend's in Oxford: he fell into the river while punting, lost the cap of his uniform in the pandemonium of the streets, climbed a fence and scrambled through undergrowth to reach his friend's college after the gates had closed for the night. The next day, in London, "I saw the King and Queen come out onto their balcony at Buckingham Palace four times; my patriotism overflowed inside me and I cheered and yelled while they were there and cheered and yelled even louder when they weren't."[10])

Charles de Gaulle celebrated the end of the European war by going to Notre Dame Cathedral for the "Te Deum," the traditional prayer of thanksgiving for victory. This time he was accompanied up the centre aisle by Cardinal Suhard. De Gaulle did not have the same taste for the purge that some of his more fiery followers had (his goal was to establish order rather than revolution, and he even brought into his government some people who had been Vichy supporters). His memoirs for this period do not mention the Catholic bishops, and Georges noted that de Gaulle had met with Suhard without consulting Georges Bidault (his cabinet minister who had called for getting rid of certain bishops, including Suhard) as early as September 1944. The Vatican had hastily replaced the papal nuncio, and de Gaulle seemed prepared to begin afresh.

The new nuncio, not the Vatican's first choice (their preferred candidate suffered from ill health), had been the papal nuncio in Turkey. He was a sixty-three-year-old archbishop of peasant stock named Angelo Roncalli, who combined a sharp intelligence with an affable personality. British ambassador Duff Cooper referred to Roncalli affectionately as a fat little Italian priest, and Georges, less spontaneously, described him as "heavy, of swarthy complexion, and quite voluble, and quite the 'diplomatic' type."[11] Over the ensuing years, the Vaniers were to establish a warm friendship with Roncalli, and Pauline acted as his hostess for formal dinners. On such occasions, Pauline, just two inches shy of six feet in height, stood beside the short, roly-poly nuncio as if she were his consort and shook hands with the line of diplomatic guests, one of whom, arriving solo, was her husband. Formality broke down in the general laughter over the strangeness of the scene. (Thirteen years after his appointment to Paris, Roncalli was to be elected to the papacy and would become Pope John XXIII. The Vaniers would remain friends with him until his death.)

For the Vanier family, the declaration of Allied victory over Japan in August meant that Byngsie, who was at Fort Benning, Georgia, training for the Pacific war, was spared. Georges wrote in his personal notes of his gratitude for the news that the war was over. He added: "With three boys, one nearing 20 and making ready for the Japanese war, a second 18½ and a third approaching 17 ... a matter of a few years might have meant for one or all (save perhaps Bernard because of his rheumatic fever) the tragic fate suffered by so many gallant young men. Am I selfish? I hope it is not merely that. There is so much good to be done in the world by young Christians and let us pray our three may be worthy of that name."[12]

Now began the family's postwar plans. A residence was eventually found at 5 rue Dosne, a three-storey house that stood on a cul-de-sac against a bank of trees and shrubs. It was decorated in a Chinese style with lacquered walls and had a drawing room that gave out onto a large balcony. Jock's schooling was coming to an end, and he was scheduled to go to sea with the Royal Navy. Twenty-two-year-old Thérèse, yet to be demobilized, had expressed a desire to study medicine. In Montreal, Bernard, having headed the list of prize winners at Loyola College, was making plans to leave for France with Michel. Byngsie too was waiting to be demobilized. Both parents had written to him several times to inquire about his future plans; Pauline had told him that if he wanted to study philosophy, "we have many friends who are quite adequate in that line, amongst others [Jacques] Maritain and [Etienne] Gilson"[13] – these being, as it happened, two of the most prominent European philosophers of the age. Georges wrote that, as a student, Byngsie could become demobilized quickly so as not to lose a year of his studies. Visiting Canada with de Gaulle in September 1945, he even offered to write to the Department of Defence on Byngsie's behalf. The usually forthright Byngsie seems not to have responded to the series of offers, although he applied for demobilization in November and was on his way to France by the end of December.

In the meantime, Pauline worried about what four-year-old Michel's reaction would be to the parents who were by now strangers to him. "Poor little chap, the ordeal of the trip is going to be bad enough without finding a mother at the other end whom he doesn't know," she wrote to Byngsie. "I do hope that he won't be too miserable. I know that it won't be long before he gets accustomed to us all, but it will be trying at first."[14] When Bernard and Michel arrived with Michel's nanny in October, 1945, Pauline was awash in tears. Bernard walked into her arms, and Michel, coming down the steps with his nanny, said, "You're my Mummy."[15] On Georges's advice, Bernard began a course of studies at the École Libre des Sciences Politiques, and Pauline was pleased to report a few weeks after their arrival that Michel had settled down better than she expected – although, she added ruefully, his nanny was the person he ran to for comfort, and he missed his grandmother's games of hide and seek. As for Madame Archer, now alone in Montreal, Pauline had advised her to stay in Canada until the spring because the fuel shortage promised another bitter winter. (When Pauline's mother did arrive in Paris the following April, she moved into a room in the ornate, old-world Hôtel Royal Monceau, where she lived until her death in 1969 at the age of ninety-five.)

Except for Byngsie, the family was once again complete for their first post-war Christmas. Jock left for sea on 4 January 1946, and three days later Byngsie arrived. This coming-and-going of their now-adult children was how it was to be from now on.

Meanwhile, the Canadian embassy was established in a building on avenue Foch that had for four years been used by the Gestapo and before that had been the abode of the Hungarian song-and-dance twins known as "the Dolly Sisters." In the latter capacity it had been outfitted with a grand staircase, a marble bathroom with gold fixtures, and elaborate boudoirs. According to the memoirs of Charles Ritchie, who came on staff at the embassy during this period, the secretaries were stuck with their typewriters in odd passages here and there, and the gilt-and-marble bathtub was filled with stacks of files and documents.

The Canadian ambassador quickly gained a reputation, as he had in London, for his Spartan work habits – this time, not allowing heat in his own office because most of the French populace was still without fuel. He was said to wrap himself up in his army greatcoat while he worked at his desk during the frigid winter. He was also reputed to be as exacting with his staff as he had been twenty years earlier at the Citadel. (Pauline wrote to Byngsie of a hapless driver supplied to the Canadian embassy by the army; the man proved to be "quite impossible and he would certainly drive Daddy nuts! He has the worst manners I have ever seen in anybody."[16]) When Georges discovered that someone had given the embassy secretaries a bottle of brandy to help keep them warm at night, Georges insisted they give it up lest they become dependent on alcohol, and he hid the wine supply of the embassy residence from the staff.

To some, Georges seemed overly fussy and perfectionist, but to those whose judgment and work skills he trusted, he gave latitude and encouragement. He took his own responsibility seriously, checking every document for accuracy before it left the embassy. Years later he told a correspondent that a magazine article described him as "a barking general" during these years. "I don't think I barked very much,"[17] he added ruefully. But if he seemed to run the embassy like a military operation, and if some of the staff chafed at the regimental work environment, the feeling was mitigated at least somewhat by the ambassador's quiet, dry wit, and his generosity in recognizing work that was well done. Charles Ritchie referred to Georges Vanier in his memoirs as a wise diplomat with "a particular brand of irony and deprecatory understatement, which often concealed a sharp point."[18]

On those outside the embassy, he made a positive, even heroic, impression. From the beginning, alone among diplomats, he had taken de Gaulle's side against what seemed to be overwhelming odds; then thanks to Canada's early recognition of de Gaulle's provisional government, he had been the first accredited ambassador to Free France. In addition, his family roots, passionate love for France, and deep knowledge of its history and culture endeared him to the French people. The Vaniers' closest French friends remained former resistance members. They severed ties with those from before the war who had stayed loyal to Pétain, most notably General Edouard Réquin, who had been Georges's French counterpart in Geneva. They also distanced themselves from members of the clergy who had supported the Vichy government. A priest who had written a book defending his friend Joseph Darnand, the executed head of the dreaded Milice, sent the Vaniers a copy of the book. In the accompanying letter, the priest said that Darnand's deputy, Jacques de Bernonville, who had entered Canada through the United States on a false passport, was also a friend of his. A politely cool acknowledgement was sent to the priest.[19] Their relationship with Cardinal Suhard of Paris, who had compromised himself somewhat, remained diplomatically cordial. In response to a letter from Suhard's biographer several years later, Georges wrote that he met the cardinal on several official occasions, but they did not become personal friends.

During the first postwar year, the main challenge facing the Canadian embassy was to explain the turbulent state of newly liberated France to External Affairs. In spite of de Gaulle's desire to bring order to the country (he was quoted as saying he did not want his government to have blood on its hands), vengeance within post-liberation France still replaced a civilized system of justice at the trials of Vichy officials. Georges and his first secretary, Saul Rae, wrote dispatches describing the trials of Pétain and his deputy, Pierre Laval, as travesties: the prosecutor, an elderly man who had come out of retirement, was ineffective, and the members of the jury often took over his role. The defence lawyer's performance was no better, and witnesses rambled on and on in an obvious effort to improve their own political standing.

In trying to sort out the tangle of forces vying for government seats, Georges turned to thirty-four-year-old Pierre-Henri Teitgen, a former member of the resistance who had become the minister of justice. Teitgen, whose pseudonym in the resistance was "Tristan," had been arrested by the Milice, beaten and put on a train heading for a camp in Germany. He escaped by cutting a hole in the roof of the compartment with a small saw hidden in the sole of his shoe, climbing onto the roof, and sliding down the side of the moving train. Georges noted in a dispatch to External Affairs that Teitgen was not a good administrator, but he was impressed with the new minister's honesty and perceptiveness.[20]

But observing and reporting on the sorry affair that the new government turned out to be required utmost tact and diplomacy. France was now being run by inept ministers who had gone into the resistance from various walks of life and had fought with courage but had no experience in governing a country. De Gaulle, though still revered everywhere, was a soldier, not a politician. He had little interest in economics, and there was no practical program in place for bringing France out of poverty and into prosperity. Power struggles still existed among various factions of the resistance in some parts of the country. Low morale and lack of confidence had settled in.

An election was held on 21 October 1945. The three parties that had gone into the election with the hope of victory – Communist, Socialist, and Mouvement Républicain Populaire (MRP) – received an almost equal number of votes, a situation that seemed to solve nothing. De Gaulle was unanimously voted head of government, but on 21 January 1946, the great hero abruptly resigned. Georges explained to External Affairs that de Gaulle was not interested in party politics and had balked at the proposal for a new constitution that would make him, as president of France, a mere figurehead with no governing authority. Georges was convinced that de Gaulle's role was not finished and that he would return to lead the country. This prediction was correct, but the return of France's wartime hero to political life would not happen for many years, until after the Vaniers had left Paris.

Although those who still worried that de Gaulle was an incipient dictator were relieved, now another fear reared its head. A shaky tripartite coalition was formed among the three parties, but the popularity of the Communist party, due to their resistance work, caused unease in some quarters. Would the Communists try to stage a *coup d'état*? The pathetic state of the country's economy made it seem ripe for a revolution of some kind, especially since the shadow of the Soviet Union now loomed in the east.

Another vexatious issue that confronted the embassy in the first year after the war was processing immigration visas, a duty that came under the direct control of the immigration branch of the Department of Mines and Resources, and not of External Affairs. But the immigration offices in Europe had closed at the beginning of the war, and now millions of migrants and refugees streamed to the Canadian embassies with requests to settle in Canada. In Ottawa, the same cumbersome bureaucracy and intransigence that had led to stalling on the refugee question in 1940 still prevailed. In Paris, the Canadian ambassador's only recourse was appealing to External Affairs to impress upon Immigration the necessity of opening up offices once again in Europe. An immigration office was eventually opened in Paris in November 1946, and Canada's policy in this regard gradually broadened. (Claims made in later years, that Georges knowingly issued visas to Vichy collaborators, have no credibility; apart from his exacting personality and strict adherence to correct procedure, as well as his pro-de Gaulle and anti-Pétain record, the process of issuing visas was not a matter for the ambassador's discretion.)

Early in 1946, the Vaniers visited Vézelay, a town in Burgundy, south east of Paris, which was quickly to become their spiritual home. Originally a Roman fortress, it was built on the side of a hill, the houses and streets interlocked in labyrinthine complexity. The main street ran up the centre of the town and ended at a twelfth-century basilica, which stood at the top of the hill. Vézelay had a dramatic and colourful history. The bones of Saint Mary Magdalene, after whom the basilica was named, had supposedly been laid to rest there. The town had been one of the starting points for the medieval pilgrimage to Santiago de Compostela, and it had featured prominently in the second and third crusades. Such historical figures as Thomas Becket and Richard the Lionheart, as well as all the kings of France, made pilgrimages there at one time or another. The light-filled basilica, a cavalcade of architectural richness and Christian symbolism, contained both Romanesque and

Gothic features and had been built in precise synchronization with the solar cycle, so that at the winter solstice the noonday sun would shine on the capitals of the north pillars and at the summer solstice it would stream straight down the centre of the nave. A park behind the basilica, which was lined with beech and oak trees, gave out on a wide vista of the forests, cultivated fields, and villages below. The Vaniers eventually leased a house near the park. This setting provided a sense of peace and beauty for the rest of their years in France, and even afterward.

During the first few months after his arrival in Paris, Byngsie had mentioned nothing of his future plans. He visited Vézelay with the rest of the family, went skiing with his siblings in Switzerland, attended a session of the Nuremburg trials, and accompanied his proud father as an aide-de-camp on official visits. Then, late in the evening of 20 August 1946, he knocked at the door of his parents' room as they were getting ready for bed. There was something he wanted to tell them, he said, before the day was over. The significance of the day was immediately apparent to Pauline: it was the feast day of St Bernard of Clairvaux, a luminary of the religious order known as the Cistercians. Byngsie announced that he had decided to enter a branch of the Cistercian order known as the Trappists. He would be returning to Canada to join the Trappist monastery in Oka, Quebec, near the Lac des Deux Montagnes, south of Montreal. The monastery was situated on property that, less than a century earlier, monks from France had transformed from a rocky wasteland into a vast farm and apple orchard. They had also established a thriving agricultural school and had become particularly known for making cheese.

But there was more to the Trappists than their ability to produce food. The Trappists were one of the most austere Catholic religious orders. Besides the farm and the cheese-making factory, at which they worked for several hours a day, they chanted the liturgical prayer known as the Divine Office at set hours. Their day began at two in the morning with chanted prayer. Meals were meatless and sparse, and in Lent, without dairy food. The monks had a strict rule of silence, and instead of speech among themselves they substituted an elaborate sign language. It was a life stripped to the bone, devoted to contemplation, a life that had come down through the centuries from early Christian hermits who had stolen away to caves to live in solitude.

Byngsie told his parents little of what had led up to this surprising decision. Trappist monasteries, especially in the United States, saw an upsurge of ex-servicemen streaming through their doors in an effort to find a life of peace after their experience of war. Byngsie had not experienced war directly, but the upheaval in their family life over the previous six years had meant that the teenage boy and eldest son was forced to grow up quickly, and, perhaps, to begin thinking deeply about the meaning of his own life.

In the first week of September the family spent a few days in Vézelay, and in personal notes, Georges recorded that he and his son walked together through the park among the enormous trees and sat on the wall overlooking the valley. He asked Byngsie what his friends would think of his decision. "They will think I'm a crackpot," his son replied.[21] In mid-October, the weekend before Byngsie's departure, Georges, Pauline, and their eldest son returned for a final trip together to Vézelay. Georges observed his son during Mass in the chapel of the great basilica as the early morning light illuminated the sanctuary: "Byngsie in his army jacket and battle dress trousers. He knelt, head slightly bowed, hands in front. At communion I was only a few feet from him and looked at him as he received communion, eyes closed, expression of great serenity," he wrote later. "I felt in the chapel that I was saying good-bye."[22] Georges and Pauline had from their first visit to Vézelay established the custom that, on leaving to return to Paris, they turned to look back as the car descended the hill away from the town. The gesture signified a literal "au revoir" – "till the next time" – to their spiritual refuge. On this occasion, they decided they would not look back at Vézelay as they were leaving; the son in the car with them would never be making this trip again.

Byngsie left for Canada on 21 October, a month before his twenty-first birthday. As they prepared to see him off at the train, Georges noticed that his son's face was "very pale and strained," and he turned away "for fear of meeting his eyes looking at me." During the awkward moments of leave-taking, Byngsie said, "It is wonderful to have such parents," and Georges wanted to reply that it was "wonderful to have such a son, but I wasn't sure enough of my voice. Instead," he wrote, "I made a gesture which was meant to convey this meaning. Then I took him in my arms and said ineptly, 'Au revoir'. At the station I meant to say 'Thank you for being such a son', but didn't dare. I kissed him and said, 'God bless you.'"

Two weeks after Byngsie's departure, Georges and Pauline returned to Vézelay for the week-end, apprehensive lest his absence loom too large for them. The weather was cold and damp, and during the night they filled gin bottles with hot water to heat the bed. They retraced the places they had been with him – the same restaurant for lunch, the same long walks, the same benches where they sat overlooking the valley, the visit to the same chapel – "but we were not uneasy or sad," Georges wrote in his notes. On Monday morning, the couple left Vézelay as a red dawn spread across the sky. They sat "quiet and serene" in the departing car, and as it headed down into the road toward the valley, away from the ancient jumble of buildings and the basilica at the crown of the hill, they turned to look back, with the feeling that, as Georges recorded in his notes, "we have not lost him."

Informing his staff at the embassy of Byngsie's decision, Georges said, with typical stoicism, "There is only strength and joy in this." In a farewell letter to his son, he wrote: "You have made us very happy, Byngsie, yes very happy. We will miss you but we will not lose you. You will be nearer to us than if you were with us in body. This I believe very deeply. There must be no sadness in the parting." In a rough draft of the letter he had added, "which does not only mean that a deep feeling of loss for a time,"²³ and then crossed out these words. They are, however, likely more telling of his true emotional state, in which admiration and pride mingled with grief as he struggled to comprehend this decision by the son he thought would follow in his footsteps.

Byngsie's decision to enter the monastery probably staggered Georges more than Pauline, who had been attracted to the ascetic lives of nuns from girlhood. Georges's ambition for his eldest son had been a reasonable one, given Byngsie's intelligence, personality, and academic achievement. The whole postwar world lay before the young man, and doors to a career in politics, diplomacy, or academia would have been readily opened to him. There would have been a father's satisfaction in man-to-man companionship with a son who, despite his parents' absence and the family's upheaval, had grown into an astonishing maturity. His brilliant son's rejection of everything that spelled worldly success marked a profound turning point in Georges's own spiritual life.

Within a few weeks, Byngsie was given a monk's habit and became known as Brother Benedict. A year after his son's departure, George made a solitary three-day visit to the monastery during a holiday in Canada (no overnight accommodation existed at the monastery for women). The trees in the surrounding woods were aglow with autumn colours, and in the monastery the silence was broken only by the soft padding of footsteps on the polished floors. During the first night Georges's stump "jumped" continuously, as if reacting to the hush (though he concluded that "the X-rays for the morning photographs had disturbed the nerve balance"). The days in the monastery were punctuated with meditation and the liturgical singing of Gregorian chant in the stark, high-ceilinged chapel, the monks filing silently in and out, dressed in their white robes and straight black scapulars. Georges was placed in an upstairs tribune, where he could see his son throughout High Mass. With chagrin, he noted that the meals given to him reflected none of the austerity of the monks' meals.

During the days he met with Brother Benedict for hour-long visits and walks to the chicken farm, and found him "smiling as usual," but also showing "a maturity so far beyond his years that one consults and confides in him as one would in the case of a man twice his years." On one occasion, the Father Abbot took him to a basement area where his son was sorting apples, "looking for bad ones – no compliment to his intelligence! ... he seemed particularly interested in the disposal of one small apple, pressing it and turning it on all sides – quite a 'cas de conscience.'" For his last day, Georges steeled himself to rise at the same time as the monks because he wanted to be able to hold in his memory the complete rhythm of Brother Benedict's day. At two am, settled in the tribune, he watched as the monks filed into the darkened chapel and the singing of Gregorian chant began. The day ended seventeen hours later at "Compline," with the monks coming one by one into the chapel "against a shaft of light from the corridor"[24] and, again in darkness, chanting the night-time prayer.

This was how it would be from now on: Brother Benedict would soon begin studying for the priesthood in this monastic setting, and would otherwise spend his days praying and meditating, working on the farm, sorting apples for cider, and cutting rounds of the famous Oka cheese. His parents would receive letters from him a few times a year and occasionally visit the monastery. Georges's feeling that he had not lost his son, perhaps initially articulated in an attempt to assuage his own grief, became a deeply held conviction. He believed that a deeper bond united them than if Byngsie had pursued a career and remained physically close by, and he relied on his monk son's prayers for the rest of his life.

* * *

As the twentieth century edged toward its halfway mark, the Vanier children continued to thrive. Thérèse was pursuing a medical degree at Cambridge University, one of only ten women allowed into the program each year. A Montreal friend, Murray Ballantyne, reported after a visit to Brother Benedict, "Although lean, he is clearly adequately nourished. He has, I think, hit his stride. He was of course subdued and restrained in manner ... but he was the old Byngsie, full of humour and fun."[25] Bernard proved to be the inheritor of his father's poetic soul: having begun to paint during his student years in Montreal, he forsook a political science degree and became a professional artist. Michel, in upper-class tradition, went off to boarding school at age eleven as his siblings had before him. His parents' choice was a Benedictine school, St Pierre-qui-Vire, in Burgundy, near Vézelay.

Jock was distinguishing himself in the navy: he was chosen to be one of the officers aboard the *Vanguard* on the 1947 trip that took King George VI, Queen Elizabeth, and their daughters, Princess Elizabeth (later Queen Elizabeth II) and Princess Margaret, to South Africa. He sent his parents a long letter bubbling over with details of the trip. Meeting the royal family for the first time, he felt "a bit wobbly" in the legs, he wrote. "I stepped forward and shook hands with His Majesty at the same time bowing my head, he said 'How do you do' and I tried to make some appropriate reply but my voice seemed to stick somewhere down in my stomach." As for Queen Elizabeth, "I have quite lost my heart to her and think that she is simply wonderful." Jock and the other young officers on board kept the royal family amused with plays and impromptu concerts and "all sorts of crazy games which were great fun ... the newsreel camera man took some shots of us and later on when we got to Capetown I was able to see myself on the film!" In South Africa, he danced with the diminutive Princess Margaret at her sister's twenty-first birthday ball. When they arrived back in England and the cheering crowds and press reporters disappeared, he felt "terribly flat" and "really quite sad now that it was all over."[26]

Sometime after the royal family's historic trip, Jock decided to transfer to the Royal Canadian Navy, sailing on the aircraft carrier *Magnificent*, a move that made his parents proud ("It was wonderful to hear that you were going to the *Magnificent*," his father wrote. "Mummy has informed 'le tout Paris' of this and I almost had to use force to prevent her from writing to the Prime Minister and the Minister for National Defence to express her appreciation of your posting to a large ship – I think she said 'big boat'. She has been telling people that a destroyer or a corvette is much too small for you who are 6'6", or is it 6'8"? In any event the height is increasing from day to day."[27])

Significant partings marked the closing years of the 1940s. General Leclerc, who had become the inspector-general of the armed forces in North Africa, dropped in frequently on the Vaniers when he was in Paris. On 25 November 1947, Georges wrote in his notes that Leclerc was leaving on an inspection tour of North Africa the next day. Three days later, word came that the plane Leclerc was on had crashed in Algeria and everyone on board was killed. His death at the age of forty-five severed a crucial link that had bound the Vaniers to de Gaulle's Free French cause from its early days.

Mackenzie King departed from the Canadian political scene by resigning as prime minister in 1948. He had always been an admirer of the Vaniers, and hoped that they might develop into friends after his retirement. In Georges's last letters to him, he addressed his former superior by the name that only friends and family used: "Rex." It is difficult to gauge to what extent Georges had changed his mind about King over the couple of decades since the constitutional debacle with Lord Byng but it is likely that, like many other Canadians, he admired the way King led the country through the Second World War. In his last letter to King, he wrote, with the ring of sincerity, if not exactly an easy familiarity, "I hope you are making good progress with your memoirs ... I adjure you to make every effort within reason to complete them. It will be a terrible loss for the country if they are not published because you alone have the material necessary to write the political – I should say the politico-national history of our country since the beginning of the century." (Pauline wrote a more effusive and exaggerated postscript to the same letter: "Dearest Rex, I think of you with infinite gratitude for your kindness to us through the years we have had the privilege of knowing you."[28]) King died on 22 July 1950, leaving no memoirs, but a valuable diary instead.

Georges remained, for the time being, pessimistic about the state of France. The immediate postwar fear in the country – that the Communists might take advantage of its widespread economic paralysis by fomenting strikes and social unrest – was alleviated by the Marshall Plan for European recovery. France was a major beneficiary of the Marshall Plan, which came into effect in 1947, and farms, vineyards, and industries began to get on their feet again. Vincent Auriol, a respected socialist, became the president of the republic. But Georges, like de Gaulle, was of the opinion that the political parties were too busy warring with each other to work for the good of the people. And there remained the specter of the Soviet Union and the fear that it would overtake the whole of Europe. A fellow diplomat recalled in a memo to Georges a scene that took place at the French president's New Year's reception for the diplomatic corps in early 1948. At the reception, the Soviet ambassador stood alone in the receiving line, avoiding eye contact with any-one. When Georges Bidault, the former foreign affairs minister, came along the line of diplomats, shaking hands with each one, there was a second of indecision as to whether or not he would shake the Soviet's hand. "Their faces," Georges's colleague wrote, "were a study in dislike and mistrust." Finally they seemed to decide that "for the sake of appearances they must shake hands and both their hands shot out although even then they did not look at each other. After a second or two of feeling around in mid-air, their hands met, touched in a handclasp and dropped away again to their sides with no further sign being given that they even knew that the other was in the room."[29] That image of mistrust and apprehension was to symbolize much of European feeling for the next several decades as the Soviet tyranny tightened its grip.

For Georges, the problem went deeper. He had hoped that the hardship and humiliation of the Vichy years and the heroic work of the resistance would bring about a spiritually revitalized France. Instead, he felt that the French people had come out of the war morally and spiritually diminished. He expressed his disappointment in his last letter to Mackenzie King in March 1950. "On the surface and for the time being things may appear brighter, but fundamentally there is no improvement," he wrote. "Slowly but surely we appear to be drifting towards a clear cut division in the world – two camps, the Marxist and 'the other.' I can say 'the other' whereas I would like to say 'the Christian,' but unfortunately it would not be true, because a great part of 'the other' camp is terribly materialistic though self-styled 'Christian.'"[30] He worried that wartime ideals and sacrifices had produced only a hunger for material comfort and soft living.

* * *

But for the Vanier family, new horizons were beginning to appear. In October, 1946, among the many letters Pauline received was one from Père Thomas Philippe, a theologian who had recently opened "L'Eau Vive," a "spiritual foyer" for students near Paris. He asked for an appointment with Pauline to find a way to invite Canadians who were studying in Paris to come to this new foundation, either as residents or as visitors. This modest request was the beginning of an association between the priest and the Vaniers that was eventually to have an enormous ripple effect.

15

TOWARD THE END OF DIPLOMACY

By 1950, Pauline Vanier had come into her own as Canada's chatelaine in Paris. As France began to prosper once again, luncheons and formal dinners replaced the earlier stripped-down diplomatic cocktail parties, and Pauline returned to the usual duties of an ambassador's wife. She shed the Red Cross uniform and began to shop at Worth's of Paris, a couturier that specialized in clothes of elegant simplicity. She now supervised a household staff of five: a butler, cook, kitchen maid, housemaid, and footman. The bear hugs Pauline gave whenever she met friends earned her the nickname "Madame L'Embrace-adrice," and during these postwar years, close friends of a younger generation (including Canadians studying in Paris) took to calling her "Maman." Variations of this form of address – paradoxically for a woman who tended to malign herself for her maternal failings – would continue for the rest of her life.

Although both Vaniers became noted, as in London, for their light-hearted humour, thoughtfulness and ability to bypass stuffiness, not everyone felt at ease in Pauline's presence. Some of the younger diplomatic wives felt daunted by her. When her white hair was swept high on her head, she cut a tall and formidable figure. She carried an aura of heroism because of her association with the resistance and her monumental post-liberation work. Her knowledge of French ways and friendship with some of the intellectual elite gave her gatherings an air of sophistication that could be intimidating to the uninitiated, newly arrived from Canada. There were some too who considered her insufficiently discreet, and thought that her talkativeness led her to express opinions inappropriate for an ambassador's wife.

For Pauline herself, what became important once again was the need for a priest as a spiritual guide. The letter that she received in 1946 from Père Thomas Philippe, looking for Canadian support for his house of studies, may not have seemed like an answer to this spiritual need at the time she received it, but seven months later, she accepted his invitation to visit L'Eau

Vive. It was situated in Soisy-sur-Seine, a short distance south-east of Paris, beside Le Saulchoir, a theological college where Père Thomas taught. Soon afterward, Pauline wrote to Mother Mary of the Cross that the forty-eight-year-old priest seemed rather over-eager in offering her spiritual counselling and inviting her to hear his sermons. The nun replied, "each fresh word of yours that I read about him put me off more and more – I might say, stiffened me up. I do mistrust people who offer themselves to help the souls of others, and also people who issue invitations to hear them preach. And from that angle I feel on my guard about him still ... I would go very slowly before I opened out to him. Frankly, I fancy he is going to help you a great deal, but I do think it is very much better to go slowly in so grave a matter. What comes to me through your letter is that he is rushing at you."[1]

Whatever initial difficulties Pauline had with the zealous priest, she decided to seek his spiritual advice, and two years later, Mother Mary of the Cross was writing, "I never cease thanking God for the help you have in Père Thomas."[2] Jock, on his navy ship, had also been embarking on a spiritual search. Pauline introduced her son to Père Thomas, and in 1950, at the age of twenty-two, Jock left the navy. He went to live at L'Eau Vive, and began studying philosophy at Le Saulchoir, which was run by the Dominicans, a religious order that had existed since the thirteenth century and of which Père Thomas was a member.

The group of old houses that formed L'Eau Vive were high-ceilinged and cold, warmed only by wood stoves, but they were surrounded by huge chestnut trees and stood among unspoiled meadows filled with wild flowers. The idea behind L'Eau Vive, besides offering a residence for international students, was to expand the teachings of Christian spirituality beyond the walls of monasteries and to help lay people find the means of contemplation as well as a bridge between theology and their everyday lives. Georges and Pauline soon became involved in the Association des Amis de l'Eau Vive, which helped to raise funds for the fledgling venture. By the early 1950s, L'Eau Vive was a hive of spiritual energy. The philosopher Jacques Maritain gave summer classes there, and the centre attracted Hindus and Muslims as well as other Christians. The American poet Robert Lax stayed at L'Eau Vive for a time, and he wrote about it with enthusiasm to his friends the Trappist monk Thomas Merton and the writer Jack Kerouac, who told the beat poet Allan Ginsberg about it. It was also to provide the seed of Jock's life's work.

But slowly, this dynamic enterprise began to come apart. Those involved with L'Eau Vive, including the Vaniers, may not have known at the time that it was being watched with suspicion by the Vatican. The new theological thinking that had been suppressed half a century earlier had risen again among a new generation, this time in the religious houses and seminaries of continental Europe. It tried to interpret Catholic teaching, which had remained static since the sixteenth century, in the light of historical events and the changes brought about by scientific discoveries and a new world order. In France itself, the worker-priest movement had been taking place, in which priests took jobs in factories in an effort to make contact with the working classes. The theological centre of the new thinking was the Dominican college of Le Saulchoir, where Jock Vanier was studying.

Several years before the Vaniers became involved, Père Thomas had been sent by the Vatican to replace the prefect of studies at Le Saulchoir, who was forbidden to teach and whose writings were suppressed. Then in April 1952, Père Thomas himself was suddenly removed, his writings on mystical spirituality having aroused Vatican distrust. Père Thomas's language, like that of the medieval mystics, was emotional rather than rational. It was not derived from the intellectual constructs of theology, and was therefore considered unorthodox. He was forbidden to minister as a priest. .

Two years later other leading Dominican priests were removed from their posts, and the worker-priest movement was dissolved. In the meantime, the students of L'Eau Vive, caught in the web of Vatican opprobrium, were forbidden to study at Le Saulchoir. Jock, like the others, enrolled at the Institut Catholique in Paris, and he was left in charge of L'Eau Vive, whose future now remained unclear. It was another reminder for the Vaniers that the Church in which they worshiped and to which they pledged their lives of service contained contradictory elements and considerable imperfection. A decade later, the forward-thinking Dominicans' work would be given new life and two of the priests who had been treated the most harshly would become consultants to the bishops at the Second Vatican Council. Père Thomas's status as a priest would also eventually be restored. But for now, at Le Saulchoir, the new theological thinking was suppressed. It was not long before L'Eau Vive was closed entirely.

Georges and Pauline were not naïve, nor were they under any illusion about the limitations of the Catholic hierarchy, but they were shaken by the injustice meted out to a priest who was their friend and a spiritual counsellor to Pauline and Jock. In addition they worried about their son, who had abandoned a promising navy career only to be left in a no-man's-land. In contrast, their oldest son had progressed steadily through his monastic studies back in Canada, and in March 1952, the Vanier family assembled in Montreal for Brother Benedict's ordination to the priesthood. (Thérèse was the one absent family member, having to stay in England for medical exams.) The ceremony took place in the same magnificent basilica where Georges and Pauline had been married over thirty years earlier.

In the meantime, the Canadian embassy carried on its business. Lester Pearson was now the minister for External Affairs within the Liberal government of Mackenzie King's successor, Louis St Laurent. In this capacity, he was also Georges's superior. At Pearson's urging, Canada joined the United States and the countries of western Europe in an alliance known as the North Atlantic Treaty Organization (NATO), whose purpose was to form a common defence against the threat of Soviet Communism. Georges met in 1951 with General Dwight Eisenhower, supreme commander of NATO. He sent to External Affairs a detailed report on the meeting, covering everything from the general's comportment and diet (behind his hearty manner lay the weariness of a man of action stuck behind a desk, and he poured a great deal of ketchup on his food) to the question of military defence against the Russians (a European army might be useful if first there was political integration), and the prospect of a re-armed Germany (they discussed whether the Germans were indeed a warlike people – Georges thought they derived "a deep satisfaction from seeing themselves marching towards conquest,"[3] but Eisenhower's view was more nuanced).

Europe was wary of the emerging American super-power status, and Georges, neither American nor European, but respected by both as he had been in Algiers, may have played a conciliatory role in some of the negotiations. Pearson wrote to him in 1952, "It was ... a great pleasure for me to see how close and friendly are the relationships between the embassy and the NATO mission and I know ... that you are largely responsible for this happy development."[4]

* * *

In 1952, plans were underway to establish a new Paris residence for the Canadian ambassador. The cramped quarters of the house on rue Dosne, with its plain rooms and awkward design, were barely adequate for embassy entertaining. Georges was particularly aware of its unsuitability because of his position as vice-dean of the diplomatic corps (he held this position because he had been the first ambassador accredited to the provisional government in 1944; the papal nuncio was *ex officio* the dean of the diplomatic corps). A splendid eighteenth-century three-storey building with tall windows and a chateau-like façade was found at 135 rue Faubourg Saint-Honoré, located in the heart of Paris, near the Champs-Élysées and the Arc de Triomphe. A filigreed iron gate led to a front courtyard, and a back garden extended to the street beyond. In the entrance hall, a sweeping staircase led up to the private quarters. The main floor contained gilded salons with rococo detailing and blazing chandeliers, a grand dining room, and a library with wood-paneled walls. The Vaniers threw themselves with excitement and energy into the project of decorating and choosing furniture. In April 1953, the new residence was ready to be occupied, and the Vaniers moved in, eager to begin receiving guests in its spacious rooms. Four days later, Georges was told that his eight-year tenure as Canadian ambassador to France was to be terminated at the end of the year.

The carrier of this unwelcome news was his old friend Lester Pearson. In fact, this was the second diplomatic disappointment for Georges in less than five years. Just before his retirement, Mackenzie King had kindled the hope that Georges might be offered the post of high commissioner in London, and Pearson had indicated a similar sentiment. Georges was thrilled by this possibility, but when Louis St Laurent succeeded King, he decided that since he was a French-Canadian prime minister, English Canada would not look favourably on having another French Canadian in the London post. And so Georges had been passed over.

Why his termination as ambassador to France came at this particular time and in such an abrupt manner remains unclear, although Georges turned sixty-five the same month as he received this notification, so the view may have been expressed within External Affairs that he should make way for a younger ambassador. Outright retirement seems not to have been a question, because in correspondence from Ottawa, the likelihood of an appointment in Canada is mentioned cryptically, and Pearson wrote that "this is the end of a chapter, but it has been a magnificent chapter, and is by no means the end of the story."[5] It is possible that a Senate appointment or the governor generalship were mentioned at this time.

More immediately, however, ambassadorships in either Spain or Switzerland were offered to him. Georges felt angry and insulted: both the French and his friends in Canada, he said, would regard a move to posts that were junior to that of France as a demotion. "A public statement to the effect that the government was most anxious not to lose my experienced services would be taken with a grain of salt,"[6] he wrote to Pearson. A final appeal for an extension of his stay in Paris, as well as a direct appeal by Georges Bidault on behalf of the French government, were both denied. He was told that his appointment as ambassador to France would end on 31 December 1953. Reluctantly, he decided that retirement was his only reasonable option, and he and Pauline prepared to leave Paris and return to Canada.

But not before certain matters, however seemingly insignificant, were dealt with. He inquired of External Affairs whether he could keep a leather portfolio and a set of bronze medals that had been given to him. And pointedly, he asked Pearson for a draft of the press release announcing his retirement: "I am sure you would wish me to see it before it is published so that we may agree on the wording."[7] When the press release arrived, he balked at the phrase "after a distinguished career of forty years" and asked that it be corrected to the actual number of thirty-eight. Forty, he said, "makes one sound terribly old."[8] More significantly, he objected to the sentence that indicated he had been seconded to the Canadian army from External Affairs. "On the contrary I have always been seconded to External Affairs from National Defence." On the eve of diplomatic retirement, he remained a soldier first.

In December came the rounds of goodbye dinners. In a ceremony on 31 December, Pauline was granted France's Legion of Honour, a tribute that regulations forbade to her husband as the representative of a foreign government. That same night, toward midnight, exhausted with emotion, they boarded a train at the Gare de Lyon, waved away by a crowd of friends, government officials, and embassy staff. Over the previous weeks they had received many accolades, none more eloquent than that of a fellow Canadian living in France: "It is Paris who must thank you, for being the most gracious stars in its diplomatic firmament for so long – for bringing friendliness and glamour to its every gathering; it is we Canadians who must say 'merci' to you who have represented us with such distinction for so long and brought honour to the name of your country. Nobody can help but be sad at your going, we shall all be the poorer for it."[9]

* * *

The Vaniers had decided to remain in Europe until the end of the school year so as not to interrupt Michel's studies. The train from Paris took them to Switzerland, where they had an extended stay while Michel recovered from a skiing accident and a bout of measles. With Bernard at the wheel of a new Citroen, they took a leisurely trip through Italy. Writing to Frances Shepherd, Pauline enthused, "This rest has been a Godsend. George is in fine form, in fact he is better than I have seen him for years and oh! me, is he in a humourous form too … in spite of Mick's mishaps we are really having a grand time. Eating, sleeping, and giggling a lot as well which helps the digestion I believe."[10]

By late spring they were in Vézelay, their spiritual home, and from there they paid a visit to Charles de Gaulle at his retirement home. Georges found de Gaulle mellowed and gracious, working on his memoirs, casting back philosophically on the crucial role he had played in the saving of France. He viewed the great general's present position with mixed feelings, noting both the beginnings of a jowl and a charming manner hitherto carefully hidden, and he missed the impassioned, fiery, uncompromising leader of former days. "On voit loin,"[11] de Gaulle told him as they stood in his study overlooking the valley from the window. Georges took this short piece of wisdom as de Gaulle's view of history and his own role in it, and the simple maxim by which he now lived.

In June, Georges and Pauline travelled to England to visit Thérèse. Pauline took the opportunity to tell her daughter, a newly minted doctor, about a lump she had recently found on her breast while bathing. Thérèse arranged for her to see a specialist, and in late June Georges wrote to Father Benedict that Pauline had just undergone "a very serious operation."[12] Breast cancer had been discovered, and the operation was a complete mastectomy. This was probably the lowest point in their lives since the fall of France, the shock of unexpected cancer coming on the heels of an unwanted retirement and the ongoing concern about L'Eau Vive and Jock's welfare.

As for all women suffering from this disease, it probably seemed to Pauline a double curse: the dreaded death-knell sounded by the word "cancer" and the mutilation that invaded a woman's sense of her femininity. The hush, bordering on shame, that accompanied this onslaught, intensified the affliction. Few people were told the nature of Pauline's surgery, and it is possible that even Father Benedict knew nothing precise about it, the intimate nature of the procedure perhaps being considered too indelicate for a monk's ears. Pauline opened up about her mastectomy many years later to only a few close women friends, when breast cancer became a subject for public discussion, and she expressed fascination with the surgical methods and treatment that had become more refined over the decades. Whatever her feelings at the time, she took this life-changing episode in stride, as she often did when met with serious adversity. Five months after the surgery, she glowed with lively confidence at a ball given by Les Fusiliers Mont-Royal in Montreal, wearing a black silk jersey gown that was cut low over the bosom. And as the years went on, she joked about needing to replace the prostheses, which she laughingly called "falsies," with larger ones as she gradually put on weight.

* * *

Georges, Pauline, and thirteen-year-old Michel arrived back in Canada in early September, 1954. They moved into a two-bedroom apartment on Sherbrooke Street in Montreal, and Michel went to study at Collège Saint-Alexandre in Limbour, Quebec. Canada had changed in the years since their wartime sojourn: the country was in the grip of the cold war and the fear of communism, but because of the postwar boom, there was also a general feeling of prosperity. In Ottawa, a Canadian, Vincent Massey, was now the governor general and the Liberals under Louis St Laurent's leadership ruled comfortably with a fifth consecutive majority government. In Quebec, a monarchical alliance between the government and the Church character-ized the premiership of Maurice Duplessis and the party in power, the Union Nationale.

The Vaniers settled into their new life, resuming relationships with old friends and making new ones. They became acquainted with the Carmelite nuns and, for Pauline especially, the monastery on avenue du Carmel would become a regular haven for meditation and retreat. They found a different sort of community under the auspices of Tony Walsh, a fifty-six-year-old Englishman who had recently opened a "house of hospitality" named Bene-dict Labre House. In this modest dwelling, he offered shelter and meals to homeless men. He gathered around him a talented group of volunteers – journalists, medical doctors, and university professors – who helped in the centre and came together regularly for prayer, lectures, and discussion. In this eclectic group of people, which included the psychiatrist Karl Stern, the Vaniers found a community similar in spirit to that of L'Eau Vive in its desire to live a basic Christian way of life. Pauline served at tables regularly, proving clumsy as a waitress, but thanks to her broad humour, succeeding in engaging the men in laughter. She also began visiting prisons and followed the progress of some of the prisoners for several years.

They were sought-after guests in Montreal society, and Pauline's unstoppable vivacity and years of experience in the rarefied world of diplomacy was to earn her the 1958 title of "Woman of the Year" from a group of Quebec women journalists. The art of being a good hostess may or may not have been high on her list of personal accomplishments (as always, she was pulled in two directions: service to those in need and a life of glamour and parties), but when she was asked about her hostessing style, she replied, "I believe that the most important thing for a hostess is simplicity."[13]

The transition from being at the centre of activity in a European capital was less easy for Georges. He was named a member of the Canada Council and helped on its investment committee, and was also made a director of the Bank of Montreal, Le Crédit Foncier, and the Standard Life Assurance Company. These activities took him into the business world, but they were not satisfying. He was also named the honorary colonel of the Royal 22nd Regiment, and in 1955 he received an honorary doctorate from the University of Montreal. Although these distinctions pleased him, he may have been disappointed that none of his three older sons had, in the end, followed in either his military or his diplomatic footsteps.

In fact, his sons had become more a source of worry than of pride. He still looked to Father Benedict as a model and spiritual guide, but Trappist austerities had landed this beloved son in the hospital with tuberculosis soon after his ordination to the priesthood, and it had taken him two years to recover. His father still considered him too thin, and he sent anxious letters to the abbot inquiring about his son's health. Bernard's life as an artist was a precarious one, and although Georges was impressed with this son's talent, he told Bernard that he would probably make more money painting houses. And Jock, now pursuing a doctorate in philosophy at the Institut Catholique in Paris, seemed to be wandering in uncertainty, a casualty of church politics. When writing to male friends, Georges had sometimes referred to one or other of his sons in the clubby phrase "my boy" ("my boy the monk," "my boy the sailor"). But now, if the subject of his children came up in the male-only bastions of leather chairs and brandy snifters, a world he sometimes inhabited, the only one of his offspring he could boast about whose accomplishments made any worldly sense was his daughter.

Thérèse had obtained an internship at St Thomas's Hospital in London – only the second woman to do so, according to her proud father – and she had begun to specialize in pediatric hematology.

Decades earlier, in a convocation address at Loyola College, he had advised the graduates to be good losers. "I am not sure that it isn't a good thing to be beaten sometimes. After all, what should an obstacle be – a thing to be overcome, an incentive, not a barrier. It is a fine but difficult thing to be a graceful winner; it is not bad training to begin by being a graceful loser."[14] But this was easier said than done. He had known professional failure only once before in his life – between 1940 and 1942, when he and Pauline had stood alone in their belief in Charles de Gaulle's leadership and he had been sidelined from war action – and even then, he had been vindicated in the end. Now failure seemed to stare him in the face, and the unaccustomed hours of idleness intensified it.

Paradoxically, the desolation of these years led to a turning point in his spiritual life. A few years earlier he had come upon a book called *Difficulties in Mental Prayer*, by an Irish Trappist monk named Eugene Boylan, and he was later to say that this discovery began a change in his life. As the title suggests, the book dealt with the struggles and setbacks in the life of prayer, and indicates the type of experiences that Georges was probably having in his half-hour of daily meditation: a sense of dryness (perhaps in his case compounded by emotional depression) that is known in Christian spirituality as "the dark night of the soul." Father Boylan had a no-nonsense approach to the spiritual life (he advised priests when counseling penitents to stop making judgements, to remember their own need of mercy, and to keep their mouths shut), and what Georges found most helpful was the monk's emphasis on the primacy of love above rules, in the sense of the all-embracing Christian term "agape."

It was a continuation of the inner turn he had made after hearing Father Steuart's sermon many years earlier. As he faced old age in a retirement that was not of his own choosing, the realization struck him, in a new way, that these particular circumstances could lead him to deeper spiritual fulfillment. The result, his son Jock would write some years later, was a trust that an unseen grace would carry him. The intransigent side of his personality, intensified by his life in the military, began to soften, and the inclination toward categorical judgments lessened. The moments when his face tightened in anger became fewer. He himself noticed that his blood pressure improved. He started reading spiritual classics such as the works of St John of the Cross and St Thérèse of Lisieux. Eventually he and Pauline would study these authors together, and some years later, when her eyes began giving her trouble, he would read aloud to her.

* * *

By 1958, Vincent Massey's term as governor general of Canada was nearing its end, and it was expected that he would be succeeded by a French Canadian. The press openly speculated about the possible appointment of Georges Vanier as representative of the crown in Canada. He had been considered as a candidate for that office many years earlier by Mackenzie King, and it is likely that Lester Pearson had suggested this possibility upon Georges's retirement from Paris. But by now two events put his candidacy for the governor-generalship into question: in 1956 he had suffered a heart attack and his health seemed uncertain. And in 1957, the Conservatives, under John Diefenbaker, had upset the long-governing Liberals with a minority government, a win that was followed nine months later by another election that gave the Conservatives the largest majority in Canadian history. Lester Pearson had become the head of the Liberal Party and was now the leader of the opposition. Georges's position as Pearson's candidate made him unlikely to be Diefenbaker's choice for governor general.

Nonetheless, in April 1959 Diefenbaker called him to Ottawa and asked if he would consent to become the next governor general. Georges may have been amused at the irony of the request, coming as it did from Pearson's nemesis, and he was doubtless aware that there may have been some political motivation involved, his appointment being intended to benefit the Conservative party in Quebec. But there was little hesitation and no looking back at the state of his health. Once again, he would be able to work for the good of Canada in the public arena.

The news, for the time being, was kept under wraps. Queen Elizabeth was due to visit Canada in the summer, and she would make the announcement then. She and the Duke of Edinburgh arrived in June, and Georges, as honorary colonel of the Royal 22nd Regiment, accompanied her on a visit to the Citadel in Quebec City. Then he and Pauline left for Europe to visit their children and Pauline's mother. On 1 August, the last day of the royal visit, while the Vaniers were still abroad, the Queen announced the name of the new governor general.

* * *

Three weeks later, at the Montreal dockside, the seventy-one-year-old governor general designate, impeccably groomed and wearing a grey suit, stepped with the help of a silver-banded walnut cane from the ocean liner *Ivernia* and into the glare of flash bulbs. His white hair, still thick, was only just beginning to recede from his forehead, and his moustache, once pencil-thin, was full and distinguished. The thick pouches under his eyes gave a look of gravitas to his fine features. Reporters flocked around him with questions and notebooks.

The short exchange that followed gave them a foretaste of what they could expect in the future from this man. Was his health up to the job? "If we believe the Lord is our strength, why not act as if we thought this was true?" he answered, and then he quoted from Shakespeare's *Hamlet*: "There's a divinity that shapes our ends, rough-hew them how we will," as if this was a piece of wisdom he lived by. Why had he returned to Canada by boat and not by air? "I wanted some time to rest and reflect." He added, with wry, self-deprecating humour, "In fact, the time may have done my character some good." And then, how did he spell his first name, with or without an s? "Suit your preference,"[15] he replied, intimating that his feet were planted comfortably in both worlds.

The Vaniers returning to Paris after the liberation, September 1944.
Library and Archives Canada/Georges P. Vanier Fonds/Acc. No. 1971-311 Box 5820

Visiting Dieppe, 1944. Library and Archives Canada/Georges P. Vanier Fonds/Acc. No.
1971-311 Box 5820

Pauline laying flowers at a Canadian war cemetery in Dieppe, 1944.
Library and Archives Canada/Georges P. Vanier Fonds/Acc. No. 1971-311 Box 5820

Georges and Pauline with Thérèse and Jock (Jean) in Paris, 1945. Library and Archives Canada/Georges P. Vanier Fonds/Acc. No. 1971-311 Box 5820

Charles de Gaulle and Mackenzie King in front of the war memorial in Ottawa, 1945. Georges Vanier stands in the background, fourth from the right. Library and Archives Canada/Georges P. Vanier Fonds/Acc. No. 1971-311 Box 5820

Pauline with her friend Lady Bigham (Drysie) and a Carmelite nun, 1948. Courtesy of Ware Carmel

Friends and family in Vézelay, mid-1950s. From the left,
Lady Bigham (Drysie), Alice Staath, Pauline, Thérèse, Georges,
Jock (Jean), Michel. Courtesy of Jean Vanier

Governor General and Madame Vanier with Dr Peter Burton, his wife
Rachel, their two children, and a friend. Courtesy of Rachel Burton

Yves Chevrier, Governor General Vanier's valet, in the
Rideau Hall ball room, 1963. Courtesy of Yves Chevrier

The Vaniers with Roland and Norah Michener; undated. Michener was speaker
of the House during the first three years of Georges Vanier's tenure as governor
general. He was also Vanier's immediate successor as governor general. Library
and Archives Canada/Credit: Bill Olson, Dominion-Wide Photographs Limited/Georges P. Vanier
Fonds/Acc. No. 1971-311 Box 5820

Bernard Vanier's children, Valérie and Laurence, watch their grandfather shave, summer, 1966. Courtesy of Yves Chevrier

16

"ONLY TO SERVE"

On the morning of 15 September 1959, a car led by three police motor-cycles pulled up slowly to the Parliament Buildings in Ottawa. The governor general designate, Georges P. Vanier, stepped out of the car wearing the gold-braided dress uniform of the Royal 22nd. He walked with a cane, his shoulders hunched, a resolute expression covering decades of struggle and pain. When he reached the podium before an assembled guard of honour, he stood to his full height and saluted, as straight and smart as the twenty-six-year-old who had donned an army uniform in 1915. The sound of a cannon split the chilly Ottawa air. He then turned and joined the prime minister to enter the Parliament Building and the Senate chamber, where he took his oath of office before the chief justice and a room full of privy council-lors, Supreme Court judges, diplomats, and parliamentarians. Pauline Vanier stood at his side with a small bouquet of white flowers in her hands, wear-ing a black taffeta dress and a small feathered hat, and watched him nervously.

Seated at the dais, he began his inaugural address. "My first words are a prayer. May almighty God in his infinite wisdom and mercy bless the sacred mission which has been entrusted to me by Her Majesty the Queen and help me to fulfill it in all humility. In exchange for his strength, I offer him my weakness. May he give peace to this beloved land of ours and, to those who live in it, the grace of mutual understanding, respect and love." He went on in a slow and ponderous voice to trace the history of Canada's two founding peoples and to express the desire that their descendents would "go forward hand in hand to make Canada a great nation, hand in hand also with Canadians of every origin, with their heritages, irre-spective of race or creed." He ended with an exhortation to all Canadians: "If Canada is to attain the greatness worthy of it, each of us must say, 'I ask only to serve.'"[1]

Some of those seated before him may have been impatient to get back to matters more pressing than the pious "governor generalities" (a term coined by one of his predecessors, Lord Tweedsmuir) delivered by the new representative of the Crown. But if they listened closely to his address, and particularly if they were personally acquainted with Georges Vanier, they would have realized that it contained everything the new governor general stood for. His words sprang from a conviction he presumed his listeners shared: that they lived as finite beings in the presence of an infinite divinity. They may not have known that the "sacred mission" he was undertaking was a continuation of his answering the call to arms during the First World War, serving the cause of freedom in the second, and representing Canada in diplomatic duties that were often frustrating, exhausting, and thankless. In proclaiming "I ask only to serve," he was announcing his intention of becoming more than a figurehead, of doing more for his country than merely showing up for ceremonial events. He intended his tenure to be marked by an inner quality of the spirit, in the manner that he and Pauline had been striving to live in their thirty-eight years together.

His wisdom had been hard won at the centre of some of the most tumultuous events of the twentieth century. But new elements had now introduced themselves, some of which would continue to engage Canada and the world for the rest of the century, long after his death. The Cold War had intensified, as had the nuclear threat that accompanied it. Within Canada, the long-serving Liberals had been upset by a Conservative victory in 1957, and in Quebec, the long reign of Maurice Duplessis had just come to an end with his death a week before Georges's installation. Quebec would soon have a Liberal government and young intellectuals such as René Lévesque and Pierre Trudeau were becoming politically active. Quebec – and Canada – would never be the same again.

Vincent Massey had set an important precedent as the first Canadian in the position of governor general. The imperial ties had been loosened in the years since the Vaniers had been confidants of Lord Byng, and as a "dominion," Canada now had equal status with Britain. Massey had brought a patrician gravity to the role and his presence as a distinguished former diplomat gave it international stature. He believed in Canada's greatness, visiting all parts of the country, including the North. His lasting legacy to the cultural life of Canada took the form of the Canada Council, which he helped to established, and the promotion of such artistic endeavours as the Stratford Festival. The challenge for the new governor general was to continue "Canadianizing" the vice-regal role in the face of new changes and developments.

* * *

Settling down in Rideau Hall, the Vaniers began a curious existence, in which they were, in a sense, both exposed to the world and shielded from it. The large rambling house at No. 1 Sussex Drive was surrounded by a park and a small village of smaller buildings, and it also housed a staff of over thirty, including a private secretary, speechwriters, attachés, aides de camp, and a French chef. The governor general's office was wood-panelled and circular in design, and had a fireplace and sitting area with leather chairs. His wife's office was near his, and both overlooked the garden. Directly above the office, in their private quarters, light filled their spacious bedroom through tall windows. One of the other bedrooms was converted into a chapel, and for an altar they used an eighteenth-century mahogany chest with nine panels featuring carvings of saints in bas-relief. They had bought the chest decades earlier from an antique shop in Albert, a town in northern France not far from where Georges fought his final battle. The red-carpeted hallways of the residence gave plenty of opportunity for walking exercise, but stairs were another matter. Governor General Vanier lost little time in requesting that an elevator be installed. When the job was finally finished, two years after he moved in, he thanked the deputy minister of the Department of Public Works, writing: "Going up these 20 steps several times each day was not only a matter of fatigue, but a frustration as well, when others were taking them four at a time!"[2]

From now on, life was dictated by protocol. They were both addressed as "Your Excellency," and when he was referred to by the staff, the governor general was called "H.E," as he himself had once referred to Lord Byng. A typical weekly log might contain meetings with the clerk of the Privy Council, the chief of Protocol, a representative from the diplomatic corps, a cabinet minister, the chairman of the chiefs of staff, receptions for various ambassadors, and perhaps a formal dinner with the designation "white tie with decorations." The Vaniers were driven in motorcades and guarded by members of the Royal Canadian Mounted Police. The governor general could no longer express a political opinion, nor did he grant interviews. As the representative of both the Crown and the people, he was to remain above controversy. Holidays, on the whole, were no longer spent in France, but closer to home in the historic resort town of Tadoussac, on the Saguenay River, where they generally spent the month of August, although Pauline made periodic visits to Paris to visit her mother, who was nearing ninety and in frail health.

Their short stays at the Citadel, the governor general's official residence in Quebec City, were in some ways a return to earlier times, only now their abode was at the other end of the long narrow stone building from where they had lived in the 1920s. This residence was much smaller than Rideau Hall, and had been the site of the 1943 Quebec war conference between Churchill and Roosevelt. As they had decades before, the Vaniers could look out on one side past the cliffs to the majestic St Lawrence River, and on the other, to the courtyard with its daily parade of the guard of the Royal 22nd. In both residences, the staff joined them for meals. They tried to establish a family atmosphere as they had known it during an earlier era with Lord Byng.

Usually, Georges's day began at eight o'clock with breakfast and the newspaper, and he was in his office by nine-thirty. Lunch was at one o'clock, and he rested between two and three o'clock in the afternoon. He and Pauline normally made their daily half-hour meditation together in the chapel, and Mass was celebrated at five o'clock. There were often late afternoon receptions for visiting dignitaries, and the evening ended with a black-tie dinner. On Sunday evenings a film was shown. Much of the day was spent in answering correspondence and deciding which requests to accept, and they came in by the dozens: to open a university or hospital or school, to speak to a charitable organization, to unveil a monument, or to espouse a cause. By the end of Georges Vanier's tenure, the couple would go on a hundred and thirty-one tours to all parts of Canada, travelling mostly by private railway car, and they would cover nearly a hundred and fifty thousand kilometres. His speeches would eventually number well over five hundred.

Some groups particularly pleased the governor general. He was delighted to discover that he was the chief of the Boy Scouts, having declared youth – representing the future of Canada – to be one of his main interests. The war amputee association, called the War Amps, and the Blood Services Branch of the Canadian Red Cross brought back sharp memories. When a fellow war veteran asked if he remembered the battle of Chérisy, he answered that indeed he did remember it: "As you know, I left a leg there."[3] And to the author of a book on blood transfusions he recounted how one such procedure, administered in 1918, left him with "a feeling of active physical resuscitation. I have no doubt whatever that the transfusion saved my life."[4]

One of the Vaniers' duties during the first months in Rideau Hall was hosting an afternoon party for two hundred members of the Ottawa Boys' Club, an event captured by the National Film Board. The party took place in the Tent Room, which had first been built as a tennis court, and the green and white striped awning that draped from the ceiling and walls gave the festivities the look of an indoor picnic. The December event had a seasonal theme, and the governor general was seen mock-wincing as he pulled a Christmas cracker with one of the boys and then smiling as he donned the paper hat that emerged from it. Madame Vanier, also wearing a paper hat, circulated among the visitors, chatting and urging more food upon them, and afterward her husband gathered the boys around him, his face wearing an unusually wide smile. No longer on stiff behaviour, the children freely exchanged corny jokes with him.

Some of the younger generation could not imagine that this limping, white-haired gentleman with courtly manners had once been a strapping soldier who had charged toward the enemy with a bayonet, but by the early 1960s the First World War had already become regarded as an important part of Canadian history, and for this reason Georges was generally admired and held in awe. Matters closer to his own heart had already begun to touch some Canadians, such as a partially blind woman from Nova Scotia who wrote: "I shall always remember the Governor General's words in his inaugurational [sic] address. I am conscious of my weakness and physical handicap, but ... I am sure his words have been a help and blessing to many other handicapped individuals as well as myself."[5]

In various areas of Quebec, he was not viewed entirely kindly, some noting that he was French only on his father's side, and that he had not always signed his name "Georges" with an "s." And one irate fellow Catholic – scandalized that the first person of his faith to represent the Crown sometimes went to religious services in Protestant churches as well as synagogues – had to be mollified by his private secretary as follows: "In private life, the Governor General is a Catholic and he worships as a Catholic both in public and in private. In public life, he is still a Catholic, but he is also Governor General of Canada representing Her Majesty the Queen for all Canadians. In this capacity there are times when duty requires his presence at the services of worship of other denominations. This official presence in no way constitutes a denial of his faith."[6]

At first the press hardly knew what to make of him, relatively unknown outside Quebec as he was. One journalist compared his "glacial dignity" and "formidable calm" to that of Charles de Gaulle.[7] (This journalist had not yet seen him in a party hat romping with children, or donning an immense Cree feather headdress as an honorary chief. And he had yet to see him in an Arctic port, carried by a fork lift perilously close to a stack of crates and calling down, "Watch out, that's the only good leg I have left!"[8]) Another noted his reserve in speech. "He doesn't hold with saying any more than is necessary. In conversation, he is restrained and moderate and he doesn't believe in using two words when one will do."[9] Others remarked on the patrician appearance of the vice-regal couple. The young photographer Roloff Beny, photographing them for *Maclean's* magazine, wrote: "My immediate impression was of a handsome couple enormously in love with each other and with life."[10]

Regardless of what others thought of him, Georges relished his job. His days of action behind him, perhaps he now felt that what remained was the opportunity to impart the fruit of reflection derived from a lifetime of spiritual experience. The exactitude of the protocol probably suited his temperament as well as his military working style, and his tendency toward correctness in everything. The staff learned to step gingerly around him during the times when his face constricted in anger and his body tensed up. There were occasions when aides de camp retreated in wide-eyed shock after an unexpected verbal explosion, such as happened once when a television crew traipsed in with too many cables and wires. He wrote to a friend that he did not mind his moments of impatience because they taught him to be humble.

The Vaniers made their first vice-regal trip to western Canada in April 1960, and returned glowing with a look of rejuvenation. Every year brought more trips, to every part of Canada. Georges's doctor, Peter Burton, became increasingly concerned for his health during these visits, although he noticed that the governor general always came back from these trips buoyed in spirit, with his face less lined than when he had left. But Georges was aware of his own ebbing strength, and steeled himself for long ceremonies. He wrote to Father Benedict to pray for him on 13 January 1960, when there would be a state dinner followed the next day by the opening of Parliament and his first speech from the throne, because "These two occasions will be physically very difficult ordeals."[11]

Meanwhile Pauline was in her element. She chose as her lady-in-waiting and overall personal assistant her cousin Thérèse Berger, who had administrative experience with the Canadian Cancer Society and other social agencies. Pauline enjoyed indulging her fondness for evening gowns, and she photographed well, especially when simple dark suits and dresses, worn with a pearl necklace, set off her cloud of white hair and fair complexion. A friend wrote to Georges that she was "a knockout" on television. Obliged by tradition to curtsy to her husband on formal occasions (the custom was dropped after the Vanier years), she practiced with great earnestness, lest she sully her dignity by looking foolish in front of distinguished guests. In a bout of nervousness on installation day, she curtsied instead to another woman who was curtsying to *her*, and afterward she recounted how the two knocked knees with each other, half-sitting in mid-air. In later years she also related the story, which varied with each telling, of how her first vice-regal encounter with old friend Lester Pearson had her rushing to embrace him, and then realizing in horror that she could no longer show favouritism to political figures, she had to find a way, in the spirit of equality, to embrace the prime minister, John Diefenbaker. "I think he enjoyed it as much as I did," she remarked enigmatically years later to one listener.[12]

She took charge of the household with gusto, and during the first year she occupied herself with decorating: replacing drapes, chair covers, and carpets, and overseeing the refurnishing of some of the rooms. She took a particular interest in the greenhouse, which was located at the end of a narrow corridor of offices, and she liked to cut and arrange the flowers herself. She also redecorated one room with pine paneling and furnished it completely with Canadiana. It was named the Canadian Room, and tea was served there every afternoon. (This room has since received a thumbs-down from interior decorators, a verdict suggesting that perhaps Pauline's talents lay elsewhere.) It was not long before her natural generosity led her to take soup to members of the household who were ill and, on cold winter days, to the police who stood outside on security duty, impulsive actions that often incurred the frustration of the kitchen staff.

In perfect health at the start of the move to Rideau Hall (her cancer had never returned), Pauline soon noticed that her eyes were failing. It was the beginning of a cataract problem, and she began to see everything in a fog. Walking downstairs became a nightmare, and on tours she required hand rails to hold on to. Her brief speeches were printed in large dark letters. The Rideau Hall staff rallied around her, making sure everything necessary was done to support her. During these months, as her eyesight inexorably failed her, her husband read to her for an hour every night, but she admitted afterwards to a journalist from the magazine *Chatelaine* that his choice of reading material did not always interest her. Her cataract surgery took place in January, 1964, and several weeks later, her vision restored, she was marvelling at the trees and the birds.

* * *

Apart from his wife and his private secretary, Esmund Butler, two people were most important in Georges's new life. One was his valet, Sergeant Yves Chevrier, who had been interviewed and then chosen from among three young members of the Royal 22nd. Upon learning young Chevrier's age, twenty-four, the septuagenarian Vanier said, "You're just a child,"[13] and then told him that he would be hired for a trial period of six months. It was the beginning of a long and intimate association. Sergeant Chevrier arrived at Rideau Hall with no knowledge of English or the fine points of protocol, and he was dazzled by the size and grandeur of the residence. But he displayed a talent for organization and a penchant for tidiness that no doubt pleased his boss, and as well, he knew instinctively how to be discreet and friendly, without crossing the line into over-familiarity. He was also a quick learner, discovering in short order the intricate sartorial meanings of such shorthand designations as "white tie," "black tie," and "morning coat." He learned the order in which medals were to be placed on uniforms. He became an indispensable part of Georges Vanier's daily life, on call from early morning until late into the evening. Sergeant Chevrier accompanied the Vaniers on all their train trips across Canada, always with a long narrow box in his arms, like the sergeant at arms carrying the mace. It was, in fact, an extra artificial leg.

The other important person in the governor general's life was the prime minister. John Diefenbaker, a populist lawyer from Prince Albert, Saskatchewan, with a head of curly iron-grey hair, an intense facial expression, and considerable oratorical skill, had become the prime minister in 1957, at the age of sixty-three, when the Conservatives came to power with a minority government. The following year he led the Conservatives to the largest majority government in Canadian history. But as a prime minister he was said to be a political loner, suspicious of civil service officials as well as some members of his own cabinet, and as a result he tended to keep his own counsel rather than consult others.

At least one journalist declared, incorrectly, that Vanier was not interested in politics. He may not have been keen on partisan rough-and-tumble, but the task of governing and his own responsibility to the country were a

different matter. Though he wrote to a friend in Europe that life "is alright
if you don't take yourself seriously, or others as well,"[14] he did in fact take
his job seriously, and foremost was the duty of making sure there was a stable
democratic government in Canada. This meant keeping *au courant* with what
was happening in Parliament and staying close at hand at election time.
Beyond that, there was the burden of having to be on guard in the case of
minority governments lest a constitutional crisis occur. As it would eventually turn out, this weight of responsibility was to become one of the marks
of Vanier's tenure as representative of the Crown in Canada.

* * *

By the time an election was called in the spring of 1962, the Conservatives
had plummeted in popularity. A charismatic young president in the United
States seemed to usher in a new era but in Canada there was a general conviction that the government was in disarray. The sense of unease generated
by the falling dollar, high unemployment, and a series of budget deficits,
was reflected in the 18 June election results. The Conservatives lost many seats
and barely held on to enough votes to form a minority government. Vanier
did not see the prime minister until a week after the election, at a dinner in
honour of the princess royal. Diefenbaker seemed relaxed, and Pauline, seated
next to him, said she had "ideas about a union [sic] government." (A short-
lived notion about the possibility of a coalition between the Conservatives
and the Social Credit seems to have been mooted at the time. About his
wife's indiscretion Georges noted: "I made no comment."[15])

The election results were not good news for anyone, and the next few
months were politically fraught. Diefenbaker and Pearson, although mutu-
ally cordial in public, regarded each other with considerable resentment and
hostility. The economy was in a shambles, and tension was rife. In late June,
the prime minister came to see the governor general in a state of high anxiety, ambivalent about wanting to lead the government. "I am not sure the
prime minister is happy to be the incumbent," Georges wrote in his notes.
Diefenbaker then seems to have gone on to discuss alternatives to forming
a government. Should he resign? The answer, according to the governor general: "He has a plurality of 21 over the Liberal party and says 'we are the
government' which is true and means that he has to try to govern but how,
only by reversing the policy he defended only recently by his 'hand outs,'
by reducing his budget, in a word by admitting that his pre-election policy

was all wrong. There is a serious loss of face here but he has no excuse for resigning and has to face the House of Commons."

When they met again in July, Diefenbaker, in a calmer frame of mind, "was very communicative, consulted me about the appointments he was to make of Ministers, spoke of the speakership of the House of Commons and the Senate." And when the governor general offered condolences on the death of Diefenbaker's best friend and confidant, Senator William Blunt, the prime minister surprised him by saying "that there was another person in the world like [Senator Blunt], almost implying that he had not met any other, then adding 'you.' I was so surprised that I was quite stunned and said with a certain amount of feeling and emotion, 'that is the greatest compliment you could have paid me.' I was perplexed because his remark was entirely uncalled for. Our relationship, although always friendly, has never justified a compliment of that kind." Georges later concluded that the prime minister must have found him to be "the type of person who could be counted upon not to reveal anything."[16]

The question of governing the country, which might have developed into a serious crisis, was thus averted for the time being, and the governor general returned from his annual holiday in Tadoussac to swear in the members of the cabinet. But the government would prove to be short-lived. One of the precipitating factors was what would later become known as the Cuban Missile Crisis. American president John F. Kennedy and his wife had visited Ottawa in May 1961, four months after his inauguration, and Kennedy had taken a dislike to Diefenbaker in the face of the prime minister's attempt to defend Canada against American pressure and encroachment, particularly in the area of defence. The prime minister refused to have Canada join the Organization of American States, and although Canada had bought the American Bomarc missile, Diefenbaker refused the nuclear warheads it was designed to contain.

On 22 October 1962 the prime minister was informed by an American envoy, with only one and a half hours' notice, that the Soviet Union was sending ballistic missiles to Cuba and that the Americans were setting up a naval blockade and wanted Canada's participation. After two days and lengthy cabinet discussions Diefenbaker finally agreed. In the end, the international crisis was settled peacefully, but Canada's late acquiescence to the American request, which Diefenbaker explained as the principled response of a sovereign nation, was interpreted as a sign of an indecisive government. From then on, questions regarding nuclear weapons, and the government's approach to them, increased – as did doubts about Diefenbaker's ability as a leader.

The main issue during the closing months of 1962 was the Bomarc missiles, and Diefenbaker's refusal to allow nuclear warheads, a decision that made the missiles effectively useless. For Diefenbaker it was a matter of principle: he wanted the Canadian government to make an independent decision rather than allow itself to be pushed around by the United States. Dissenting voices from the opposition (and, as it turned out, from within his own cabinet) increased. The catalyst in finally helping to bring down the government was a press release on 30 January 1963 from the US State Department, saying that a continental defence was necessary in the face of possible nuclear attack. The statement was later interpreted as a clarification of the American need to secure all its allies against the threat of Soviet aggression, but Diefenbaker took it as a public criticism of one sovereign nation by another, and as a personal rebuke.

The situation hardly needed a catalyst, however. It was clear that the government would not last much longer. In the press, the rumour was circulating that the prime minister would ask the governor general to dissolve Parliament before a vote of non-confidence could be taken. Georges read these reports with more than heightened interest. Was he going to be forced into the same position as his friend and predecessor Lord Byng had been forty-six years earlier? Lord Byng's refusal of Mackenzie King's request to dissolve Parliament had kept constitutional experts in disagreement ever since.

The prime minister's phone call came at eleven fifteen am on 31 January. He asked if he might come to see the governor general in twenty minutes. At eleven forty-five, he phoned again to say that he was still in cabinet and that they were discussing "the unprecedented action taken by the State Department of the United States." While he waited, Georges was left to wonder about the purpose of the phone call and concluded that the prime minister intended to ask for dissolution of Parliament. "Otherwise why want to see me?" he wrote. "He certainly wouldn't ask me for advice about how to handle the situation. I imagine that after talking over the matter with his cabinet he came to the conclusion that in any event it would be better for him to make a statement in the House first."

The afternoon of the next day, Friday, 1 February, the prime minister, looking tired and admitting that the previous two days had been hard on him, did come to see the governor general, who was no doubt primed to give his opinion on dissolving Parliament. But Diefenbaker spoke instead about President Kennedy, "who had told him once in the course of conversation that Canada would have to do what the United States wanted. Mr Kennedy had talked to the press about getting tough with American allies as well as with adversaries."[17]But Diefenbaker still did not bring up the question of dissolving Parliament. Instead, he said he would be back the next day. Vanier was convinced that he would request dissolution then.

The weekend passed, but Diefenbaker did not appear. On the morning of Monday, 4 February, the governor general heard that Douglas Harkness, the minister of National Defence, had resigned from the cabinet because of differences with Diefenbaker over nuclear arms. "This will be a severe blow for the government," Georges wrote. Indeed, events from then on moved quickly. On Tuesday, 5 February, the government was defeated by a vote of non-confidence. And at twelve forty-five the next day, Diefenbaker arrived at Rideau Hall bearing, for the governor general's signature, documents proclaiming the dissolution of Parliament. No records exist of the twenty-minute conversation that followed.

A question does remain, however: did Diefenbaker actually consider asking the governor general to dissolve Parliament in order to pre-empt a non-confidence motion, or was this merely press speculation? If he did intend to do so, why did he not? In his notes following their 1 February meeting, Georges indicated that he thanked the prime minister for not asking for dissolution the previous day, and Diefenbaker said enigmatically, "I have to be restrained sometimes." At any rate, Georges was, perhaps fortunately, spared the decision which – no matter how he would have decided – would have landed him in a constitutional controversy.

By now Diefenbaker would have been aware of Georges's close attention to detail and proper procedure. So it was likely no surprise when he received notification later in February, after two more cabinet ministers (George Hees and Pierre Sévigny) resigned, that the governor general had not given the requisite approval to their resignations because they had not been properly sent to him, or that the governor general had questions about appointments requiring his approval that were made after Parliament had been dissolved. Although the prime minister still had the authority to make such appointments, Georges indicated that, if necessary, he "would certainly exercise his prerogative to warn."[18] On 29 March, he wrote to remind Diefenbaker of a conversation they had had on this matter. "I told you then that the question of appointments by a government which had been defeated in the House was one which had given me great concern, and that after a careful study of precedents, of constitutional practice, and of political evolution in our constitutional monarchy, I decided to base my appreciation of any appointment recommended on whether a delay in making the appointment could possibly be detrimental to the public interest." He had signed his approval to the appointments in such cases as returning officers, members of the world fair commission, and the ministers replacing those who had resigned, but told the prime minister that at this late date, with the election just over a week away, he balked at signing his approval of Senate appointments: "I feel that, as the Senate is not sitting, there could result no possible detriment to the public interest."[19]

To an ordinary citizen, the precision of his points might have been regarded as nit-picking, but to Georges Vanier they reflected the responsibility that was part of his office.

Indeed, if his office were to have any meaning at all, it was important to not only observe correct procedure, but to exercise that responsibility, limited (and virtually non-existent) as his actual authority might be. He might have said too that his major responsibility – that of ensuring a democratically elected government in Canada – relied on having small matters done properly.[20]

* * *

The election was set for 8 April 1963. Early that day, Georges woke with a sensation of breathlessness that he later described as "a small setback." It was a mild heart attack, the first concrete indication since he had assumed office that all was not well with his health, and perhaps the first physical sign of the toll the tense political situation had taken on him. He was ordered to take several weeks of bed rest. The next day he learned that the Liberals had upset the Conservatives with a minority government, and on 22 April, the changeover of government took place in his bedroom, with the governor general propped up against pillows. At eleven fifteen he accepted John Diefenbaker's resignation. At noon Lester Pearson was sworn in as the prime minister, and then came the swearing-in of all the ministers of the new government.

By the fall of 1963, Georges was back in full gear again. His renewed vigour may partly have been inspired by the reappearance in his life of the man who became the new prime minister. The son of a small-town Ontario Methodist minister, Pearson had retained his homespun roots. He was warm and friendly, with a boyish smile, a puckish sense of humour, and a pudgy and somewhat rumpled appearance. His intellect was sharp; he had studied at Oxford University on a scholarship, and his decades of work in diplomacy had given him a broad understanding of international affairs and a vision of Canada's place in the world. The high point of his international achievement had been as the president of the UN General Assembly, when he diffused the Suez Crisis by the creation of the UN peace troops, for which he received the Nobel Peace Prize in 1957. His friendship with the Vaniers extended back decades. Pearson was nine years younger than Vanier, and the two men had always worked together in an atmosphere of mutual respect, if not always agreement.

But if Georges had a more relaxed relationship with the new prime minister, he also had to contend with the uncomfortable fact of a minority government, which produced an ongoing need for vigilance. A minority government meant that a constitutional crisis might develop at any time, and as the months of 1963 wore on, the question of national unity and Canada's future would compound the burden on the governor general and would introduce a new fragility to his role and office.

As he approached the age of seventy-five, some of his most challenging years were still ahead.

17

THE FINAL CHALLENGE

According to a Vancouver journalist who was part of a small crowd waiting for the Vaniers outside a church one day, a man came up to him and asked what was going on. "The governor general is at Mass," was the journalist's reply.

"But he went yesterday," the man said.

"He goes to church every day."

"He must have been a pretty wild fella when he was young and now he's trying to make up for it," the man said, walking away.

The journalist went on to remark in his article that Georges Vanier, in affirming his religious faith on a daily basis, preached "a compelling sermon" in an age when agnosticism was gaining ascendency and faith was looked upon "as quaint if not passé."[1]

Reading the anecdote, Georges may have chuckled, especially given the irony that he had in fact loosened up considerably since his moralistic, rule-bound youth. His faith was summed up by the motto he had chosen for his coat of arms, *Fiat Voluntas Dei* ("May God's will be done"), which indicated that divine will had placed him in the position he was in, and he owed it to his fellow citizens to do the best job possible for as long as his health and strength held out. From the outset, he had let it be known that matters of the spirit were the most important to him, and he had been bothered, ever since the end of the Second World War, by the ascent of materialism over spiritual values.

What did he mean by "this rather nebulous conception of Spirit?" he asked himself in a 1960 speech to the Canadian Club of Vancouver, and then he defined it as "that which lends dignity to man, enabling him to transcend his limitations." He went on to outline the advances in science and technology, marvelling at them and at the same time, recognizing the danger in humanity's becoming slaves to them. "Lethal weapons of a frightening character exist, without there being any evidence, on the spiritual side, that man has reached the state of, at all times, loving his neighbour," he said. "We are able to probe the outer reaches of space while we remain unable to see into the inner recesses of man's mind. We devote much time and energy to mastering the forces around us, but the forces within still go, in large measure, undeveloped."[2] In the same speech, he asked himself rhetorically if he was speaking like "something out of the Middle Ages." By the mid-1960s, it may have sounded to some as if he was merely an old man, past his prime, an anachronism in a world of change. But what he saw about him was making him concerned; in particular, the breakdown of society's most fundamental unit, the family.

In a speech to the Club Richelieu in Ottawa-Hull, Georges said that "the qualities which make for good relations between members of the family also make them good citizens of the larger community," and added that "society must have citizens with open hearts, able to dedicate themselves to the common good, and such citizens will be found first and foremost among members of families where the spirit of generosity and service has taken root."[3] He went on to enumerate some of the social ills that stemmed from disharmony in the home: alcoholism, delinquency, prostitution, drug addiction, the school drop-out rate. In four years of travelling about the country, visiting schools, jails, hospitals, and other institutions, the Vaniers had seen for themselves the effect of those ills on Canadian society. With the help of such eminent professionals as Montreal neurosurgeon Wilder Penfield, they held a conference on the family at Rideau Hall in June 1964 and the Vanier Institute of the Family received its charter in the spring of 1965. To his old army friend J.P. Cathcart Georges wrote, "We have no illusions about transforming the family situation in the world or in Canada but we are trying to impress on people the necessity for each one of us in life to do what he can, however small, and in whatever sphere, to alleviate the present unfortunate family crisis."[4]

Of their own far-flung family, all except Father Benedict spent part of their summer holiday with them each year in Tadoussac. Their Trappist son's health had returned, and Georges enjoyed telling groups of nuns that "When we go to see him, he only smiles or laughs ... and so, you see, he's not a serious man!"[5] Thérèse, now a haematologist, continued to practise medicine at St Thomas's Hospital in London. Bernard, who was still producing paintings, and Michel, who had embarked on an academic career in political science, had both married and each had two children. The Vaniers took particular pleasure in their grandchildren, and in the young children of staff members and friends. "If I weren't in my present job, I'd like to be – what do you call it – a babysitter,"⁶ Georges told Dr Burton, and, as he had done years earlier with his own children, he liked to play the trick of having them stick a pin into his artificial leg. A letter describing Bernard's eight-month-old daughter Laurence as she watched him shave showed that his dry wit remained intact. "She was full of something called 'pablum.' It is a Latin drink which they have invented over here for babies. Laurence would just lie there like a female Buddha full, so full, of pablum that I didn't dare shake her, otherwise she would have bubbled over. To keep her amused I gave her various things to play with: shaving stick, aftershave lotion, and any odd razor blades that might be lying about. She's wonderful, she didn't cut herself once!"⁷

Jock had completed his doctoral thesis in philosophy in 1962. His father, not above pulling out a well-worn cliché at his son's expense, wrote to a friend that Jock had "just written a large book on Aristotle, the only part of which I understand is the introduction. The rest is Greek to me!"⁸ Jock seemed to be living like a vagabond, "roving about as usual,"⁹ his father wrote in 1963. Before his son's visits, Georges had to alert the security guard at the gate about the identity of the young man in worn clothing with a rope around his suitcase. Jock's parents had wondered for some years whether their third son would ever settle down. In the meantime, he himself had remained close to his spiritual mentor from the days of L'Eau Vive, Père Thomas Philippe. A letter from Thérèse to her parents in May 1964 indicates the beginning of what was to be her brother's life's work; Jock, she wrote, was "very busy over some new project which he may have mentioned to you – he only briefly said something to me about it – a plan to set up some sort of house or houses near Compiègne for des débiles mentaux – it sounds just like him and Père Thomas. And I hope it works out alright."¹⁰

Two months later, after she had been to France and seen Jock's new project for herself, their daughter wrote, "I think it is a splendid idea in every way and he is going about it very realistically ... The property he hopes to get (almost settled) seems ideal and the house promising."ˣ¹ This new venture, which Jock called "L'Arche," was a small community for people with mental handicaps in the village of Trosly, on the edge of the Compiègne Forest in north-east France. When his parents learned more details about the fledgling work, they became supportive and proud of their son, if somewhat anxious about the responsibility he was laying upon himself. But Georges would not live long enough to see L'Arche become an international movement and the name "Jean Vanier" known throughout the world.

* * *

As a Canadian whose paternal roots ran centuries-deep in Quebec's history, Georges Vanier was aware of a double responsibility in his vice-regal role: to continue the work of Vincent Massey in bringing the position of governor general out of the era of British imperialism so that it became representative of the Canadian people, and to remind the country of its rich French heritage. One of the first things he had noticed when he first entered the gates of Rideau Hall as governor general was that the sign in front was in English only, and he requested that a French sign be placed there as well. He had never forgotten the challenge of his old mentor, Père Gaume, to identify himself as a French Canadian, and in his daily activities he spoke and wrote in French as much as possible. From the start, he had known that maintaining the unity of Canada was a crucial element in the task before him. In speeches across the country, he made subtle references to his years in the trenches with the 22nd battalion, his experience with striking miners during that long-ago summer in Nova Scotia, his work as a diplomat trying to ease the worldwide wheat crisis of the 1930s, and his pride in the Canadians who fought to liberate Nazi-occupied Europe – making it clear that his love of his country ran deep.

For ordinary Canadian citizens seeking redress for perceived injustices of one kind or another, he acted as an unofficial ombudsman, having no authority to act on their requests, but sending them on to the appropriate federal departments, asking for replies to each case. One of his most agonizing duties was the signing of death penalties, and it may have been a deep regret that he had no power to overturn such punishments; he could only ratify with his signature the decision of the federal cabinet. Seven prisoners were hanged for murder in Canada during Georges Vanier's tenure, the last (indeed, the last in Canada)[12] on 11 December 1962. He received at least one written plea to use his influence in having the sentence reviewed. In such cases, he referred the matter directly to the minister of justice.

* * *

It was a historical irony that while Canada's first governor general of French origin was criss-crossing the country with impassioned words of unity, the first serious rumblings of the call for the separation of Quebec from Canada were heard in what came to be known as the "quiet revolution." After the Liberal government replaced the Union Nationale in 1960, a movement to take Quebec's power companies and other economic resources from English-Canadian interests and put them into provincial hands had developed rapidly into an overall critique of traditional values and established customs in the province. The Catholic clergy were said to have kept the rural population in a peasant-like state of pliable ignorance; they were accused of having too much control over daily life, and their domination of the province's educational system was declared to be oppressive and backward-looking. By 1964, the Catholic Church was no longer at the centre of most Quebecers' lives, and many people were identifying themselves, not with the Church, but with Quebec itself, as if it were a national entity. The word "separatist" entered the Canadian vocabulary.

A group calling themselves Rassemblement pour l'Indépendence Nationale (RIN) was gaining prominence, and young intellectuals were beginning to talk of Quebec as a republic. Splinter organizations formed, among them a Marxist group called Front de Libération du Québec (FLQ) who held to the belief that change could come only through violent revolution. A week after the swearing-in of Lester Pearson and his cabinet in Vanier's bedroom in April 1963, a watchman by the name of Wilfred O'Neil was killed by a crude home-made bomb at a Canadian army centre in Montreal. This act was soon followed by a series of mailbox bombs in the city's Westmount district. Although Pearson was probably not influenced by fear of a terrorist fringe group, he knew that the time had come to open up the overdue question of Canada's French heritage, and one of his first acts as prime minister was to appoint a royal commission on bilingualism and biculturalism. It was the beginning of the shift to official bilingualism.

As governor general, Georges could not directly express his opinions in the face of the seismic changes that were taking place in his native province and among the citizens he had identified himself with all his life. It is reasonable to suppose that he regarded Quebec's economic self-determination as a welcome move, and that he approved of the attempt to bring the province's education system into the twentieth century. But his own commitment to a united Canada was too great to allow him to support any vision of the country as divided into two separate nations. As he often did, he deepened the question to the level of the spirit. "Our world is becoming more and more conscious that true peace requires first a spiritual disarming, the expulsion from our hearts of any feeling of hate, jealousy, violence. Outer peace involves first a unity of hearts and souls," he said in his 1964 New Year's address to the nation. He then became specific. "The cry for unity in Canada is great. It is inconceivable that the heirs to the two great Western civilizations, Anglo-Saxon and French, should be unable to find a brotherly way of life based upon respect for rights conferred by history, a respect also for conventions freely accepted nearly a century ago but adapted to the exigencies of our time."[13]

But his words fell on deaf ears in some quarters. When an invitation came to take part in the Montreal parade marking the annual celebration of Quebec's patron saint, St Jean Baptiste, on 24 June 1964, he accepted, even though there were strong indications that he might not be entirely among friends. On the afternoon of the day itself, the RIN staged a sit-down strike in the square at Place Ville Marie, and then about a hundred and fifty protesters marched through the city shouting revolutionary slogans. A plane flying low over the city dropped similarly worded leaflets along the parade route. The parade, consisting of bands and floats celebrating various aspects of French-Canadian history, was a night-time event. It extended along a four-mile route on Sherbrooke Street, from Maisonneuve Park to Atwater Avenue. Governor General and Madame Vanier as well as other dignitaries were to be seated on a reviewing stand in front of the Municipal Library.

At nine thirty pm, the vice-regal couple were escorted to their front-row seats, Georges dressed in a business suit with a white carnation in his lapel. A group who had positioned themselves in the crowd directly across the street immediately began booing and waving placards that read "Vanier Vendue," "Vanier pour Angleterre," "Canada Monarchie – Québec République." At about ten thirty pm the parade reached the reviewing stand, led by eleven Montreal policemen on horseback and a bank of others on motorcycles.

The parade proceeded without incident until the RIN members appeared, two hundred and fifty strong, carrying the blue and white Quebec flags featuring the fleur de lis. As the marchers approached the reviewing stand, rather than lowering their flags in the customary salute to the governor general, they turned their heads away from him, dipped the flags slightly in the direction of the protesters across the street and then raised them as they marched past the Vaniers. Then some moments later, when the soldiers of

the Royal 22nd marched past the reviewing stand, their band in full dress
uniform with red tunics and bearskin hats, the slogan-bearing placards were
raised high across the street, and as Georges, the honorary colonel of the
Royal 22nd, rose from his seat and returned the contingent's salute, the
protesters booed loudly. A phalanx of policemen moved in, demanding that
the demonstrators hand over their placards. When they refused, the police
grabbed the placards. In the scuffle that followed, three protesters were carried off by the police, shouting "Québec Libre!" The crowd, in turn, booed
the protesters and cheered and clapped as the police dragged them away.

The rest of the parade proceeded peacefully, but for the rest of her life
Pauline Vanier was to remember this as a night of terror. It had been only
seven months since the assassination of President Kennedy in the United
States, and for a year Montreal had been sitting on a knife-edge of violence
because of the mailbox bombings. From moment to moment during the St
Jean Baptiste parade, as the Vaniers sat exposed on the reviewing stand, the
atmosphere felt electric, as if the crowd might easily turn ugly.

In a blistering editorial, the *Globe and Mail* mocked the "pathetic little
effort ... to insult this distinguished soldier and diplomat, and the high office
he holds."[14] But when it was all over and the Vaniers were safely back in
the calm of Ottawa and Rideau Hall, Georges relished the opportunity to
write to his children that the crowd's cheers had drowned out the protesters' catcalls. As much as he lamented the discourtesy done to the institution
he represented, as well as the insult to his French-speaking regiment, he may
also have enjoyed hearing that in a sideshow to the main event, a protester
ran onto the veranda of a house and pulled down a Red Ensign flag that
was flying beside a Quebec flag. A sixty-year-old man sitting on the veranda
grabbed and pummelled the protester with punches until police moved in
to break up the fight.

If the Vaniers needed more perspective on the situation, it probably helped
to receive Thérèse's reaction. "How horrid for you both, but I can just see
Daddy rising above the whole thing (not necessarily levitating!)."[15] And in
a further letter she wrote, "Good old Daddy – I can't imagine a better chap
to have around at the moment – for the communal good anyway if not for
his own – and even that I consider enhanced – you know you thrive on
'problems'!"[16]

Lester Pearson seems to have agreed that the best chap to have around
was Georges Vanier, and he possibly knew that this particular governor gen-

eral was still up for a challenge. When his five-year term was coming to a close, in the middle of 1964, the prime minister asked him to stay on for another year. He wrote to his friend J.P. Cathcart: "It is a great blessing to be active at my age in a way which gives me an opportunity of carrying on at a time when Canada is experiencing some growing pains."[17]

Plans had already been made for Queen Elizabeth and Prince Philip to visit Canada on the hundredth anniversary of the 1864 talks in Charlottetown and Quebec City that had culminated in Confederation. The royal couple were to come to Canada for nine days in October 1964, to visit Charlottetown, and then to travel by the royal yacht up the St Lawrence River to Quebec City, where the celebrations would continue. But controversy over the visit and fears for the queen's safety ran high. The terrorist tactics of the FLQ in the Montreal area had not let up, and the scuffles of the St Jean Baptiste day in Montreal, although relatively harmless, had shown the kind of discourtesies that might be inflicted upon the queen. Also, press commentaries recalled in ominous tones the assassination of President Kennedy, as if a similar deed might be attempted in Canada. Anything could happen.

As the royal visit approached, pamphlets distributed by the FLQ gave instructions on how to infiltrate crowds, touch off riots, and cause hysteria in crowds, and how to provoke the police in order to make them seem to be Gestapo-like militia. The RIN planned passive tactics, less inflammatory but equally disruptive, which consisted in staging "sitting" events, allowing themselves to be carried off by the police. A RIN leader further inflamed speculation by saying publicly that if someone assassinated Queen Elizabeth, there could be civil war in Canada. As the days of her visit to Quebec approached and the royal yacht steamed up the St Lawrence River, unprecedented precautions were taken by the combined forces of the RCMP, the Quebec police, and the Canadian army. Roads, streets, railways, and the airport were under close surveillance. All vehicles were stopped for inspection on the highways leading to Quebec City. All the major figures taking part in the official ceremonies, including the governor general, were placed under twenty-four-hour police protection.

The result, as it turned out, was a welcome anti-climax. When Queen Elizabeth stepped out from the yacht on the chilly morning of 10 October, met by the Vaniers, the worst that could be said was that the Quebec crowds were sparse. There was no action by the FLQ, and the RIN had at the last moment called off their protest, because the heavy police presence would have made it ineffective. Although in some cases there may have been a protest by absence, the press reported that many people were simply afraid to come out in public in case violence erupted. By the time the royal party arrived in Ottawa, the unpleasantness was over and the only sobering sign was the sight of the RCMP standing guard on the tops of the surrounding buildings. The crowds came out, banners waved, and a placard bearing the words of a Beatles song, "We love you, yeah, yeah, yeah," drew a smile from the queen.

* * *

The federal election of 8 November 1965 returned another minority government for Pearson's Liberals, now with the inclusion of three new members of Parliament from Quebec – Jean Marchand, Gérard Pelletier, and Pierre Trudeau – all of whom became cabinet ministers and would help to change the face of Canada. But an important wrinkle had begun to emerge in Quebec's relationship with the federal government: France. Specifically, Quebec's relationship with France. Charles de Gaulle, at the age of sixty-eight and in spite of weakened eyes and an increasingly wide girth, had come back to power in 1958 in the wake of the crisis provoked by the Algerian nationalist movement. He was following the nationalist aspirations in Quebec with interest.

In the early 1960s, in an effort to establish itself internationally as a sovereign country, Quebec had begun to make quasi-official ties with France as one nation with another. De Gaulle was happy to deal with Quebec directly as if it were a nation, bypassing the internationally accepted diplomatic route of going through the Canadian embassy. When the Canadian ambassador in Paris, Jules Léger, delicately suggested that relations with Quebec should be made through the auspices of the Canadian government, he was not only ignored but actually left out of official functions, and otherwise treated as a nonentity. In 1965, France and Quebec signed a number of agreements. Pearson and External Affairs Minister Paul Martin were aware that if Quebec further established itself internationally as a sovereign nation, Canada's constitution would be threatened. They moved to create an allowance for provinces to sign agreements with foreign governments on matters that fell under provincial jurisdiction, thus legitimizing Quebec's agreements with France and at the same time treating Quebec as a province like the others.

But Canadian efforts went nowhere. Canada's ambassador continued to be snubbed while Quebec representatives who visited France were treated like royalty. Finally, in a last-ditch effort to smooth relations, the government decided in February 1966 to approach France with the suggestion that Governor General Vanier make a state visit, ostensibly to return the visit that de Gaulle had made to Canada in 1960.

Six months earlier, when his year's extension in office was up, Georges had been asked by the prime minister to remain in that position for an indefinite period. "Indefinite" at the time may have meant until the end of Canada's centennial year, 1967. But it also was probably clear that, given the throes of a France-Quebec alliance now added to a call for Quebec's separation, there was no one who better personified the Canadian state than Georges Vanier. Pearson sent him hand-written good wishes for his seventy-eighth birthday in April 1966: "My birthday greetings are from the heart and with them goes unbounded admiration and gratitude to Pauline and you for the work you are both doing, and so magnificently, for our country. Canada is so fortunate to have you in your present post at this time."[18]

Together, Georges and Pauline Vanier appeared to be the living embodiment of the co-existence of the two cultures. Each of them had a strong family connection to Quebec and to the history of French Canada. What was more, the couple's personal ties with de Gaulle extended back to the summer of 1940 when Georges, alone among foreign diplomats, had stood by the general in his lonely effort to save France, and had pressed the Canadian government to do the same. For years, Georges had sent a message to de Gaulle on the hallowed anniversary of 18 June, to commemorate the then-unknown general's radio broadcast after France had fallen to the Nazis in 1940. De Gaulle was said to have enjoyed renewing his friendship with the Vaniers during the 1960 visit, and in early 1964 he had written to Georges to congratulate him on being named an honorary general in the Canadian army. "Your elevation to the highest Canadian military level ... is just recompense for a magnificent career in the army and in diplomacy. Allow me to add how pleased I am to have had the privilege, over the course of difficult years, of being able to count on the faithful friendship that you have always shown toward France."[19]

Planning began immediately for the governor general's visit to France. He would travel as head of state, a designation that required the queen's approval, which was readily given. There had been precedents to such a visit: governors general in the past had been given full head-of-state reception in

Washington, and so, although no governor general had ever before visited a
European country on such an official mission, the trip would not stand out
as anomalous in any way. There had also been such visits on the part of other
Commonwealth governors general.

For six months letters went back and forth between the governor general's office and the queen's private secretary, and between the governor
general's office and the Canadian embassy in Paris, in a manner that, if symbolic importance and the future of Canada had not been at stake, could have
been viewed at times as a farce. For the French, the sticking point was that
the queen, rather than the governor general, was actually the Canadian head
of state. From Canada, the counter-argument ran that while not *exactly* the
head of state, the governor general *represented* the head of state, and therefore expected to be given the marks of respect and the degree of ceremony
normally rendered to a head of state. And besides, a communiqué suggested
gently, it was not up to a foreign government to decide who was, and who
was not, Canada's head of state.

This argument was not accepted by France. De Gaulle looked forward
to the visit, but since the governor general only *represented* the head of state,
the French government was not sure exactly what treatment he should be
given. In Ottawa, the treatment was more or less clear: at the very least, the
governor general should be greeted at the airport like any other head of state
and he should stay at the Élysée or some other official residence and not at
a hotel. There were other questions of protocol: would the Canadian flag
be flown? Would the president accompany the governor general to lay a
wreath at the Arc du Triomphe? Specific answers were not forthcoming.
Then, on the Canadian side, a sign of desperation: if the French were willing to receive the governor general in a manner *approaching* the visit of a
head of state, and to consider his visit as a return of de Gaulle's state visit to
Canada, this resolution would be satisfactory.

Questions of protocol and semantics went back and forth during the
winter of 1966. But while matters were still under discussion, de Gaulle suddenly withdrew France from NATO's military alliance and, on 21 February,
demanded that Canadian forces leave French soil. This demand prompted
Pearson to wonder aloud bitterly whether the hundred thousand Canadians lying in war graves should leave too. Obviously, de Gaulle, now aged
seventy-six, was becoming more and more erratic and increasingly alienat-
ing himself from his usual allies.

In June, a new development raised the separatist stakes: the Union Nationale was re-elected, with Daniel Johnson becoming premier of Quebec. On and on the letters continued to go between Canada and France. Would the governor general be received as a head of state or would he not? De Gaulle remained firm, if vague: he would welcome a visit from an old friend in some undefined manner, but it would not be a state visit. On 20 July, the governor general's office wrote to External Affairs: "General de Gaulle's stand that the governor general may not be accorded Head of State treatment makes our position extremely difficult. If we accepted these terms, it would create a precedent which would have grave implications for the future. Previous governors general have paid State visits to Washington and have received all the marks of respect normally given to Heads of State. To accept less than this for a visit to France might well prejudice our position should visits to other countries be proposed in the future. Under the circumstances, it has been decided that the question of an official visit must, we regret, be dropped for the time being."[20] And so that was that, and for Georges Vanier, no such opportunity would come again.[21]

* * *

In early November 1966, three months after the cancellation of his state visit to France, Georges underwent surgery for an enlarged prostate. Up until then, his health had been reported as excellent. But he had been finding his strength failing and wrote to a friend that reading the Speech from the Throne at the opening of Parliament was a particular ordeal, and his heart specialist, Paul David, had some ongoing concerns. Still, he looked forward to a full recovery and participation in Canada's centennial celebrations.

In the meantime, Pauline answered all the get-well messages that poured in for her husband. She also substituted for him in opening schools, visiting churches, and laying wreaths and cornerstones, as she had after his heart attack three years earlier. She managed everything with an appearance of aristocratic ease that hid the anxiety and lack of confidence that had dogged her all her life. The couple had become loved and admired across Canada, and as many had observed years earlier, her effervescence, spontaneity, and effortless ability to draw people into conversation complemented his quiet thoughtfulness, dry wit, and serenity. As the years progressed and Georges's energy sagged on lengthy public occasions, she kept an eagle's eye on him, and whenever he began to fade, she moved seamlessly to his side to light-heartedly engage the circle surrounding him. At their annual Tadoussac holiday in August, she had written her forty-fifth – and as it would turn out, final – letter to her husband, commemorating the 28 August anniversary of his wounding. "This annual letter, instead of becoming more difficult to write is becoming easier because I still have more things to tell you ... It's that after these long years that we've lived together, I've learned and am still learning every day to appreciate you more and more. My admiration for you, and even more, the love that I have for you, has always been profound."[22]

She had received honorary doctorates from various universities and, in 1965, had been named the chancellor of the University of Ottawa, the first non-member of the clergy to hold that position (she laughingly told friends in later years that in her ermine-trimmed red academic gown she looked like Mrs Santa Claus). She was also named "Woman of the Year" by the Canadian Press in the same year. But even as she was revved up by the fuss, she felt undeserving and inadequate. She wrote to her mother that she was ashamed to discover faults in herself that she hadn't previously known about: bouts of irritability and a tendency to haughtiness toward people she disliked or toward those who took the limelight from her (her lady-in-waiting, Thérèse Berger, who was a near-equal to Madame Vanier in charm and attractiveness, left Rideau Hall in early 1966, ostensibly because the period of time she had committed herself to was now over. But Pauline wrote to a friend in France that "it was the only possible solution because it was clear that we didn't altogether understand each other, and I was certainly unjust toward her, the poor thing."[23]) After receiving a self-castigating letter from her, her daughter Thérèse wrote briskly, "Dear Ma, when you feel yourself lapsing into an inferiority complex, remember a number of things: when different people meet they leave a mark ... What Daddy is today and what your children are today is, in larger measure than you apparently realise, your doing."[24]

Father Benedict received similar missives of self-reproach, but stayed away from the fray, preferring a gentle teasing approach: "Is there any truth in the report that your new address is as follows: 'The Lord High Chancellor and Mr. Vanier, Résidence du Chancellerie'? Congratulations on those baskets of degrees; may the crop prosper, because it will help support Mr. Vanier."[25]

* * *

By December 1966, Pauline was reporting to some friends that her husband was well on the way to recovery and would soon be active again, although to others she admitted her smiles masked considerable worry over the state of his health. Thérèse spent Christmas with them, and two days later Vanier was well enough to tape his 1967 New Year's message to the nation. The address, which had been written and re-written as he lay on his sick bed, began with a reflection on Canada's achievements in the first century of its existence, and then he moved on to the future – the next century – and he outlined his belief on the need to seek the common good: "If we imagine that we can now go our separate ways within our country; if we think that selfish interests can now take precedence over the national good; if we exaggerate our differences or revel in contention; if we do any of these things, we will promote our own destruction ... But if we remain united, if we seek first and always the greater good, if we cherish, not the digressions which divide us, but the major bonds of shared heritage and common values which unite us; if we do these things, then we can look forward to a future which will make the progress of this century seem pale by comparison."[26]

When the new year of 1967 was rung in, most of the country looked forward to Expo 67 in Montreal. The heads of sixty states had been invited, and it would be a splendid showcase of Canadian unity. It may have been sheer force of will, or perhaps an element of wishful thinking, that made Georges write to friends that he was feeling stronger every day and looking forward to a full recovery. He was described as "convalescing" on New Year's Day when it was Madame Vanier on her own, her strained face breaking into a forced smile, who set off the centennial train on its celebratory trip across Canada. When, later in the month, he was pulled, wearing a toque, on a toboggan to a Rideau Hall skating party for the press, some reporters were moved with emotion at the sight of his thin and drawn appearance. He rarely appeared in the dining room for meals, preferring to eat in his bedroom.

But there were still days when he seemed to be improving, his strength returning. By the middle of February he was well enough to send a spirited letter to Pearson regarding the use of the governor general's quarters at the Citadel, where he was planning an extended stay later in centennial year. Pearson had offered the Citadel residence to Quebec's lieutenant governor for receptions during the visits of heads of state, but Georges thought that this gesture might in the end send an undesired message. "May I recall that I consider it not only important but essential that at all costs we must prevent the Citadel being made use of as if it were provincial property in connection with visits of heads of state, etc.," he reminded the prime minister. "This would give the obvious impression to these guests that the Citadel was the property of the Quebec government and not under federal jurisdiction,"[27] he continued, adding that proper protocol was crucial where such delicate matters were concerned.

He also took issue with a statement made by the journalist Charles Lynch in *Canadian* magazine speculating that he "might not be a really convinced monarchist." "Such completely irresponsible speculation is unworthy of comment by one whose life has been and continues to be a life of service and sworn allegiance to the monarchy,"[28] he wrote to Lynch. The journalist apologized publicly, and a few days later, he was invited to Rideau Hall for a goodwill chat with the governor general. Lynch noted afterward that the old man's handshake was still firm.

During February Georges presided at four receptions, the last of which was the signing of an agreement to affiliate the Boy Scouts of Canada with Les Scouts Catholiques du Canada. This occasion was particularly dear to his heart. In French, he repeated sentiments that various Canadian groups had been hearing from him for over seven years: "The three main questions which occupy me, which pre-occupy me, which haunt me, are youth, national unity and spiritual values. In the Scouts, I find the synthesis of all three."[29] On the morning of Thursday, 2 March, he met with a group of seventy-five political science students from the University of Montreal and their professor, Dale Thomson. The governor general arrived downstairs in a wheelchair. Notes for remarks had been prepared for him, but he chose to speak directly without them. Appropriately, he spoke of the spiritual power that draws a people together into a nation, a power founded on love which finds its expression in respect for law and the rights of others, and willing service and sacrifice for the good of one's fellow citizens. It was a simple legacy, delivered in a slightly trembling voice to a youthful group representing the future of the province he loved. His exhortation finished, he became relaxed and chatted briefly with them. He gave a cheerful wave as he was wheeled from the room.

The prime minister had, since the beginning of the year, been worried that Georges's health would not stand up to the demands of the centennial celebrations in the months ahead, and the slight progress during the first few weeks of 1967 did not carry much conviction. Pearson arranged for a heart specialist from Boston, Dr Paul Dudley White, to examine him. Dr

White arrived on Friday, 3 March, and gave his opinion that indeed, the governor general's heart was not up to the task required by the centennial's public duties. The next day, Pearson suggested to him that he might take on a quieter role, moving to Quebec as "keeper of the Citadel" for the rest of centennial year. Perhaps he now felt as he had fifteen years earlier when he had been offered a lesser diplomatic position in Europe: better to leave the scene immediately, make a clean break rather than hanging on. Or perhaps he knew that his end was rapidly approaching. In any event, he answered that he would prefer to resign. That evening, he and the prime minister watched "Hockey Night in Canada," the hallowed Saturday evening program beloved of men across the country. The Montreal Canadiens were up against the Detroit Redwings, and Georges fell asleep with the happy knowledge that the Canadiens won the game.

Sometime earlier, Dr Burton and Sergeant Chevrier had moved him from his own bedroom to a room across from the chapel. Sergeant Chevrier affixed a mirror in the doorway in such a way that from his bed the invalid could see the altar. Sunday, 5 March, was "Laetare" (Latin for "rejoice") Sunday, marking the mid-point of Lent, when the Scripture readings, breaking the usual sombre Lenten pattern, sound a note of joy. The chaplain, Father Hermas Guindon, arrived at ten thirty for morning Mass. Pauline was already in the bedroom with her husband, as were their sons Jean, who had come to Canada on a lecture tour, and Michel. Dr Burton had also arrived. Father Guindon brought communion, and then Pauline and her sons went into the chapel for Mass. When the patient indicated that his oxygen mask was irritating and tried to remove it, Sergeant Chevrier wiped it out and then gently replaced it and gave him a sip of water. Georges said a faint "Merci." By the time the family returned to his bedside, he was already dying. Dr Burton felt his pulse becoming increasingly weaker, and quietly announced at eleven twenty-two that he was dead.

* * *

The governor general's coffin was brought to the Rideau Hall ballroom on the afternoon of his death. Thérèse and Bernard flew in from Europe, and Father Benedict received permission to come to Ottawa from his monastery. Of Georges's own siblings, only his sister Eva survived to mourn him.

The next day, the coffin was removed to the Senate chamber in the Parliament buildings, draped in the red and white Canadian flag that had come into existence only two years earlier. On it were placed his Royal 22nd cap and his medals. Crowds filed past the coffin, which was flanked at the four corners by four servicemen (at one point in the lying-in-state, in a move that would have delighted him, the guard was replaced for a time by four boy scouts). Flags across the country were lowered. Letters of condolence arrived from across Canada; children, prompted by their teachers, sent pictures and poems in touching tribute.

On Wednesday, 8 March, in frigid weather, a muffled roll of drums led the military gun carriage carrying the governor general's body from the Parliament building down Wellington Street and onto Sussex Drive, on its way to Notre Dame Cathedral, followed by a riderless horse with reversed boots. A seventy-eight gun salute, one for each year of Georges Vanier's life, shot through the air. Pauline Vanier, wearing a grey mink coat against the bitter cold, led the procession into the cathedral for the funeral.

From Ottawa, the coffin and mourners took the train to Quebec City. After Mass in the Quebec basilica, the coffin was placed in a crypt and later in the spring was transferred to the small memorial chapel in the Citadel. Tributes to Georges Vanier after his death mentioned the youthful spirit that had remained intact inside an ailing body; the noble bearing combined with a simple and unaffected manner; the distinguished service as a soldier and diplomat. One journalist lamented the passing of the singular generation of Canadians who had served their country in two world wars. The *Globe and Mail* editorial spoke of the "reason, restraint and true affection for his country" that Vanier had shown in the face of Quebec's fledgling separatist movement: "Had we been served by a smaller man, one with less understanding of the turbulent forces that had been set in motion, Canada could well have been set asunder."[30]

Two years after Georges's death, in a letter to the biographer Robert Speaight, Michael Pitfield (who had been an attaché in Rideau Hall during the Vanier years) wrote that "Georges Vanier had a more difficult time, in terms of constitutional issues, than any of his predecessors since Byng; even in comparison with Byng, he had a longer time of it. For all the months of minority government, there were a thousand and one little things all compounded by the aura of uncertainty that the crisis in national unity brought to bear upon the office. It was not that crisis occurred, but that the governor general had to be constantly on guard to prevent one, and to deal with one if he could not prevent it. This was very hard to do and a tremendous burden."

Pitfield went on to say how Georges Vanier carried on from Vincent Massey in trying to "Canadianize" the Crown, "rarely dwelling upon personal loyalty in order to give greater emphasis to the things the Crown can symbolize: unity, justice, excellence, service and so forth ... I would venture that more than eighty per cent of his attention to the office had to do with its strictly Canadian implications, with its being representative of the Canadian people and their experience, rather than with its being representative of the British, or even Commonwealth, experience and traditions ... The man, by demonstrating in a thousand ways that the office is a Canadian thing, did much to perpetuate it and the country it serves and, in doing so, secured in the only way possible a continuing link with the Crown."[31]

More personally, the heart specialist Dr Paul Dudley White wrote to Madame Vanier from Boston, "How quickly fate decided for us all! ... During the few hours that I had gotten to know your husband I developed a deep and abiding affection and esteem for him, and I shall never forget him. It is spirits such as his that make the doctor's life an inspired one." He ended his letter: "Happily for him he did not live to suffer more, but for you his loss will indeed be grievous; yet your spirit too will survive this blow."[32]

Pauline had no idea how correct his prediction was, or how far she would move beyond merely surviving.

18

THE END: FULL CIRCLE

The former mayor of Ottawa, Charlotte Whitton, led a movement to have Pauline Vanier appointed to be her husband's successor, but this effort was short-lived. Prime Minister Pearson paid tribute to the important role she had played throughout the previous eight years and considered her briefly as a possible candidate, but because of the uncertainty surrounding his minority government, he decided against it.

Pauline left Rideau Hall a month after her husband's death, two weeks after her sixty-ninth birthday. Sergeant Chevrier and his brown mongrel "Friday" joined her; together they moved into a brick townhouse at 27 Redpath Place in Montreal. They established a harmonious household, with moments of tension dispelled by a sense of humour on both sides (he found her to be a liability in the kitchen, dirtying every dish and making messes everywhere, and the dog Friday often made messes of another kind), but the adjustment to life away from the public eye was difficult. Her extroversion had responded readily to the activity of Rideau Hall, and in spite of her desire for Christian simplicity, she had enjoyed the attention and the pomp. No longer did people dance attendance on her. No longer was she surrounded by protocol or official functions that had provided the stimulation of meeting people from various walks of life and visitors from other countries. Most of all, there was no longer the supportive presence of her husband. She wrote to a friend in France that at Easter, three weeks after his death, "I felt an 'Alleluia' in the fullness of my heart, but my tears were flowing the whole time."[1] Still, as she had done on other traumatic occasions, she displayed courage and resilience in moving into private life.

But not before a final encounter with the formidable Charles de Gaulle. In the summer of 1967, Pauline took a trip to England and France to visit her children, and was invited to lunch with President de Gaulle and his wife, Yvonne, with whom she had remained on warm terms. De Gaulle had sent only a low-level official to represent the French government at Georges Vanier's funeral, had sent her only a formal letter of condolence, and a month later, had refused to send a government representative to the fiftieth-anniversary commemoration of Canada's battle of Vimy Ridge. He had, however, accepted Canada's invitation to Expo 67, a visit that was scheduled for later in July.

The lunch to which de Gaulle invited her took place on 7 July at the Élysée Palace. It turned out to be a private affair at which only de Gaulle and his wife were present. After some pleasant small talk, de Gaulle began to speak of his upcoming trip to Quebec and Montreal. No mention was made of Ottawa, to which, as the capital of Canada, all heads of state would be paying an official visit. Pauline took mental note of this omission. She was also aware that de Gaulle was treating her with an excessive cordiality that unsettled her. Then he broached the question of the future of Canada, and told her that he foresaw an independent Quebec. Yvonne de Gaulle, she noticed, looked down at her plate and at her husband, saying nothing and avoiding eye contact with Pauline.[2]

Pauline was still in France when, on 23 July, de Gaulle steamed into the Quebec City port on a French cruiser. At the Citadel, his first act was to place a wreath inside the memorial chapel. (Did he also notice, immediately inside the chapel, the grave of the one diplomat who had stood by him during the dark days of 1940?) It may have been a surprise to Pauline when, the next day, he declared that the drive to Montreal past cheering crowds was comparable to his triumphant march down the Champs-Élysées after the Nazis had been driven from Paris. But it was likely not a surprise to her when he uttered the notorious declamation, "*Vivre le Québec libre!*" from the balcony of the Montreal City Hall. And the irony was probably not lost on her that this extraordinary breach of protocol was made in the province where, a quarter of a century earlier, she and her husband had spent more than a year trying to convince Pétain supporters to transfer their allegiance to de Gaulle.

* * *

Over the next five years, during which she was in demand for speeches and appearances, she returned to her pre-Rideau Hall volunteer work, helping at Benedict Labre House and visiting prisoners. Through Thérèse's weekly letters, she received regular news about what was happening in Trosly, France.

It was clear that Jean's work was blossoming, and soon "the house" became "houses." In 1969, Pauline travelled to Richmond Hill, Ontario, to assist at the opening of the first L'Arche house outside of France. L'Arche was now an international movement.

That same year, her mother, Thérèse de Salaberry Archer, died at the age of ninety-five in her old-world hotel in Paris. Jean, the grandchild living in closest proximity, had taken on the role of caregiver to the diminutive and fragile Madame Archer. Even as she began to sink into senility, his grandmother remained interested in Jean's L'Arche project, and she gave him money to buy her a house so that she could live in the community as well. It was an untenable proposition, and her grandson was probably relieved when Madame Archer died as the house was being prepared for her. The house, left in her will to her daughter, now stood empty.

In 1972, approaching the age of seventy-four, Madame Vanier decided to try living in her mother's house in Trosly for a trial period of six months. She held an auction of some of her possessions, the highest bid going for a pencil drawing of her at the age of eleven by the Quebec artist Marc-Aurèle de Foy Suzor-Coté, and she offered furniture and family mementoes to her children. The seventeenth-century mahogany chest that had formed the altar in the Rideau Hall chapel was given to the Trappists at Oka, and soon became the altar in their renovated church. She bade a tearful goodbye to Sergeant Chevrier (who was to find his inestimable services put to use by Governor General Jules Léger, and a succession of other incumbents of Rideau Hall) and left for France on 29 February, just before turning seventy-four years of age. Except for yearly visits to Canada, she remained there for the rest of her life.

Trosly, situated north-east of Paris, was a village of stone buildings, many of which, modest to the point of poverty, still did not have indoor plumbing. White lace curtains and window boxes full of bright geraniums brought colour and gentility to its otherwise dreary atmosphere. In the eight years since Jean had moved there, the L'Arche community had expanded from one house to a community of more than two hundred in homes they called "foyers." The "boys," as the mentally handicapped men were then called, were the core members of the community – its heart and spirit – but to help them, as "assistants," Jean had recruited young people mainly from Canada, but also from France and the United States.

"Les Marronniers," the house that Pauline inherited from her mother, stood behind large chestnut trees at the end of a long gravel walkway across the narrow street from Jean's original house. The interior was unpretentious. At the back, a narrow bedroom, to which a bathroom had been added, was partially divided from a small sitting area. French windows gave out to trees and a garden, and in the front was a small kitchen and eating area and a room where she could entertain a small number of guests.

In spite of the bone-chilling weather, the damp house and the inconveniences (she had to have her bath at six-thirty in the morning so as to get the only hot water of the day), her letters of the time indicate that she settled in relatively well almost from the beginning. She fell into the gentle rhythm of country life, setting off with her basket to the village's only general store and, when spring arrived, picking vegetables from her own garden. When she had been at Trosly less than a month, she spent a day in Paris visiting friends, and found the experience dislocating. "This will be my last visit to Paris for a long time. It is no longer my life,"[3] she wrote to a cousin.

But her presence – possibly because of the mystique of being Jean Vanier's mother (a reaction she would make fun of in later years, drawing a long face, wide-eyed with mock admiration), but also because of her own outgoing personality – brought many visitors. "She doesn't act like a madame at all!"[4] remarked the mother of one of L'Arche's American assistants. A few weeks after arriving, she found a local woman to cook and clean four hours a day. She was amused at herself as a former *grande dame* who took pride in being able to prepare her own breakfast, pleased and flattered whenever anyone praised her coffee. She was also happy to report that her newfound domestication extended to washing the dishes herself and sweeping the black and white tile floor. Eventually she became known to everyone as "Mamie," a short form of "Maman," a name that would remain with her for the rest of her life. As the life of glamorous society receded into her past, she became less interested in fashionable clothes. Her only jewellery now was her plain gold wedding band.

What she did not mention in letters (and perhaps it did not even register with her at the time) was an incident during her first few weeks at L'Arche. As she described it years afterward, she was alone in the chapel one day in tears, at one of her lowest emotional points, when she felt a hand on her shoulder. She looked up to see a mentally handicapped man from one of the foyers. Without speaking, he took her hand and led her silently out of the chapel and to the door of her home. This small gesture was to be one of many upside-down lessons of unconditional acceptance she would learn in what she called "the school of L'Arche" during the coming years.

Anxiety about her lack of usefulness remained a leitmotif in spite of her general contentedness. Worries about her faults may have increased as her physical strength diminished and her world grew narrower. She worried that, having co-founded the Vanier Institute of the Family, she was guilty of hypocrisy because both her married sons had become divorced from their wives. She wrote pages to Father Benedict of what she called *"poubelle"* (garbage), litanies of her failings: she became haughty and demanding over small matters such as inelegant meal presentations; her spontaneity, once considered charming, now sometimes burst out in flashes of anger; she grew depressed and impatient in the face of her waning energy; she sometimes fell into self-pity at no longer being the centre of attention. She worried from time to time that she did not fit in at L'Arche and that she was somehow at fault for being a failure. Her son responded with soothing reminders ("Remember, all the faculties – even the most spiritual – have their 'substratum,' their roots, in our body, our 'neurology,' and so it is not surprising that with age, even outside of specific illness, there will be a 'slowing down.'"[5])

In the mid-1980s her eye problems resurfaced, and by 1986 she could no longer read or see well enough to write. She relied on cassette tapes for reading material, and her letters were dictated. The damp cold of the winters in northern France seeped into her bones, aggravating the arthritis in her back, and the unremitting grey skies tended to lower her spirits. She wrote that although L'Arche "is a peaceful place it is in some ways very super active and I get so fed up with the goings and comings. Here am I a grumbly old woman. Actually, I am very happy here but the old carcass is beginning to creak and moan and that makes me cross."[6] Inability to read meant that she was now more dependent on others. Anxieties from earlier years manifested themselves in new ways; she feared loneliness and panicked whenever she was left alone. She sometimes said she was afraid to die, but at other times complained that God had forgotten to come for her. And when her hearing, too, began to fail, she feared that she would become senile, and an impossible burden on the community.

Through it all, the old humour and spunk continued to surface from time to time. When she managed to bend down sufficiently to tie her shoe laces, she flashed a V-for-victory sign. When homecare help was requested from the nearby town of Pierrefonds and a male nurse presented himself as the person sent to bathe her, she gave a momentary start, and then laughed and shrugged off her feminine modesty. And in spite of her increasing infirmity, she still travelled to Canada every year. In 1989, at the age of ninety-one, she made her last trans-Atlantic trip.

The end came quickly. On Thursday, 21 March 1991, she was found curled up in bed, sobbing and in physical agony. At the hospital in Compiègne, tests revealed intestinal cancer, and she was operated on the next day. On Saturday, 23 March, full of tubes and surrounded by machines, she opened her eyes briefly and recognized Jean at her side, and then she lapsed into unconsciousness and died shortly afterward. It was five days before her ninety-third birthday and the day before Palm Sunday, the beginning of the most sacred week in the Christian calendar. It would have pleased her to know that her funeral Mass in Trosly was celebrated on 25 March, the anniversary of Father Benedict's ordination to the priesthood.

Pauline Vanier's body was returned to Canada on an armed services plane, and on 3 April another funeral took place in Notre Dame Basilica in Quebec City. The Canadian flag was draped over her casket. Her body was later buried in the memorial chapel of the Citadel beside that of her husband.

* * *

The graves of Georges and Pauline Vanier, beneath the floor of the memorial chapel on the Citadel grounds in Quebec City, bear inscriptions that are barely visible in the tiny, cramped space. On the stone over Georges Vanier's grave is written the first two lines of Psalm 121: *J'étais dans la joie quand on m'a dit: Allons dans la maison du Seigneur* ("I rejoiced when I heard them say: Let us go to God's house"). These words form the Introit, or opening invocation, of the Mass for the Fourth Sunday of Lent, the day he died. On the stone over Pauline Vanier's grave, the remainder of the verse from the same psalm is inscribed: *Et maintenant devant tes portes notre marche prend fin* ("And now our feet are standing within your gates"). The one completes the other, as the couple completed each other in life.

It is not known exactly how they came to be buried at the Citadel. It may have been the stated wish of Georges Vanier, but official documents from the time suggest that the decision in the end was a hasty one, made by Pauline Vanier and Jean Pierre Allard, the chief of General Staff, in the emotion-filled hours after the governor general's death.

In 1998, *Maclean's* magazine published a list of the hundred most important Canadians in history, and Georges Vanier came out at the top. He was the country's "moral compass," the magazine said. If this is so, it is not because of what he accomplished alone. It is because he and his wife Pauline – herself no less an exemplar – carried out their lives of service, in the midst of day-by-day struggles, human imperfection, and sometimes failure, by embracing the life of the spirit above all. Without in any way imposing their own beliefs, they represented the best of all faiths and spiritual traditions. The Vanier name lives as a symbol of all that is noble in Canada; of what Canadians themselves could become.

ACKNOWLEDGMENTS

The assistance of many people has been vital in the preparation of this book. Thanks first of all to the wonderful staff of Library and Archives Canada for their patient help and competence. In particular, archivists Lucie Paquet and Victorin Chabot eased the way for me, and historians Paul Marsden and Paulette Dozois directed me to material I would not have found on my own.

Other archivists were also helpful in providing information and, in some cases, primary materials: Marie-Hélène St-Cyr Prémont of the Musée Royal 22e Régiment, Quebec City; Sister Veronica of the Ware Carmel Archives, Ware, Herts, England; James Hodkinson SJ of the British Jesuit Archives, London, England; and Paul Spaeth of the Robert Lax Archives, St Bonaventure University, St Bonaventure, NY. Thanks as well to Charlene Elgee, librarian at Citizenship and Immigration Canada, Ottawa.

The following books paved the way for me by telling various aspects of the Vanier story: *In Weakness, Strength: The Spiritual Sources of Georges P. Vanier, 19th Governor-General of Canada* by Jean Vanier; *Vanier: Soldier, Diplomat and Governor General* by Robert Speaight; *One Woman's Journey: A Portrait of Pauline Vanier* by Deborah Cowley and George Cowley; *Georges Vanier, Soldier: The Wartime Letters and Diaries 1915–1919*, edited by Deborah Cowley; and my own book, *The Hidden Way: The Life and Influence of Almire Pichon.*

After the deaths of Georges and Pauline Vanier, Monsignor Roger Quesnel of Ottawa was asked to begin an investigation process into their lives with a view to the possible introduction of their cause for beatification as a married couple. Although this book is unrelated to that process, Monsignor Quesnel was generous in sharing his material and his knowledge of the Vaniers, and encouraged me throughout the time of research and writing. I am most grateful to him.

The manuscript was read by Luanne Armstrong, Patricia Cain, and Wayne Grady. Their suggestions helped to improve the text, and I thank them for

their time and thoroughness. The constitutional expert Edward McWhinney
graciously agreed to read the chapters covering the period during which Georges
Vanier was the governor general of Canada. My sincere thanks to him for
his wide-ranging comments. Thanks also to Judith Robertson for permission to quote from the writings of Charles Ritchie and to the Hon. Michael
Pitfield for permission to quote from his correspondence to Robert Speaight.

Individual people helped me in various ways in the preparation of this
book, and in particular I would like to acknowledge the assistance of John
Baker, the late Dr Peter Burton and Rachel Burton, Elizabeth Buckley, Yves
Chevrier, Michel de Salaberry, the late Marguerite Eudes, the late Mario
Galeazzi, Pierre Gratton, Margaret and Ed Holubowich, Sidney Madden,
Anne McCarthy, Elizabeth Oliver, Bernard Parkin SJ, and Bernard Poirier.
Also, I am grateful to editors Mary-Lynne Ascough, Joan McGilvray, and
Susan Glickman for their editorial skill and friendly guidance.

Finally, I owe a debt of gratitude to the children of Georges and Pauline
Vanier: Thérèse, Benedict, Jean, Michel, and the late Bernard Vanier. This book
could not have been written without their generous co-operation. I offer
them my profound thanks.

NOTES

CHAPTER ONE

1 Library and Archives Canada, MG2 A2, Box 3 file 25, 18 June 1916.
2 Box 2 file 15.
3 Box 1 file 15.
4 Box1 file 20.
5 Box 1 file 25.
6 Box 1 file 24.
7 Box 1 file 17.
8 Box 1 file 28.
9 Box 1 file 28.
10 Box 1 file 29, 5 June 1908.
11 Box 1 file 31.
12 Box 1 file 35.
13 Box 1 file 34.
14 May 1911, Box 1 file 34.

CHAPTER TWO

1 Box 4 file 13, 1 February 1919.
2 *The Montreal Standard*, 12 December 1914.
3 *Amherst Daily News*, 15 March 1915.
4 Box 2 file 7, 21 May 1915.
5 Box 2 file 7, 6 June 1915.
6 Box 2 file 7, 8 August 1915.
7 Box 2 file 7, 14 September 1915.
8 *The Listening Post* 8, 25 November 1915.
9 Box 2 file 13, 24 May 1915.
10 Box 2 file 13, 1 December 1915.
11 Box 2 file 13, 18 January 1916.
12 Box 2 file 10, 2 August 1915.
13 Box 2 file 10, 6 September 1915.
14 Box 2 file 13, 24 November 1915.
15 Box 2 file 8, 1 December 1915.
16 Box 2 file 8, 16 December 1915.
17 Box 2 file 15, 13 November 1915.

18 Box 2 file 15, 6 December 1915.
19 Box 93 file 3.
20 *Christian Science Monitor,* 16 May 1916.
21 Box 3 file 4.
22 Box 3 file 4, 18 January 1916.
23 Box 3 file 25, 27 January 1916.
24 Box 2 file 25.
25 Box 3 file 3, 12 February 1916.
26 Box 3 file 4, 2 March 1916.
27 Box 2 file 25, 27 May 1916.
28 Box 3 file 3.
29 Box 3 file 2, 18 June 1916.
30 Box 3 file 2, 15 June 1916.
31 Box 3 file 2, 1 August 1916.
32 Box 3 file 2, 16 August 1916.
33 Box 63 file 1.

CHAPTER THREE
1 Box 3 file 3, 4 October 1916.
2 House of Lords Record Office, B7, 14.
3 Box 3 file 12, 14 April 1917.
4 Box 3 file 12, 10 August 1917.
5 Box 3 file 14, 28 August 1917.
6 Box 93 file 4.
7 Box 4 file 7.
8 Box 3 file 19, 27 February 1918.
9 Box 93 file 5.
10 Library and Archives Canada, Government of Canada Files, RG24,
    National Defence Series C-1-b, Reel C-5053, File 649-D-12250.
11 Box 3 file 23.
12 Box 3 file 19, 11 August 1918.
13 Box 3 file 20, 6 September 1918.

CHAPTER FOUR
1 Box 3 file 20.
2 Box 3 file 20, 6 September 1918.
3 Box 93 file 5, 6 September 1918.
4 Box 3 file 20, 10 September 1918.
5 Box 3 file 20, 18 September 1918.
6 Box 3, file 20, 26 September 1918.
7 Box 3 file 22, 20 September 1918.
8 Box 4 file 4.
9 Box 3 file 21, Charles Sullivan, 16 October 1918.

10 Box 3 file 21, 1 November 1918.
11 Library and Archives Canada, RG150, Box 9905-46.
12 Box 4 file 12, 18 January 1919.
13 Box 4 file 12, 1 February 1919.
14 Box 4 file 13, 8 February, 1919.
15 Box 4 file 3.
16 Box 3 file 21, 15 December 1918.
17 Box 4 file 12, 28 March 1919.
18 Box 3 file 20, 7 September 1918.
19 Box 3 file 21, 28 November 1918.
20 Box 4 file 12, 21 February 1919.
21 Box 4 file 12, 24 April 1919.
22 Box 4 file 12, 21 February 1919.
23 Box 4 file 12, 13 May 1919.
24 Box 4 file 12, 22 May 1919.
25 Box 4 file 12, 14 July 1919.
26 Library and Archives Canada RG150, Box 9905-46.
27 Box 4 file 13, 22 May 1919.
28 Box 4 file 12, 13 May 1919.
29 Box 4 file 17.
30 Library and Archives Canada RG150, Box 9905-46.
31 Box 35 file 4, 26 November 1965.
32 Box 4 file 17, 23 September 1919.

CHAPTER FIVE
1 Box 113 file 4.
2 Box 113 file 5.
3 Box 113 file 6.
4 Box 113 file 6.
5 Box 113 file 6.
6 Box 113 file 6.
7 Box 113 file 6.
8 Interview with the author, 22 April 1988.
9 Ibid.
10 Ibid.
11 Box 113 file 7.
12 Private correspondence, 3 January 1921. Most of the letters between Georges and Pauline were written in French. Translations are by the author.
13 Private correspondence, 27 January 1921.
14 Box 4 file 22.
15 Box 4 file 22, 23 September 1921.
16 Box 4 file 21, 15 September 1921.
17 Private correspondence, 24 March 1921.

18 Private correspondence, 13 April 1921.
19 Box 4 file 19, 18 March 1921.
20 Private correspondence.
21 Ibid.
22 Box 4 file 20, J.H. MacBrien, 27 August 1921.
23 Box 4 file 20, 28 August 1921.
24 Box 4 file 20, J.H. MacBrien, 2 September 1921.
25 Private correspondence, 1 September 1921.
26 Private correspondence, 22 September 1921.

CHAPTER SIX
1 Box 4 file 19, 18 July 1921.
2 *The Montreal Standard*, 1 October 1921.
3 The cathedral was renamed Mary Queen of the World in 1955.
4 Box 113 file 7.
5 Private correspondence, 6 January 1922.
6 Box 113 file 7.
7 Box 113 file 8.
8 Box 4 file 31, 4 March 1923.
9 Box 4 file 29.
10 Box 113 file 8.
11 Box 4 file 27, 29 December 1922.
12 Box 4 file 27, 18 September 1922.
13 Box 4 file 27, 18 November 1922.
14 *The Staff and Staff College*, xi
15 Box 4 file 31, 3 January 1923.
16 Box 4 file 29.
17 Box 4 file 29, 19 March 1923.
18 Box 5 file 1.
19 Box 4 file 30, 15 January 1923.
20 Box 5 file 1.
21 Box 4 file 32, 17 December 1923.
22 Box 5 file 23, 10 November 1924.
23 Box 4 file 31, 3 January 1923.
24 Box 5 file 18, 30 November 1925.

CHAPTER SEVEN
1 cf *American Notes*, St Martin's Press, 1985, 191.
2 Box 6 file 4, 20 December 1925.
3 Box 6 file 5, 11 March 1926.
4 *Time* (Canada Edition), 21 September 1959.
5 Box 6 file 33, 7 January 1928.
6 Box 4 file 31, 24 March 1923.

7 Box 6 file 8, 12 September 1926.

8 Box 6 file 1, 8 November 1926.

9 Box 6 file 18, 4 April 1927.

10 Box 11 file 6.

11 Library and Archives Canada, Henry Willis-O'Connor papers, MG30 E78, 25 October 1926.

12 Box 6 file 9, 4 December 1927.

13 Box 6 file 21.

14 Private correspondence, 28 August 1928.

15 Box 6 file 9, 15 February 1928.

16 Box 6 file 31, 20 October 1928.

17 Box 6 file 31, 2 November 1928.

18 Box 6 file 31, 3 October 1928.

19 Box 6 file 25, 9 November 1928.

20 Box 6 file 24, 14 September 1928.

21 Box 6 file 31, 11 October 1928.

22 The painting was eventually donated to Canada's National Art Gallery and now hangs in Rideau Hall in Ottawa.

23 Box 7 file 6, Philip de Laszlo, 29 December 1929.

24 Box 6 file 28, Walter Curran, 16 December 1928.

25 Box 7 file 22, 17 March 1929.

26 Box 7 file 22, 18 March 1929.

27 Box 7 file 17, 28 April 1929.

28 Box 7 file 4.

29 Box 7 file 4, 10 July 1929.

30 Box 7 file 4, 10 August 1929.

31 Box 7 file 13, 5 August 1929.

32 Box 7 file 4, 29 December 1929.

33 Box 7 file 4, 29 December 1929.

34 Box 7 file 23, 10 January 1930.

CHAPTER EIGHT

1 Library and Archives Canada, Lester B. Pearson Diary, MG26 N8, Boxes 1–2.

2 Box 8 file 12, 12 April 1930.

3 Box 7 file 27, 15 July 1930.

4 Box 7 file 28, 18 April 1930.

5 Lester B. Pearson Diary, MG26 N8, Boxes 1-2.

6 Private correspondence, 26 April 1930. This letter is one of the few that Pauline wrote to Georges in English.

7 Private correspondence, 27 April 1930.

8 Private correspondence, 28 April 1930.

9 Private correspondence, 28 April 1930.

10 Private correspondence, 4 May 1930.
11 For years afterward, Pauline bitterly regretted having destroyed Georges's
   letters. Later, after the years had become several decades, she laughed about it.
12 Private correspondence, 8 May 1930.
13 Private correspondence, 10 May 1930.
14 Box 8 file 10.
15 Box 7 file 4, 29 December 1929.
16 Private correspondence, 10 May 1930.
17 Box 8 file 12.
18 Box 8 file 12.
19 Box 8 file 8, 6 February 1931.
20 Box 8 file 4, 15 November 1930.
21 Box 7 file 26, 1 November 1930.
22 Box 8 file 19, 1 March 1931.
23 Box 8 file 22, 23 April 1931.

CHAPTER NINE
 1 Box 8 file 16, 23 April 1931.
 2 Box 8 file 14, 5 January 1931.
 3 Private correspondence, 8 March 1931.
 4 Box 8 file 17, 30 March 1931.
 5 Box 8 file 26, 6 February 1931.
 6 Box 8 file 19, 1 March 1931.
 7 Box 8 file 32, 19 January 1932.
 8 Box 1 file 1, undated.
 9 Box 9 file 11, 23 February 1933.
10 Inglis, *Documents on Canadian External Relations*, vol. 5, 14.
11 Box 8 file 29, 14 September 1932.
12 Box 10 file 2, 27 March 1936.
13 Box 8 file 26, 12 August 1932.
14 Box 8 file 33, 17 October 1932.
15 Box 8 file 33, 11 November 1932.
16 Private correspondence, 23 April 1934.
17 Private correspondence, 22 April 1934.
18 Private correspondence, 8 June 1934.
19 Box 111 file 13.
20 Box 9 file 19, 19 June 1934.
21 Private correspondence, 16 June 1934.
22 Private correspondence, 17 May 1934.
23 Box 9 file 30, 3 March 1935.
24 Box 9 file 32, 21 June 1935.
25 Box 9 file 34, 6 June 1935.
26 Box 9 File 31, 6 September 1935.

27 Private correspondence, 23 September 1936.
28 Box 10 file 21.
29 Box 16 file 2.
30 Private correspondence, 12 August 1935.
31 Private correspondence, 27 August 1936.
32 Private correspondence, 1 March 1937.
33 Private correspondence, 2 March 1937.
34 Private correspondence, 15 March 1937.
35 Box 9 file 38, 21 December 1935.
36 Box 10 file 8, 27 March 1936.
37 Box 10 file 16, 2 April 1937.
38 Box 10 file 24.
39 Box 10 file 30, 15 February 1938.
40 Private correspondence, 6 March 1937.

CHAPTER TEN

 1 Box 10 file 26, 6 October 1937.
 2 Box 9 file 31, 6 September 1935.
 3 Private correspondence, 26 September 1936.
 4 Private correspondence, 20 August 1935.
 5 Private correspondence, 28 August 1935.
 6 Private correspondence, 28 August 1935.
 7 Private correspondence, 26 September 1936.
 8 Private correspondence, 26 September 1936.
 9 Basset, Bernard, *The English Jesuits,* 448.
10 Vanier, Jean, *In Weakness, Strength,* 8.
11 Speaight, Robert, *Vanier,* 190.
12 Private correspondence, 11 May 1938.
13 Private correspondence, 28 August 1938.
14 Private correspondence, 29 August 1938.
15 Box 10 file 33, 15 April 1938.
16 Box 10 file 31, 10 July 1938.
17 Private correspondence, 30 August 1938.
18 Private correspondence, 31 August 1938.
19 Box 10 file 34, 7 September 1938.
20 Box 10 file 34.
21 Box 10 file 34.
22 Box 10 file 34, 21 December 1938.
23 Box 11 file 2, 14 December 1938.

CHAPTER ELEVEN

 1 Box 11 file 26, 16 February 1939.
 2 Box 11 file 11, 2 May 1939.

3 Box 106 file 10, 23 March 1939.
4 Box 11 file 12, 11 February 1939.
5 Box 11 file 23, 11 April 1939.
6 Private correspondence, 19 July 1939.
7 Box 11 file 23.
8 Box 12 file 7, February 1940.
9 Box 12 file 22.
10 Library and Archives Canada, MG26 J1 Box 298, reel C4576.
11 Box 12 file 22.
12 Box 12 file 16.
13 Box 12 file 22.
14 Box 12 file 5, 14 June 1940.
15 Box 12 file 22.
16 Box 12 file 22.
17 Box 12 file 22.
18 Box 12 file 22.
19 It seems that Mrs Massey eventually managed to stifle such irritating outbursts and helped admirably with relief work in London during the rest of the war years.
20 Library and Archives Canada, Lester B. Pearson, MG26 N8, Boxes 1-2.
21 Massey College, Vincent Massey Archives, 23 June 1940, B87-0082/310.
22 Box 12 file 17.
23 Box 13 file 28.
24 Box 13 file 28.

CHAPTER TWELVE
1 Box 12 file 17.
2 Box 12 file 12, 27 June 1940.
3 Box 12 file 7.
4 Box 12 file 7, 28 July 1940.
5 Box 13 file 1, 17 July 1940.
6 Box 12 file 7.
7 Box 13 file 28.
8 Box 21 file 51, 16 December 1952.
9 Box 12 file 8, 1 September 1940.
10 Box 12 file 17, 28 August 1940.
11 Box 12 file 17, 31 August 1940.
12 Library and Archives Canada, Mackenzie King Diary, 7 October 1940.
13 Carmel Archives, 21 February 1940.
14 Mackenzie King Diary, 19 August 1941.
15 Box 12 file 24.
16 Box 13 file 25.
17 Box 13 file 23, 17 May 1941.

18 Mackenzie King Diary, 23 May 1941.
19 Box 13 file 50.
20 Box 13 file 39.
21 Private correspondence, undated.
22 Mackenzie King Diary, 24 March 1942.
23 Mackenzie King Diary, 12 October 1942.
24 Box 13 file 51, 11 November 1942.
25 Box 12 file 5, 23 December 1942.
26 Box 14 file 22, undated.
27 Private correspondence, 31 March 1943.
28 Box 14 file 21, 21 October 1943.
29 Box 14 file 20, 1 September 1943.
30 Box 14 file 20, 11 July 1943.
31 Box 14 file 21, undated.

CHAPTER THIRTEEN

1 Box 15 file 45.
2 Box 15 file 46.
3 Box 15 file 26, 30 March 1944.
4 Box 15 file 41, 21 August 1944.
5 Box 15 file 26, 30 March 1944.
6 Box 15 file 26, 28 March 1944.
7 Box 15 file 26, 23 May 1944.
8 Box 15 file 26, 1 April 1944.
9 Box 15 file 26, 28 March 1944.
10 Box 15 file 26, 24 April 1944.
11 Carmel Archives, 4 June 1944.
12 The subject of the French Jews and the Vichy government is covered in
    depth by Michael Marrus and Robert Paxton in *Vichy France and the Jews*.
13 Box 15 file 26, 16 May 1944.
14 Box 16 file 32.
15 Box 15 file 16.
16 Box 15 file 26, 19 June 1944.
17 Box 15 file 27, 12 June 1944.
18 Box 15 file 25, 11 May 1944.
19 Box 15 file 27, 17 July 1944.
20 Box 15 file 26, 10 June 1944.
21 Box 15 file 26, 24 August 1944.
22 Box 15 file 22.
23 Box 15 file 22, 18 September 1944.
24 Box 106 file 17, 6 September 1944.
25 Box 106 file 17, 11 September 1944.
26 Box 15 file 22, 9 September 1944.

27 Box 15 file 24.
28 Box 15 file 26, 22 August 1944.
29 Box 106 file 17, 11 September 1944.
30 Box 16 file 32.
31 Box 15 file 26, 16 September 1944.
32 Box 106 file 18, 4 February 1945.
33 Box 17 file 33.
34 Collaboration and post-war justice is the subject of *Long Shadows: Truth, Lies and History*, by Erna Paris.
35 Box 15 file 26, 25 September 1944.
36 Box 15 file 26, 29 September 1944.
37 Box 16 file 5.
38 Box 15 file 26, 29 September 1944.

CHAPTER FOURTEEN

1 Box 15 file 26.
2 Box 106 file 18, 30 May 1945.
3 "Ambassador's Wife," Gwenda Thompson, *Mayfair*, June 1945.
4 Box 17 file 6, 12 January 1945.
5 Box 106 file 19, N.K.A. Miller, 6 March 1945.
6 Box 17 file 34.
7 Box 106 file 19, 8 June 1945.
8 Box 106 file 18, 21 April 1945.
9 Box 17 file 33.
10 Box 17 file 6, 29 May 1945.
11 Box 17 file 33, 4 January 1945.
12 Box 17 file 5, 10 August 1945.
13 Box 106 file 18, 30 August 1945.
14 Box 106 file 18, 14 October 1945.
15 Box 106 file 18, 4 November 1945.
16 Box 106 file 18, 4 September 1945.
17 Box 24 file 13, 8 December 1959.
18 Ritchie, *Diplomatic Passport*, 14
19 Pauline's memory of the notorious Bernonville having been vetted and allowed into Canada through the Canadian immigration services in Paris, as recorded in *One Woman's Journey* by Cowley and Cowley, was incorrect. Bernonville was never granted a Canadian visa.
20 A misconception has arisen over the years about the Vaniers' relationship with Teitgen. The impression is given elsewhere (Cowley and Cowley, *One Woman's Journey*, 117–18, and Speaight, *Vanier: Soldier, Diplomat and Governor-General*, 302) that with Teitgen's help, Pauline Vanier gave advice about who might or might not be granted admittance to Canada,

and that she advised some of those accused of collaboration to "go into hiding." In fact, the process of immigration was under the jurisdiction of the Canadian Department of Mines and Resources at that time, and beyond the influence of the ambassador's wife. In an interview with Msgr Roger Quesnel, 25 June 1993, Teitgen said, "Elle est intervenue effectivement auprès de moi à plusieurs reprises pour ces gens ou pour des consultations. Elle n'avait aucune fonction officielle, elle était moins gênée de me consulter. Tandis que le Général ne me disait rien de ce qu'il faisait. Je lui disais que pour telle personne dont la culpabilité était doutouse, elle pouvait aider, que je notais cela. Pour d'autres, je lui disais de ne pas intervener." ("She actually contacted me several times on behalf of those people or to ask my advice. She had no official position, so she was less constrained in consulting me. Whereas the General told me nothing of what he was doing. I told her that she could help the persons whose guilt, according to my notes, was in doubt. For others, I told her not to intervene.")

21 Father Benedict Vanier, private papers.
22 Box 23, file 45.
23 Father Benedict Vanier, private papers.
24 Box 19 file 32.
25 Box 20 file 6, 23 February 1950.
26 Box 23 file 29.
27 Box 20 file 5, 29 October 1949.
28 Box 20 file 37, 30 March 1950.
29 Box 20 file 1, 3 January 1948,
30 Box 20 file 37, 30 March 1950.

CHAPTER FIFTEEN

1 Ware Carmel Archives, 18 June 1947.
2 Ware Carmel Archives, 4 October 1949.
3 Box 21 file 7, 9 November 1951.
4 Box 21 file 39, 21 September 1952.
5 Box 22 file 6, 21 December 1953.
6 Box 22 file 6, 24 June 1953.
7 Box 22 file 6, October 22 1953.
8 Box 22 file 6, 9 November 1953.
9 Box 107 file 21, Alice Hemmings, 11 January 1954.
10 Box 22 file 29, 11 February 1954.
11 Box 22 file 34.
12 Private correspondence, undated.
13 *La Presse*, 20 December 1958.
14 Box 6 file 7.
15 "Call Me George(s)," *Time*, 7 September 1959.

CHAPTER SIXTEEN

1 Cowley and Vanier, *Only to Serve*, 3–5.
2 Box 27 file 19, 20 December 1961.
3 Box 27 file 7, 22 March 1965.
4 Box 25 file 7, 3 March 1966.
5 Box 27 file 7, Vera Graves, undated.
6 Box 27 file 17, 3 December 1959.
7 "The Governor General," *Time*, 21 September 1959.
8 Box 103 file 8, John Keirstead, 27 December 1967
9 "A Marked Scarcity of Anecdotes," Frank Swanson, *Ottawa Citizen*, 4 August 1959.
10 *Maclean's*, 26 September 1959.
11 Private correspondence, 10 January 1960.
12 Michel de Salaberry, interview with author, 19 December 2007.
13 Yves Chevrier, interview with author, 20 July 2006.
14 Box 27 file 16, 18 January 1963.
15 Box 23 file 29.
16 Box 31 file 2.
17 Box 31 file 2.
18 Box 31 file 2, 9 February 1963.
19 Box 31 file 2, 29 March 1963.
20 Georges Vanier used as a guide Walter Bagehot's nineteenth-century text, *The English Constitution*, as had Vincent Massey. That work set forth the rights of the Crown as "the right to be consulted, the right to encourage and the right to warn."

CHAPTER SEVENTEEN

1 Undated article, "Mr Vanier Goes to Church," by Joe Cunningham, Box 24, file 11.
2 Cowley and Vanier, *Only to Serve*, 100–1.
3 Ibid., 7.
4 Box 24 file 10, 8 June 1964.
5 Box 26 file 13.
6 Dr Peter Burton and Rachel Burton, interview with author, 2 August 2007.
7 Box 27 file 16, 18 January 1963.
8 Box 24 file 13, undated.
9 Box 27 file 16, 12 June 1963.
10 Box 110 file 5, 17 May 1964.
11 Box 110 file 5, 8 July 1964.
12 The death penalty was abolished in Canada in 1976.
13 Cowley and Vanier, *Only to Serve*, 74.
14 "The RIN's Big Mistake," *Globe and Mail*, 26 June 1964.
15 Box 110 file 5, 8 July 1964.

16 Box 110 file 5, 26 July 1964.
17 Box 24 file 10, 13 April 1965.
18 Box 26 file 12, 22 April 1966.
19 Box 22 file 5, 17 January 1964.
20 Box 103 file 7, 20 July 1966.
21 Georges Vanier's successor, Roland Michener, and all succeeding governors general have made state visits to various countries around the world.
22 Personal correspondence, 28 August 1966.
23 Personal correspondence, 26 February 1966.
24 Box 110 file 3, 7 January 1964.
25 Box 27 file 1, 20 June 1966.
26 Box 46 file 6.
27 Box 103 file 7.
28 Box 26 file 8, 21 February 1967.
29 Box 47 file 16, 22 February 1967.
30 "Georges P. Vanier," *Globe and Mail*, 6 March 1967.
31 Box 103 file 18, 19 February 1967.
32 Box 87 file 3, 7 March 1967.

CHAPTER EIGHTEEN
1 Box 113, file 12.
2 Box 114, file 4. Pauline Vanier reported her encounter with Charles de Gaulle to the Canadian embassy in Paris.
3 Ibid., 21 March 1972.
4 Elizabeth Buckley, interview with author, 25 August 2009.
5 Private correspondence, 5 March 1983.
6 St Bonaventure Archives, 16 February, undated.

BIBLIOGRAPHY

Abella, Irving, and Harold Troper. *None Is Too Many: Canada and the Jews of Europe 1933–1948*. Toronto: Lester and Orpen Dennys, 1982.

Allen, Louis. "Resistance and the Catholic Church in France." In *Resistance in Europe: 1939–1945*, edited by Stephen Hawes and Ralph White, 77–93. London: Allen Lane, 1975.

Amyot, Eric. *Le Québec entre Pétain et de Gaulle: Vichy, la France libre et les Canadiens français*. Quebec: Editions Fides, 1999.

Andrews, Allen. *Brave Soldiers, Proud Regiments: Canada's Military Heritage.* Vancouver: Ronsdale, 1997.

Armstrong, Elizabeth. *The Crisis of Quebec, 1914–1918*. Toronto: McClelland and Stewart, 1974.

Arnold, Gladys, *One Woman's War: A Canadian Reporter with the Free French*. Toronto: James Lorimer and Company, 1987.

Basset, Bernard. *The English Jesuits: From Campion to Martindale*. London: Burns and Oates, 1987.

Beevor, Antony, and Artemis Cooper. *Paris after the Liberation: 1944–1949*. New York: Doubleday, 1994.

Bissell, Claude. *The Imperial Canadian: Vincent Massey in Office*. Toronto: University of Toronto Press, 1986.

Byng, Evelyn, Viscountess. *Up the Stream of Time*. Toronto: Macmillan, 1945.

Charmley, John. *Duff Cooper*. London: Weidenfeld and Nicolson, 1986.

Christie, Norm. *The Canadians at Passchendaele*. Winnipeg: Bunker to Bunker Books, 1996.

– *The Canadians in the Second Battle of Ypres*. Ottawa: CEF Books, 2005.

Christofferson, Thomas R., and Michael S. Christofferson. *France during World War II: From Defeat to Liberation*. New York: Fordham University Press, 2006.

Coady, Mary Frances. *The Hidden Way: The Life and Influences of Almire Pichon*. Norwich: Darton, Longman, and Todd, 1999.

Cook, Don. *Charles de Gaulle: A Biography*. New York: G.P. Putnam's Sons, 1983.

Cooper, Duff. *The Duff Cooper Diaries*. London: Weidenfeld and Nicolson, 2005.

Cowley, Deborah. *Georges Vanier: Soldier: The Wartime Letters and Diaries, 1915–1919.* Toronto: Dundurn Press, 2000.

– and George Cowley. *One Woman's Journey: A Portrait of Pauline Vanier.* Ottawa: Novalis, 1992.

Cowley, George, and Michel Vanier, eds. *Only to Serve: Selections from Addresses of Governor-General Georges P. Vanier.* Toronto: University of Toronto Press, 1970.

De Gaulle, Charles. *The War Memoirs of Charles de Gaulle.* New York: Simon and Schuster, 1960.

De Lubac, Henri. *Christian Resistance to Anti-Semitism: Memories from 1940–1944.* San Francisco: Ignatius Press, 1990.

Diefenbaker, John G. *One Canada: The Memoirs of the Right Honourable John. G. Diefenbaker.* Toronto: Macmillan, 1977.

Eastman, S. Mack. *Canada at Geneva: An Historical Survey and Its Lessons.* Toronto: Ryerson, 1946.

English, John. *Shadow of Heaven: The Life of Lester Pearson, 1897–1948,* Vol. 1. Toronto: Lester and Orpen Dennys, 1989.

– *The Worldly Years: The Life of Lester Pearson 1949–1972,* Vol. 2. Toronto: Random House, 1992.

Ferguson, Niall. *The Pity of War: Explaining World War I.* New York: Basic Books, 1988.

"For King and Empire." Canada: Viewer Plus Inc., Alliance Atlantis.

Gagnon, Jean-Pierre. *Le 22e bataillon (canadien-français) 1914–1919: Étude sociomilitaire.* Quebec: Les Presses de l'Université Laval en collaboration avec le ministère de la Défense nationale et le Centre d'édition du gouvernement du Canada, 1986.

Galloway, Colonel Strome. "Georges Vanier: A Hero in Two Tongues" (unpublished). 1974.

Glazebrook, G.P. de T. *A History of Canadian External Relations.* Toronto: Oxford University Press, 1950.

Godefroy, Andrew B. *For Freedom and Honour? The Story of the 25 Canadian Volunteers Executed in the First World War.* Nepean, Ontario: CEF Books, 1998.

Godwin-Austen, Major A.R. *The Staff and Staff College.* London: Constable and Company, 1927.

Granatstein, J.L. *Mackenzie King: His Life and World.* Toronto: McGraw-Hill Ryerson, 1990.

– *Nation: Canada since Confederation.* Toronto: McGraw-Hill Ryerson, 1990.

Halls, W.D. *Politics, Society and Christianity in Vichy France.* Providence, R.I.: Berg, 1995.

Hastings, Adrian. "Some Reflections on the English Catholicism of the 1930s." In *Bishops and Writers: Aspects of the Evolution of Modern English Catholi-*

cism, edited by Adrian Hastings, 107–25. Wheathampstead, Hertfordshire: Anthony Clarke, 1977.

Hawkins, Freda. *Canada and Immigration: Public Policy and Public Concern.* Kingston and Montreal: McGill-Queen's University Press, 1988.

Hilliker, John. *Canada's Department of External Affairs, Volume 1, The Early Years: 1909–1946.* Montreal: McGill-Queen's University Press, 1990.

Hutchison, Bruce. *The Incredible Canadian: A Candid Portrait of Mackenzie King; His Works, His Times, and His Nation.* Toronto: Longmans Green, 1952.

Inglis, Alex J., ed., *Documents on Canadian External Relations.* Ottawa: Department of External Affairs, 1971.

Jackson, Julian. *Charles de Gaulle.* London: Haus Publishing, 2003.

– *France: The Dark Years.* London: Oxford University Press, 2001.

Karsh, Yousuf. *Karsh Canadians.* Toronto: University of Toronto Press, 1978.

Kendall, Katherine. *Father Steuart: A Study of His Life and Teaching.* London: Burns and Oates, 1949.

Linteau, Paul-Andre, René Durocher, and Jean-Claude Robert. *Quebec: A History 1867–1929.* Toronto: James Lorimer, 1983.

Marrus, Michael R., and Robert O. Paxton. *Vichy France and the Jews.* Stanford, California: Stanford University Press, 1995.

Massey, Vincent. *What's Past Is Prologue: The Memoirs of Vincent Massey.* Toronto: Macmillan, 1963.

McLean, Eric, and R.D. Wilson. *The Living Past of Montreal.* Montreal: McGill University Press, 1993.

McWhinney, Edward. *The Governor General and the Prime Ministers: The Making and Unmaking of Governments.* Vancouver: Ronsdale, 2005.

Monet, Jacques. *The Canadian Crown.* Toronto: Clarke, Irwin, 1979.

Morton, Desmond. "French Canadian Officers and the First World War." In *Limits of Loyalty*, edited by Edgar Denton III, 79–97. Waterloo, Ontario: Wilfrid Laurier University Press, 1980.

– "The Supreme Penalty: Canadian Deaths by Firing Squad in the First World War." *Queen's Quarterly* 79, no. 3 (Autumn 1972): 345–52.

– *When Your Number's Up: The Canadian Soldier in the First World War.* Toronto: Random House, 1993.

Murphy, Terrence, and Roberto Perin, eds. *A Concise History of Christianity in Canada.* Toronto: Oxford University Press, 1996.

Newman, Peter C. *Renegade in Power: The Diefenbaker Years.* Toronto: McClelland and Stewart, 1973.

Paris, Erna. *Long Shadows: Truth, Lies and History.* Toronto: Knopf Canada, 2000.

Paxton, Robert O. *Vichy France: Old Guard and New Order 1940–44.* New York: Alfred A. Knopf, 1972.

Pearson, Lester B. *Mike: The Memoirs of the Rt. Hon. Lester B. Pearson*. Vol. 1.
    Toronto: University of Toronto Press, 1972.
Pickersgill, Frank. *The Making of a Secret Agent: Letters of 1934–1943*.
    Toronto: McClelland and Stewart, 1978.
Putkowski, Julian, and Julian Sykes. *Shot at Dawn: Executions in World War
    One by Authority of the British Army Act*. Barnsley, England: Pen and Sword
    Books, 1998.
Ritchie, Charles. *Diplomatic Passport: More Undiplomatic Diaries, 1946–1962*.
    Toronto: Macmillan, 1981.
– *The Siren Years: A Canadian Diplomat Abroad, 1937–1945*. Toronto:
    Macmillan, 1974.
Roberts, Leslie. *Montreal: From Mission Colony to World City*. Toronto:
    Macmillan, 1969.
Scott, Frederick G. *The Great War as I Saw It*. Toronto: Clarke and Stuart, 1934.
Slade, Arthur. *John Diefenbaker: An Appointment with Destiny*. Montreal: XYZ
    Publishing, 2001.
Speaight, Robert. *Vanier: Soldier, Diplomat and Governor General*. Toronto:
    Wm Collins Sons, 1970.
Spink, Kathryn. *The Miracle, the Message, the Story*. Toronto: Novalis, 2005.
Steuart, Robert. "A Reality of War." *The Month*, April 1921.
Vanier, Jean. *In Weakness, Strength: The Spiritual Sources of Georges P. Vanier,
    19th Governor-General of Canada*. Toronto: Griffin House, 1969.
– *Our Life Together: A Memoir in Letters*. Toronto: HarperCollins, 2007.
Williams, Jeffery. *Byng of Vimy: General and Governor General*. London: Martin
    Secker and Warburg, 1983.
Willis-O'Connor, H., as told to Madge MacBeth. *Inside Government House*.
    Toronto: Ryerson, 1954.

INDEX